POLICING THE RACIAL DIVIDE

Policing the Racial Divide

Urban Growth Politics and the
Remaking of Segregation

Daanika Gordon

NEW YORK UNIVERSITY PRESS
New York

NEW YORK UNIVERSITY PRESS
New York
www.nyupress.org

References to Internet websites (URLs) were accurate at the time of writing. Neither the author nor New York University Press is responsible for URLs that may have expired or changed since the manuscript was prepared.

Library of Congress Cataloging-in-Publication Data
Names: Gordon, Daanika, author.
Title: Policing the racial divide : urban growth politics and the remaking of segregation / Daanika Gordon.
Description: New York : New York University Press, [2022] |
Includes bibliographical references.
Identifiers: LCCN 2021039797 | ISBN 9781479814046 (hardback ; alk. paper) |
ISBN 9781479814053 (paperback ; alk. paper) | ISBN 9781479814060 (ebook) |
ISBN 9781479814077 (ebook other)
Subjects: LCSH: Police—United States—Case studies. | Police-community relations—United States—Case studies. | Segregation—United States—Case studies. | Urbanization—Social aspects—United States—Case studies. | Urban policy—United States—Case studies. | Equality—United States—Case studies. | United States—Race relations—Case studies.
Classification: LCC HV8139 .G67 2022 | DDC 363.2089/00973—dc23
LC record available at https://lccn.loc.gov/2021039797

New York University Press books are printed on acid-free paper, and their binding materials are chosen for strength and durability. We strive to use environmentally responsible suppliers and materials to the greatest extent possible in publishing our books.

Manufactured in the United States of America

10 9 8 7 6 5 4 3 2 1

Also available as an ebook

CONTENTS

Introduction

On a warm night in June, police officer Cory Snow anticipated that we would be sent to a shooting.[1] Conventional wisdom held that violence spiked with the heat. As the evening progressed and no shootings occurred, Snow told me it must be a slow shift. Yet, after ten months of accompanying officers during their shifts, this ride-along with Snow and his partner, Travis Foster, was one of the busiest I had observed. We drove from call to call all evening, responding to a wide array of assignments: five reports of gunshots fired; two calls for medical observation of a mental health crisis; one fight; one noise nuisance call; one call regarding a suspicious automobile; and five calls involving either trouble with a subject or a check on an individual's welfare. Snow and Foster handled these varied assignments with a sense of hurry. Foster explained that it was rare to have a break between assignments and, even when dealing with a call, the squad car could be pulled if a more serious incident arose. The officers saw this workload as characteristic of the district they patrolled. Snow described the officers' assigned sector as "the worst of the worst": the most violent sector of the city's most violent district. He periodically pointed to the intersections, blocks, and streets, describing "shit" or "garbage" areas where crime was common. These specters of potential violence, unending work, and pathological places haunted the shift. The officers raised these types of concerns before and after their many interactions with district residents, nearly all of whom were Black.[2]

Snow and Foster—both white men in their late twenties—had worked in the West District since joining the River City Police Department (RCPD). After graduating high school, Snow served in the military and had recently finished an associate's degree in police science. He had been an officer for just over a year. While we sat in the idling squad car at the beginning of his shift, I asked if police work had been what he had expected. Snow paused, equivocated, and then suggested it had

1

not. Explaining how things could get wild in the sector, he described his last homicide scene assignment: two hundred people had been in the street, fighting one another and fighting the police.[3] When I asked if he had requested to work in the West District, he said that he had, for the experience. Snow mused that you could police differently in the West District. I probed further, and he replied vaguely, "You can just talk to people differently."

Like Snow, officer Foster wanted the West District assignment. He had joined the department right out of high school through a civilian position and was later admitted into the police academy. Upon completing his training, he figured he would learn a lot in the West District in a short time frame. This had proven to be the case. Foster explained that "working in West could suck," but he hoped it would pay off. He then mentioned a seasoned officer who had recently been transferred from a slower district, noting how she seemed very inexperienced despite her many years on the force. By contrast, Foster had been handling complex assignments like shootings within weeks of starting the job.

During the shift, Snow and Foster not only responded to calls but also worked proactively. The River City police chief's strategy for intervening in crime relied on investigatory traffic and pedestrian stops. In contrast to stops that focused on traffic safety enforcement, investigatory stops served as a pretext to search for contraband like guns or drugs. As Snow and Foster patrolled their sector between calls, they spotted a gray sedan with heavily tinted windows. The officers became suspicious after the car disappeared down an alley, so they turned on the squad-car lights and initiated a stop. The police spotted a pistol resting on the passenger seat when they approached the car. They asked the driver, a young Black man, to step out of the vehicle. The driver explained that he had a gun permit, and Snow said that they would verify this information. The officers returned to the squad car with the gun and confirmed that it was, indeed, licensed. But they discussed the gun's extended magazine with concern. Snow counted that it had a capacity of twenty-six bullets. He and Foster wondered why someone would need a gun like that, speculating that the driver's alley-cruising behavior meant that he had been searching for someone. Though the officers returned the gun and let the driver go, they appeared visibly agitated after their second encounter. They said they had seen gang-related tattoos on the driver's hands and had asked about the extended clip. Although the man claimed he liked to go to the shooting range, he failed to name the location of one. After the stop, Snow drove the squad car down the block and pulled over. He glanced anxiously in the rearview mirror and noted that the gray car appeared to be following them. With one brief remark—"we're going to get the hell out of this area"—he drove away.

Snow and Foster's experiences and perceptions reflected a widely shared sense of the West District's reputation among the police. Officers often mentioned violent crime and an array of other social problems when characterizing the district. Their perceptions were tied, in part, to the structural conditions of the West District, which included many of the city's most poverty-stricken neighborhoods. Residents had to call on the police to respond to crises around health emergencies, addiction, housing insecurity, family conflicts, and other problems that reflected a dearth of institutional resources. But the West District's reputation also stemmed from a long history of criminalization. Targeted law enforcement had swept many district residents into the carceral system and stamped the area with an indelible mark of social pathology.

The combination of service needs and crime control mandates created a challenging work environment for officers to navigate. Police leaders directed officers to make proactive traffic stops with the goal of ferreting out and preventing violent crime, but these officers often faced an overwhelming volume of calls for service that sent them, like Snow and Foster, hurtling from assignment to assignment. Some officers were proud of their ability to handle this workload and "do more with less." They also touted the West District as the place where the "real police work" of crime fighting occurred. However, others looked to different districts, longing for a slower routine. Regardless of how they adapted to the work, many officers explained that the district was "all garbage." This pernicious insinuation overlaid another reality: over 75 percent of residents in these neighborhoods were Black—the highest proportion of any district in the city.

* * *

Days later, in the adjacent East District, Officer Doyle Alport was sent to a single call during his eight-hour shift. But dispatch canceled this assignment to meet an ambulance with a combative subject before

Alport even arrived. Alport later volunteered as a backup unit for graffiti in progress at the downtown train station. However, when he arrived, two of the district's patrol squads and a supervisor were already at the scene. Toward the end of his shift, Alport volunteered to take a call in lieu of another officer. The assignment involved trouble with a subject, again at the train station. Alport resolved the situation by encouraging two individuals to leave the premises, which they did. As Alport had time to kill between these calls, he set about doing the preventive work that the district leadership promoted. He made several traffic safety stops at a busy intersection. He later parked the squad car and started a foot patrol, walking along a popular bar-and-restaurant corridor. As he passed pedestrians and bar patrons, Alport would give a friendly nod and say hello. He explained that police work in the district had a public-relations component: residents liked to see foot patrol through their neighborhoods. His feelings about this mirrored a common sentiment among the police: the East District's residents might be demanding, but they were also deserving. They were taxpayers, professionals, and law-abiding citizens whose contribution to the city made them worthy of police service.

Alport, a white man in his forties, had worked in the East District for eight years, though he had been with the department for nearly twenty. He had spent four years in the Air Force and remained in the Air Force reserves after joining the police force. Alport had worked in several districts, including the West District, where he had started his policing career. He described the East District as "definitely unique," explaining that most issues revolved around the downtown entertainment corridors and the daily influx of people to the business district. Thefts and problems around homelessness were common. Alport drew a contrast between the West District and the East District: while the West District was more violent, the East District had more variety. For example, he said he had once helped deliver a baby, and he had been the first officer to respond to a sinkhole. Alport mused that you really had to treat victims better in the East District: assignments required a great deal of follow-up, thoroughness, and report writing; many officers would not like this aspect of the work. In contrast, Alport said you could "really blow anything off" in the West District, short of a shooting. When I probed further, Alport said that people have different expectations. A victim in the East District might be a business owner who is paying ten grand in taxes and who *wants* to be called back.

Since Alport had few calls during the shift, he spent considerable time in his idling squad car at a busy downtown intersection, periodically conducting traffic-enforcement stops. Unlike the investigatory stops in the West District that I had observed, these stops were concerned with traffic and equipment violations that could pose a safety hazard. At one point, Alport noted a blue hatchback that appeared to have something dangling from its undercarriage. The car was also missing a front license plate and had only one taillight. When Alport turned on the squad-car lights, the driver—a white woman in her late twenties—pulled over to the left. Alport groaned and explained that everyone is supposed to pull over to the right as a basic rule of the road. He ran the car's license plate through the in-squad computer system and found that the plates had been suspended. Alport muttered that this was probably going to re-sult in a ticket. However, when he returned from his initial conversation with the driver, Alport sheepishly explained, "actually, she's really nice," following with, "I'm such a softie." I asked if the woman could account for the condition of her car; Alport said that her boyfriend primarily drives the car, and she would sell it at the end of the month. Alport then ran the woman's driver's license information, noting that it was valid and that she lived just around the corner. He went to return the woman's license and ended the stop with a verbal warning.

Alport's experiences and perceptions were consistent with the East District's reputation. The area included River City's downtown, several middle-class and affluent residential neighborhoods, a university cam-pus, and the city's major entertainment corridors. For many stakehold-ers, these areas constituted the "heart" of River City, seen as vital to its prospects for growth and home to its most well-connected and influ-ential residents. For officers, this environment imposed different pres-sures and constraints. Though the police responded to fewer calls, and assignments often involved minor incidents compared to those in the West District, many insisted that it did not mean there was *less* work in the East District. The work was qualitatively different. Residents had demands and wielded the political and economic leverage to ensure that their needs were met. Officers felt that they needed specialized people skills to engage these "clients," who expected prompt responses and thorough investigations. Notably, the demanding yet deserving clientele of the East District were over 80 percent white.

* * *

For thirteen months, I rode along with officers in two adjacent police districts in a profoundly segregated Rust Belt city that I call River City. As a twenty-seven-year-old Asian American woman, whose knowledge of urban policing came largely from academic scholarship on the subject, I had much to learn about how the police operated on the ground. I found officers navigating two worlds: one characterized by punitive social control, a sense of relentless work, and antagonistic attitudes toward the public; the other by responsive police service, ample resources for preventive work, and a sense of citizens' worthiness. Officers conducted different forms of traffic stops and responded to different types of calls in both degree and kind. District-level policing practices overlaid the city's racial geography and reinforced foundational inequalities. Residents of predominantly white neighborhoods described effective and friendly relationships with the police, while those in predominantly Black neighborhoods worried about aggressive stops and slow response times to their 911 calls. These racialized patterns were driven by organizational practices rather than the racial animus of individual officers. The police generated disparities simply by carrying out their routine activities in work environments characterized by vastly different pressures, priorities, roles, and resources.

While such differences in the policing of Black and white neighborhoods may come as no surprise, what is puzzling about this case is that these two worlds were constructed *by design*. During the first decade of the twenty-first century, the River City Police Department redrew the boundaries of several police districts, aligning them with the city's existing racial segregation boundaries. Superficially, police executives framed redistricting around "coherent neighborhoods" as part of the department's embrace of community policing and other lauded strategic innovations. By enabling neighborhood-based approaches, they argued, the redistricting would facilitate local problem-solving and address the needs of specific communities. However, as I spoke with police leaders, elected officials, business elites, and representatives of community groups, I also discovered that the logic of redistricting preeminently focused on improving policing downtown and in middle-class neighborhoods—predominantly white areas with comparatively low crime rates. Police executives drew on widely circulating frames that saw these places as vital to the city's economic fate. As I delved deeper into this story, I arrived at the central argument of this book: through redistricting and other strategic priorities, the police embraced an active role in the city's growth politics; in doing so, their institutional activities reinscribed many long-standing race- and class-based inequalities that characterize segregation.

Though the River City Police Department's redistricting process and its consequences may appear unique, this story's implications extend beyond a technocratic administrative reform. The redistricting offers a window into how the police department, as one of the most visible public entities in the city, grappled with, defined, and regulated a segregated landscape in ways that impacted the everyday lives of the city's residents. While police executives designed the redistricting to respond to the exigencies of segregated and unequal neighborhoods, they also sought to *craft* neighborhoods in response to evolving visions of the city, what it does, and what it could be in the future. These visions flowed from a powerful and pervasive revitalization discourse embraced in River City and across the Rust Belt by urban growth coalitions—groups of public and private actors, including mayors, elected officials, urban planners, business leaders, and others.[4] Growth discourse emphasized the exchange value of certain neighborhoods and the criminal and civic threats to that value posed by others. These ideas of value and threat were neither free-floating nor arbitrary. They were embedded in a history that forged indelible links between race and urban space.

Hence, River City tells a bigger-picture story. This is a story about the rise and decline of industrial cities and the fate of the Rust Belt. It is about the way global structural transformations produced urban growth strategies that affirmatively depend on uneven development. This is also the story of how Black-white racial inequalities have been encoded onto urban space as part of the United States' long legacy of constructing and enforcing racial difference and hierarchy. It is about how race serves as a foundational axis in the organization of urban life, so that contemporary projects of urban governance necessarily intersect with the realities of racial segregation. Finally, this is a story about the police. It is about a specific police department and a broader professional field confronting a history of racism and striving for innovation while navigating pressures from the surrounding political-economic environment. When woven together, these threads reveal the central role that policing plays in the urban growth politics of postindustrial cities and the spatial and racial inequalities that result.

Urban Growth, Race, and Policing

During the latter half of the twentieth century, the United States' industrial cities experienced profound changes. This history of growth and decline conjures a series of sharply contrasting images: once-bustling factories of the Fordist manufacturing line sitting shuttered and abandoned; once-lively neighborhoods peppered with foreclosed properties; downtown skylines once filled with novel opportunities now portrayed as symbols of disorder. Such contrasts were wrought through macro-level shifts like white flight, the globalization of trade, and deindustrialization. Many of these economic changes dovetailed with neoliberal ideologies of open markets and limited state interference.[5] This ethos reconfigured the role of the state in urban life, with the federal government retrenching social welfare spending and aid to cities.[6] Structural transformations devastated the economic foundations of formerly vibrant industrial hubs, and they fundamentally altered their race and class composition and the corresponding meanings attached to urban space. Stable work opportunities evaporated for many Black residents who had relied on manufacturing jobs. Middle-class families continued to out-migrate to the suburbs, which concentrated problems of joblessness and poverty in urban cores.[7] New political projects constructed cities as sites of crime and disorder. The state turned to the criminal justice system in response, giving rise to mass incarceration.[8] Industrial collapse and its aftermath particularly devastated poor communities of color.

As cities' economic foundations eroded, many local governments turned to austerity measures, cutting back on public services to stave off fiscal crises.[9] They also chased a neoliberal vision of private investment and entrepreneurial development to stay economically viable.[10] While postindustrial cities suffered economic and population decline, the rise of financial and high-end service sectors required new nodes of management; central business districts in cities like New York, San Francisco, and Los Angeles saw their highest growth in decades.[11] Growth coalitions of public officials and private actors in the Rust Belt began to model their development strategies on the success of these global cities.[12] In this paradigm, cities are no longer merely spaces of production but are also "entertainment machines," replete with high-end urban amenities.[13] Globalization made flows of both people and capital highly mobile, and young professionals, developers, and tourists would simply move on to another place if a city could not offer what they desire.

Redesigning urban space around "consumption, pleasure, and affluent residency" is thus seen by local governments as the key to the postindustrial city's survival.[14] Revitalization projects focusing on enhanced financial districts, entertainment corridors, sports stadiums, convention centers, and luxury housing have proliferated as a result.[15] Hence, the abandoned warehouse is converted into artists' lofts or a local distillery. A foreclosed property is marketed as an economic opportunity for the next set of newcomers. Downtown is revitalized so the skyline once again heralds regional cultural amenities and entertainment options. River City, too, joined this competitive entrepreneurial development.

This vision of urban growth also intersects with entrenched racial segregation.[16] Black-white segregation in postindustrial cities solidified through both overt and subtle discrimination. Patterns of institutional investment and neglect overlaid racial landscapes with vastly unequal resources, and neighborhood conditions grew further apart with deindustrialization.[17] As divergent neighborhoods developed, a variety of political projects—from Progressive-era interventions to urban renewal to law-and-order rhetoric—defined space in dualistic terms. Dominant representations positioned predominantly Black inner cities as crime-ridden, disorderly, and violent, in contrast to white, more affluent neighborhoods with "'good' schools, safe streets, and moral values to match."[18] Contemporary urban growth projects unfold in this context of segregated and unequal cities. They also actively seek to shape these landscapes, creating and re-creating group differences in the process.

Indeed, extant scholarship has highlighted how urban development can amplify social inequalities. In declining cities with limited resources, growth discourse encourages "strategic uneven development" or "urban triage":[19] the allocation of scarce resources to neighborhoods considered savable and the relegation of others to inevitable decline. Growth logic identifies downtowns, entertainment districts, and high-end residential neighborhoods—often historically white and already better-off areas—as key sites for enhancing exchange value through further development. This growth logic also represents marginalized Black neighborhoods as economically unproductive and civically problematic. As a consequence, these spaces are overlooked as sites of public and private investment, on the one hand, and used to contain troublesome populations, on the other. The geographer David Wilson argues that a new kind of "ghetto" has emerged as a consequence: disadvantaged Black neighborhoods "have become one-dimensional apparatuses for the naked isolating and warehousing of those deemed cancerous to real-estate submarkets and downtown transformation."[20] As material conditions in central city neighborhoods worsened in the aftermath of deindustrialization, media accounts and the narratives of planners and politicians have framed inner cities as noncontributory, pathological, and, critically, threatening to revitalization efforts. Such rhetoric suggests the need to isolate and contain these areas while protecting areas of "value." With distinct capacities to regulate space, the police are obvious participants in these projects.

The Role of the Police

How the police engage with the political economy of the city has implications for racialized policing more generally. Concerns over race and policing are not only embedded in US history but have taken on greater urgency in recent years, as millions of people have mobilized through and alongside the Black Lives Matter movement to protest police killings and other forms of anti-Black state violence.[21] The history of policing is rife with ties to institutions like slavery, Jim Crow, and other overtly racist state projects.[22] Citizens have had profoundly different relationships with the police on the basis of race, and vast gulfs in experiences and perceptions persist.[23] However, the endurance of racial inequities in policing needs to be explained in light of the state's legal and normative commitments to nondiscrimination and the history of police reform.[24] For instance, many police agencies now incorporate formal policies that seek to prevent racial profiling and elevate responsiveness to historically marginalized communities.[25] In light of these dynamics, certain racial logics and outcomes in policing may be more discernable in the way the police regulate space.

Trends in the field of policing hint at affinities between law enforcement modalities and neoliberal urban governance. The restructuring of municipal finances bears directly on policing resources. As cities cut public expenditures for housing, health care, education, jobs programs, and other services, problems that were previously under the purview of social service agencies have fallen increasingly to the police and prisons.[26] This trend is an integral part of the country's punitive turn. Beginning in the 1970s, governments at all levels retrenched welfare spending and instead turned to the criminal justice system for social regulation.[27] For example, major legislation like the 1994 Violent Crime Control and Law Enforcement Act offered municipalities the chance to expand their policing resources, even when cities were otherwise financially strapped.[28] The growing reliance on carceral logics and practices has increased the average proportion of city budgets devoted to law enforcement.[29] It has also expanded the state's punitive reach into the management of homelessness, addiction, education, and many other realms.[30] In short, cities rely on the police as agents of social control *and* as frontline responders to a vast array of social challenges that find little redress through other state services.

While the police are clearly entangled with the public imperatives of neoliberal urbanism, they have also cultivated its private side. As cities are increasingly reliant on attracting and retaining mobile capital, urban leaders leverage the police to protect areas deemed economically valuable. These include middle-class and affluent residential communities, where officials note that reducing fear of crime can improve property values.[31] These areas also include gentrifying neighborhoods and downtowns—places seen as vital to attracting entrepreneurial development and the "creative class."[32] In such parts of the city, the police aim to *prevent* crime and impact *perceptions* of crime rather than merely respond to crime. They often realize these goals through order-maintenance policing, which targets minor disorder under the assumption that it will lead to increasingly serious criminal problems.[33] As Katherine Beckett and Steve Herbert describe in their book *Banished:*

The New Social Control in Urban America, local governments have facilitated order-maintenance policing in downtowns and other public spaces through a host of legal tools like civility laws, revamped trespass laws, and exclusion zones.[34] These tools enable the police to "banish" undesirable populations and maintain spaces that feel secure and appealing to tourists, developers, and affluent current and prospective residents.

On the flip side, policing in marginalized areas has also been shown to serve political-economic interests. As uneven growth amplifies divides between spaces of worth and those of decline, dominant political representations frame race- and class-subjugated communities as "wellsprings of 'underclass' disorder and danger," and they have been treated as such.[35] Campaigns like the War on Crime and the War on Drugs, in combination with new strategies like hotspots policing and zero-tolerance policing, saturated marginalized neighborhoods with police and subjected their residents to intrusive forms of surveillance and social control.[36] Residents of such communities describe long-standing patterns of overpolicing and underprotection.[37] Aggressive policing has found justification, in part, through "the guise of reclaiming spaces from social disorder and promoting urban development."[38]

This is not the only tie between policing and race- and class-subjugated communities. In a particularly harmful phenomenon, predatory policing extracts revenue from these same neighborhoods. As was shown in Ferguson, Missouri, the police generated money for the city by targeting vulnerable communities through fines and fees, asset forfeiture, and legal financial obligations.[39] Low-income Black and Latinx neighborhoods are treated not only as sites of criminal threat but as sources of capital to ease municipal financial pressures.

All of the preceding trends are place-based given the deeply uneven landscape of segregation and urban redevelopment. And intentionally divergent policing across neighborhoods is increasingly likely as the national field of policing embraces *localism*, another tendency of neoliberal urban governance. Many strategic innovations—including community-based policing, problem-oriented policing, hotspots policing, and others—home in on the neighborhood or even smaller geographic units as the target of intervention.[40] This model contrasts with the goals and tactics of the incident-based response model, which reigned throughout most of the twentieth century, prioritizing consistent response to calls for service and preventive patrol.[41] In the twenty-first century, many police departments purposefully tailor their approaches to specific areas. In theory, doing this can enhance democratic policing and ensure more equitable outcomes, which is a common argument in support of community policing, one of the most lauded and embraced of strategic innovations. While a broadly defined paradigm, community policing entails "in essence, a collaboration between the police and the community that identifies and solves community problems."[42] Proponents see this approach as opening the door for greater public voice and democratic control over the police.[43] But, by inviting additional spatial variation, the turn toward localism in policing can also amplify disparate practices and racial inequalities. This is particularly the case when policing strategies are linked to urban growth politics.

A Relational Analysis of Policing Space and Race

In this book, I use a *relational* approach to trace the processes in River City that produced just such linkages between growth regimes and racialized policing. I argue that an overlooked but critically important facet of police participation in growth politics and the construction of urban space lies in the *coevolution* of policing in white, more-advantaged neighborhoods and policing in race- and class-subjugated neighborhoods. As described earlier, much of the research on the role of the police in the transformation of the city focuses on the way they suppress the marginal, either in contested spaces like gentrifying neighborhoods or in contained areas like "skid row" or the "ghetto."[44] Fewer studies explore the policing of dominant people and places. When they do, research finds that residents of white, higher-income neighborhoods see the police as a service amenity, summoning officers to address issues with neighbors, traffic accidents, and downed power lines.[45]

This book analyzes the *ties* between policing dynamics in these divergent urban spaces. What happens in one kind of place has consequences, both anticipated and unanticipated, in others. If empowered residents demand more officers in their neighborhoods, which neighborhoods lose officers? If certain people or places are constructed as criminal threats, what is in need of protection? Police executives answer such questions in the way they choose to distribute resources, which depends on their contingent ideas of sociospatial boundaries and strategic priorities.

In the process of making these choices, the police define and construct the very nature of urban space and the social differences encoded onto it. While recognizing that histories of racial exclusion and economic transformation have shaped the conditions of segregated neighborhoods, this book sees these conditions as actively maintained and transformed. Policing is one of many institutional arenas that construct spatial and racial difference through processes like classification, boundary drawing, resource distribution, and patterned interactions. A relational or transactional perspective encourages an analysis of these constitutive processes—rather than assuming static existing "entities"—by recognizing that "the very terms or units involved in a transaction derive their meaning, significance, and identity from the (changing) functional roles they play within the transaction."[46] Categories of "Black" and "white," criminal and noncriminal, worthy and undeserving, and the like are social and political constructs that are legible through their contrasts. Distinctions between these categories can be blurry, overlapping, or shifting, and the meanings attached to them vary across time and place. To understand the ongoing institutional production of sociospatial difference through policing and other institutions, we need to examine multiple presumed racial and spatial categories and ask how the boundaries and differences between them emerge and endure.

Such an inquiry can help us see how policing is implicated in racial formation—"the sociohistorical process by which racial categories are created, inhabited, transformed, and destroyed."[47] Scholars have long understood race as a socially constructed and evolving concept used to "divide populations, define the terms of their relations, and subject them to different modes of governance."[48] The police and the broader criminal justice apparatus participate in constructing racial difference, meaning, and hierarchy through their practices. Legal actors sort citizens into institutionalized racial categories.[49] This classification lays the foundation for divergent routine encounters that communicate messages about who counts as a citizen in full standing and who will be subject to routine surveillance and punishment.[50] Experiences of disparate policing solidify racial differences in attitudes toward the state, and even racial identities themselves, by enhancing the perception that race is salient to individual and collective fates.[51] Contact with the criminal justice system and its collateral consequences reify racial hierarchies by driving inequalities in many other realms, from employment to housing to health.[52] Official crime statistics and databases generated by police departments naturalize racial difference, when many such statistics amplify prior surveillance patterns or capture discretionary enforcement practices that often target race- and class-subjugated communities.[53] The manifold racial consequences of policing result from contingent institutional priorities and spatially embedded practices. This book focuses on how such priorities and practices in policing contribute to the ongoing construction of spatial and racial categories and boundaries.

Redistricting as a Window into Institutional Logics and Practices

Police redistricting reforms render many oft-hidden assumptions in policing administration explicit. Redistricting reforms are literal cases of "boundary work": these reforms identify contingent and possibly contested symbolic boundaries between places and then institutionalize them as administrative boundaries that impact resource distribution.[54] Moreover, redistricting requires police executives to define the role and function of the police. These reforms operationalize police work in an era when strategies and priorities can vary widely, from community-based policing and neighborhood problem-solving to aggressive investigatory stops to rapid response to calls for service.[55] Thus, redistricting offers insights into how officials define the work of the police within heterogeneous and unequal urban landscapes. Because redistricting affects neighborhoods and may require the approval of other city entities, it is also a site where pressures from the surrounding political-economic field enter into police administration. Powerful stakeholders or grassroots community groups attempt to influence police administrators with varying degrees of success. Once undertaken, redistricting creates work environments that substantially shape day-to-day police-citizen encounters. Districts define the geographic scope and workload of patrol officers, and the criminal and social conditions within a district can produce distinct normative expectations and styles of policing.[56] District boundaries can thus give rise to unique systems of policing within the same jurisdiction.

In focusing on redistricting, this book contributes to a literature that sees widely legitimated institutional practices, rather than individual biases, as central to racial outcomes in policing. For instance, in *Pulled Over*, Charles Epp, Steven Maynard-Moody, and Donald Haider-Markel describe how the scripts and procedures associated with investigatory police stops (as opposed to traffic safety stops) produce patterned racial differences in stop experiences: Black drivers are disproportionately subject to stops seeking out "suspicious" activity.[57] Similarly, the sociologist Amada Armenta illustrates how laws and organizational practices associated with the 287(g) program implicate local police in racialized immigration enforcement, even as officers maintain that their work is colorblind.[58] Scholarship in this vein highlights the significance of the meso-level in shaping racial inequality.[59]

I build on this research through an analysis across macro-, meso-, and micro-levels of social organization. I connect macro-level structural attributes of the urban environment, such as racial segregation and socioeconomic inequality, to the development of meso-level organizational priorities and practices in policing. Police institutional decisions subsequently shape micro-level interactions between officers and citizens. In turn, patterns in routine practices reconfigure the macro-level structural character of neighborhoods. Police-citizen interactions communicate messages about whether a place is safe or dangerous, secure or threatening, further defining the experiences and meanings attached to place.

In sum, this book extends typical accounts of racial and spatial variation in policing in several ways. First, I move beyond a single level of social organization toward the interactions across levels to highlight how institutional practices contribute to racial outcomes in policing. Second, I look beyond the policing of marginalized communities to the policing of dominant communities, showing how the two are integral to each other and to the relational construction of neighborhoods themselves. Finally, I look past the logics of contemporary policing strategies and toward the logics of urban governance and economic development to describe the current role of the police in the city. These combined insights provide new lenses for investigating racial inequality in policing and in segregated urban space more generally.

Studying Policing and Growth Politics in a Segregated City

"River City" is a pseudonym for one of many segregated, postindustrial urban centers of the Rust Belt. The city has a nearly equal ratio of Black to white residents, who constitute a vast majority of the population. It also includes a growing Hispanic population and a small Asian and Asian American population. These groups live in relative separation from one another; their spatial distribution reflects a confluence of factors, including the timing of migration and immigration flows, the development of the city's built environment and the socioeconomic resources of newcomers, and discriminatory policies and practices that limited residential options for nonwhite populations. River City's stark history of Black-white segregation typifies the trajectories experienced by industrial centers throughout the Rust Belt. The city experienced growth sustained by the industrial sector through the 1960s, followed by the decline accompanying economic transformation. As Black Americans migrated to the city, housing discrimination produced and entrenched residential segregation patterns. The spatial inequalities associated with segregation compounded with suburbanization and deindustrialization. Unemployment and poverty rates grew in predominantly Black neighborhoods. Mass incarceration affected these same communities by drawing many Black men into the criminal justice system. By the 2000s, the city was characterized by deep Black-white racial disparities across nearly every sector, including employment, education, and incarceration.

The River City Police Department's redistricting reform presented a compelling opportunity to examine how the police responded to the exigencies of this segregated landscape and how their responses further shaped urban space. I explore the redistricting and its consequences through process tracing, a method that examines how events unfold to result in particular outcomes within a historical case. Process tracing focuses on key political actors, provides rich description of various points in time, and identifies the mechanisms that link intervening moments.[60] It is facilitated by triangulation among several data sources and the testing of "diagnostic evidence" against preliminary accounts.[61] This study draws on several forms of data that connect initial conditions, organizational decisions, and eventual outcomes.

I began my inquiry into the redistricting with a review of publicly available materials including media accounts, documentation from public meetings, and other reports and evaluations of the police department. Public records capture two important facets of the redistricting and its aftermath. First, they reflect the official organizational logic driving the police department's reforms, as communicated to other powerful stakeholders. For instance, the chief of police presented the redistricting plan before two governing bodies: the Safety Committee of the City Council and the Civilian Review Board, a public entity that oversees the police department's administration. These meetings' video footage and minutes include stated motivations for the reform and its approval process. Second, documents like news articles and evaluations represent widely circulating public endorsements and critiques of the police department's strategic choices.

I delved further into the motives and interests that drove the redistricting and policing strategies in its aftermath through in-depth interviews with thirty-seven decision-makers and stakeholders. I first sought to access the police executives and city officials who had most directly driven the reform. I shortly found that many elected officials perceived the reform as a top-down, technocratic initiative—attributed to the chief of police, even though it had been reviewed by the City Council and approved by the Civilian Review Board. I interviewed fourteen representatives from these public entities, including two of the police executives who directed the reform. Interviews capture the goals and processes of the reform, as well as the interests, stakes, and pressures driving the police department's initiatives. I contextualized the organizational goals of the police department by comparing them to a broader landscape of interests that I described through additional interviews with twenty-three representatives of agencies serving neighborhoods across the city. These agencies included neighborhood associations, business improvement districts, housing or economic-development agencies, community centers, and youth-serving organizations. My interviews focused on evaluations of the redistricting, local policing initiatives, and police service more generally. By including community representatives with a stake in policing, I could compare the priorities centered by the police department to the needs and interests of groups across the city.

Next, I examined the development of local policing strategies through an ethnographic comparison of the East District and the West District. I provide a detailed account of this project's ethnographic component in the methodological appendix at the end of this book. There, I describe how I gained permission from the highest levels of the police administration to observe and how I navigated my relationship with the police department over time. I delve into my role as a nonparticipant observer during ride-alongs, and I reflect on what my presence meant for interactions with officers and civilians. I also situate myself in the project personally, as a multiracial Asian American woman, and politically, as an individual with her own assumptions and subjectivities. I provide a candid account of epistemological and ethical questions that I faced over the course of the project, many of which attended to the complexities of researching powerful entities and individuals, or "studying up."[62] By detailing these choices in the appendix, I offer additional context for evaluating my findings and conclusions.

I selected the East District and the West District because they emerged as central to decision-makers' accounts of the redistricting process. While the redistricting had also affected two other districts in the city, much of the official discourse circulated around the importance of the East and West Districts. Beyond their emergent substantive significance, these districts offered compelling opportunities for comparison. The two districts were relatively comparable in geographic size, population, and residential land-use patterns. Yet they diverged considerably along demographic lines: the East District had the highest proportion of white residents of any of the city's districts, while the West District had the highest proportion of Black residents. The average assessed property value in the East District was more than four times that in the West District. While the East District included middle-class and affluent areas, the West District contained some of the city's poorest neighborhoods. These two districts represented two sides of the city's stark segregation and typified the dynamics underlying the logic of the department's reforms.

Black-white distinctions emerged as particularly enduring and powerful in my preliminary investigations into the way space was understood, experienced, and regulated in River City, so my selection of the

East District and the West District resulted in a focus on Black-white dynamics.[63] This focus does not suggest that the multifaceted relationships between policing, urban inequality, and race can or should be understood solely in Black and white terms. Indigenous, Latinx, and Asian American communities have also been subjected to myriad state projects rooted in spatial exclusion and containment, and they have had fraught relationships with the police.[64] Read alongside work that examines the experiences of other minoritized communities, the case of Black-white dynamics in River City adds to a growing account of how policing and segregation contribute to processes of racialization and racial subordination.

Indeed, by comparing the East District and the West District ethnographically, I could unveil the links between citywide policing priorities that interpolated growth politics and on-the-ground practices that reinscribed racial inequalities. I focused on organizational processes like (1) how the goals of local policing manifested themselves in district-level priorities and resource allocations, (2) how these priorities and resources structured the daily work of officers, and (3) how officers made sense of the people and places they encountered. In describing these pathways, I sought to document the processes through which power and governance were exercised. Hence, my primary focus during fieldwork was on the activities and attitudes of the police instead of the people they policed. I describe this decision further in the methodological appendix.

After I gained permission to observe, I began regularly visiting each district and scheduling ride-alongs with officers and supervisors. To describe the activities occurring in each district as thoroughly as possible, I sought to observe across as many different types of units and assignments. Between August 2014 and August 2015, I conducted a total of seventy-five ride-alongs, approximating five hundred hours of observation. I alternated between the districts on a weekly basis to capture seasonal variation over the year. I observed across all shifts and geographic sectors in both districts, and I rode along with officers engaged in several kinds of units and work: patrol officers responding to calls for service, community-based policing initiatives, and special deployments that only operated within each district. In order to situate officers' daily work within district-level processes like priority setting, scheduling, and communication, I interviewed district captains and the lieutenants who oversaw each shift. I also shadowed sergeants, who supervised officers on the street. By observing across the chain of command, I captured how department-level priorities filtered down to street-level practices.

During my ride-alongs, I shadowed a total of sixty-one individuals. Most were white. Five were Black, seven were Latinx, and two were Asian American. I observed twelve women and forty-nine men. Demographically, this group reflected the police department's general composition: approximately 65 percent white, 15 percent Hispanic, 20 percent Black, and just over 80 percent male.[65] Because shift assignments varied with seniority, I encountered officers with wide-ranging degrees of experience, from day-shift officers with decades on the job to officers in their first year of policing. Many officers had grown up in the city or the surrounding suburbs and identified as having working-class or middle-class backgrounds. As I rode with these officers, I aimed to capture the nature of their perspectives on the work. Officers' eight-hour shifts permitted a great deal of talk, ranging from casual conversation to semistructured interviewing. I learned about officers' career histories, experiences in the district, perceptions of social and criminal problems, and comparisons between their district and other parts of the city. In addition, officers often explained their decision-making processes. This talk revealed how the police described and interpreted their work, providing an opportunity to compare perceptions to situated actions.

While observing, I jotted notes that expanded into typed fieldnotes when I returned home. These fieldnotes captured all the activities that the officer engaged in and paraphrased our conversations. I did not audio-record ride-alongs in most cases. While the nuances of discussion might have been lost, this method facilitated more open conversation, particularly given some officers' displeasure with how the police were already recorded by the public and by their supervisors. Given the structure of the ethnographic data, I generally paraphrase discussions; quotations should be interpreted as very close approximations of an individual's words rather than verbatim quotes. Overall, the ethnographic fieldwork provided an in-depth picture of how officers' routines and attitudes were shaped by district-level priorities and the unique conditions of their work environments. By contextualizing these findings in relation to other sources, I forge links between the political economy of the city, the institutional evolution of policing strategy, and everyday realities of police work.

As a brief note, I am often asked whether my presence as a researcher altered what officers did and said in ways that preclude an accurate representation of police work. While I delve more deeply into this question in the methodological appendix, I will note that I did encounter evidence that officers' routine work was occasionally altered in organizational and normative ways when I was around. In general, I assumed that my presence reduced the likelihood that officers would exhibit socially unacceptable behaviors or attitudes. Yet, even assuming this, I was able to see and hear a great deal. Indeed, I was often surprised by how forthcoming the police could be in conversation with me and by the way their interactions with civilians seemed to unfold in relation to enduring scripts and imperatives. Given my overarching interests in organizational processes, rather than officers' potential hidden biases, I am certain that the ethnographic data answers major questions about the conditions of work within each district. I ultimately observed several institutional practices that contributed to widening racialized inequalities in policing, even if my observations were limited in some regards.

The final empirical aspect of this project situates the case of River City within the broader national landscape of police reform. Working with a student research assistant, I analyzed twenty-first-century police redistricting reforms in dozens of major cities. We searched for publicly available materials on police redistricting in the fifty largest cities in the United States. These materials include, among other things, official documents from police departments and local governments; reports prepared by academics and consultants; media articles and op-eds; documentation from public meetings; and neighborhood association newsletters and minutes. In total, we found information on forty-two implemented, planned, or proposed police redistricting reforms in thirty-four cities. I use this data to shed light on what is distinct about the River City Police Department's redistricting reform, while highlighting shared underlying connections between police administration and contemporary urban governance.

Overview of the Book

What follows in this book is an account of the way the River City Police Department responded to and participated in the growth politics of the city, shaping segregated neighborhoods and enforcing their boundaries in the process. Chapter 1 situates River City in a broader historical trajectory, tracing the dynamics that laid the foundations for augmented inequalities in the policing of Black and white neighborhoods. I argue that these foundations emerged through a convergence on the idea of "the local" in both urban governance and policing strategy. As police departments increasingly focus on tailoring their activities to particular neighborhoods, they are susceptible to pressures from growth coalitions that push for ever more investment into "valuable" areas. Urban revitalization projects intersect with historical patterns of racial segregation and discrimination, often to the effect of widening inequalities between neighborhoods. This chapter describes how popular policing reforms can ironically invite the retrenchment of spatial and racial inequities by forging new links between the police and the political, economic, and racial interests of urban governance.

Chapter 2 describes the promises and pitfalls of the River City redistricting reform. It begins by explaining the significance of the police district as an administrative and geographic unit. It then accounts for the easy success of the reform in River City. The redistricting was one of many changes undertaken by the new chief of police that were rooted in the shift toward community-based policing and problem-oriented policing. Police executives explained that aligning district boundaries with neighborhood lines would enable tailored approaches to local problems. This logic found widespread buy-in from public officials across the city. However, the redistricting also contained the seeds of further disparate policing. It provided a framework for devoting *more* resources to the new "low-crime" districts. Powerful stakeholders saw the downtown and middle-class residential neighborhoods in the East District as vital to the economic and social fate of the city. Police executives embraced an active role in protecting and serving these areas. By contrast, widely circulating discourses emphasized problems of violence in the new "high-crime" districts. Divergent district-level priorities and resources set the stage for policing practices that eventually amplified the divisions between segregated neighborhoods.

Subsequent chapters describe how on-the-ground policing further configured segregated neighborhoods and enforced and defined the boundaries between them. Chapter 3 traces the ties between urban development goals and practices in the East District, including rapid and thorough police response to citizens' calls for service, police collaborations with neighborhood associations, and a special deployment in the downtown entertainment corridors. These practices shared an economic logic. Responsive service and neighborhood problem-solving sought to retain a middle-class and affluent residential tax base, while special deployments aimed to cultivate a downtown that is desirable to conventions, tourists, and developers. Policing priorities and resource allocations in the East District cohered around a community-service ethos that explicitly—and, many would say, effectively—contributed to the city's growth project.

However, as argued in chapter 4, cultivating these areas of consumption and residential comfort in the East District resulted in corollary projects of suppression and neglect in the West District. Policing in the West District took on a fragmented and layered approach in which several different policing modalities overlayed the same geography, subjecting district residents to many different kinds of potential encounters with the police. While the district's community policing unit made inroads, the emphasis on violent crime corresponded to a proactive strategy of investigatory stops that impacted many residents and, ultimately, heightened racial tensions. The West District also did not have proportional allocations of patrol officers given its high volume of calls. Officers described an exhausting and relentless workload, while residents noted long response times and flagging service. In the aggregate, policing in the West District amplified residents' sense that their neighborhoods were simultaneously overpoliced and underprotected. In tracing widening disparities between districts, these chapters highlight the relational nature of racialized policing outcomes.

Following this account of the way district-level policing further crafted segregated neighborhoods, chapter 5 explores how policing practices were implicated in defining and enforcing the boundaries of segregation. While the police insisted that their work was race neutral,

I watched them pay attention to "race out of place." The police collaborated with private establishments to exclude, contain, and control Black people in the city's downtown entertainment corridor; officers marked Black bodies entering predominantly white spaces and potential sources of criminal threat and disorder; and organizational practices in routine traffic enforcement targeted vehicles that signaled race and class. Police scrutiny of Black people in the downtown revealed that the city's revitalization was not for everyone. Ideas of commercial viability, worth, and order, on the one hand, and those of threat, criminality, and disorder, on the other, mapped onto *people*, as well as places. Hence, projects of spatial regulation in service of political-economic goals were also projects of racial regulation.

Chapter 6 focuses on the policing of white people in the West District to show how segregation as a social structure simultaneously endures and shifts. Proactive officers assumed that white people in predominantly Black neighborhoods were drug users who could be turned into confidential informants. They drew on segregation as a heuristic that problematized any boundary crossing. However, not all white people in the West District were considered to be "out of place." In a gentrified, predominantly white neighborhood on the edge of the West District, residents sought to define their neighborhood as more akin to those in the East District. They drew on common narratives that distinguished between places of economic value and those afflicted by crime to do so. The neighborhood association's successful advocacy for additional police service within the West District showed that segregation boundaries could shift and the meanings and resources that maintained material inequalities between Black and white neighborhoods would follow. Collectively, these chapters highlight the role of the police in ongoing articulation of the boundaries and realities of racial segregation. Segregation, policing, and urban growth projects all reinforced distinctions between places of whiteness, value, and worthiness, versus those of Blackness, criminal threat, and civic noncontribution.

The book concludes by reiterating central empirical and theoretical contributions. As the police participate in postindustrial urban growth politics, their activities contribute to the dynamic and relational production of racial segregation and its attendant material and symbolic inequalities. While this book focuses on River City, evidence from police redistricting reforms in other cities highlights pervasive ties between police administrative decisions and neoliberal urban governance. This reality has meant that the police play many different roles in cities; they are called up to be community problem-solvers, crime fighters, and service providers. Various organizational barriers in River City contributed to the uneven distribution of these roles across urban space, and the conclusion identifies potential leverage points for change within policing. But it also invites broader questions of the way cities manage structural inequalities and the way they could move toward racial and economic redress. It suggests that, ultimately, many answers may lay beyond the police.

1

Urban Governance, Policing, and the Making of a Segregated City

The story of police redistricting and strategic innovation in River City would vex police reformers. How did a police department that appeared to embrace cutting-edge and progressive strategies produce intensified racialized policing? This chapter traces the foundations laid for increased inequalities in the policing of Black and white neighborhoods. I argue that a central part of this story lies in the links between urban governance and policing, which have both converged around an idea of *the local* in recent decades. Shifts in the political economy have made cities and the neighborhoods within them key sites of governance and growth, while reforms within policing have opened the door for place-based regulation in service of political-economic interests. These trends emerged at the intersection of global economic shifts, national and local political projects, and distinct regional histories that simultaneously transcend and situate River City as a specific site.

In urban governance, the rise of the local reflects shifting relations between various levels of the state. While the federal government had a heavy hand in urban life through much of the twentieth century, it retracted aid to cities with the turn toward neoliberalism in the 1970s and 1980s. In the midst of fiscal and social crises stemming from deindustrialization, cities became primary sites of governance and economic development. Many fundamental state functions are carried out at the local level, and municipal governments have become increasingly reliant on securing their own financial prospects. These dynamics have elevated the importance of place and produced a system of subnational mercantilism in which urban growth coalitions compete to render their specific cities attractive to mobile entrepreneurial and creative classes. In this context of local governance, place-making and place-marketing efforts focus on specific spaces *within* the city—often downtowns, gentrifying neighborhoods, entertainment districts, and other spaces thought capable of generating economic value. Thus, the differences between neighborhoods are particularly salient in urban growth politics. Localism simultaneously elevates city governments as key actors and targets governance priorities toward specific localities within the city.[1]

Meanwhile, policing has also embraced the idea of the neighborhood in recent decades. Policing in the United States has always been highly fragmented: separate departments cover thousands of city, county, state, and federal jurisdictions. Beyond being local in this sense, contemporary innovations in policing concentrate on neighborhoods *within* a jurisdiction. Historically, policing strategy in the United States has been characterized by a pendulum-like swing between two poles of citywide and centralized, on the one hand, and decentralized and neighborhood-based, on the other. Current strategic innovations like community policing and problem-oriented policing embrace the latter and elevate the preeminence of place. These innovations hold that as neighborhood problems vary, the police should tailor their activities accordingly. Many scholars, organizers, and police executives see place-based strategies like community policing as an opportunity for police to redress legacies of unequal treatment by responding to residents' needs in marginalized neighborhoods. The shift toward local policing indicates an openness to reforms leading to greater democratic inclusion.[2]

Yet police reform does not preclude the retrenchment of racial inequities. Reform efforts often target the shortcomings of the previous era's spatial arrangements, but new spatial methods also invite new hazards. The focus on the local has opened the door for affinities between urban growth coalitions and policing. As the police aim to be more responsive to surrounding communities, visions of place emanating from the city's most powerful stakeholders can be interpolated into strategic priorities. Neighborhood-based approaches risk reproducing and reinforcing the symbolic meanings and material inequalities that have long characterized segregated urban space.

Indeed, in River City, as in cities across the Rust Belt, the context and consequences of localism cannot be separated from the realities of entrenched Black-white racial segregation and its accompanying social and economic disparities. In northern industrial cities, race was encoded onto urban space through decades of discriminatory policies and practices. Segregation reflected the country's legacy of anti-Black racism, and it defined unequal opportunity structures that shaped generations of city residents. The inequalities between Black and white neighborhoods morphed alongside processes like suburbanization, urban renewal, deindustrialization, and the rise of mass incarceration. These phenomena articulated deep divides between neighborhoods, setting the stage for contemporary local governance.[3] As urban growth coalitions and police departments respond to and seek to reconfigure distinct places, they necessarily take up racial meanings and produce racial consequences. Thus, the story of place-based policing and its ties to urban growth politics in River City begins with the origin story of the city's segregated landscape.

Constructing the Segregated City

As this section describes, segregation in Rust Belt cities emerged from overlapping economic, political, and racial projects. Economically, cities have been central sites of production and consumption since the industrial revolution, and their fates have changed along with deindustrialization and the transition to a globally networked economy. Cities have also experienced major political shifts. From the New Deal to the War on Poverty, the federal government took on an active role in social welfare provision. Redistributive policies afforded new economic opportunities in cities, but they also provided frameworks and resources that local governments and private actors used to build segregation. With the rise of neoliberalism in the 1970s, the federal government retracted aid for social welfare programs while expanding resources for punitive regulation. Local governments were increasingly left to secure their economic prospects by competing for private investment and growth. Meanwhile, the management of social problems started to fall under the purview of the criminal justice system. Race and racism inflected all these projects. Segregation, mass incarceration, and urban revitalization each have reinforced racial differences and hierarchies. Economic and political projects in cities have relied on overt discrimination and subtle mechanisms of exclusion and containment to maintain racial inequality. These intersecting economic, political, and racial projects played out in River City.

Industrialization, State Expansion, and the Rise of Racial Segregation

River City emerged as an industrial hub in the 1800s. As was the case across the country, the land where River City developed had been home to Native American tribes for centuries, and the birth of the city was preceded by the systematic dispossession of Native Peoples through treaties and land cessions.[4] Europeans initially established trading posts that expanded into permanent settlements in the early 1800s. Soon after, burgeoning local villages incorporated into a single city. The pace of growth picked up rapidly by midcentury, as River City joined in the region's industrialization. New technologies and improving transportation infrastructures facilitated flows of goods and people, linking regional cities to one another and to broader national and even global markets.[5] River City saw the development of several major industries, including metal manufacturing, agricultural product processing, textile production, and the construction of heavy machinery.[6] The city's labor pool expanded with a steady influx of newcomers; its population increased more than tenfold during the latter half of the 1800s. By the turn of the century, River City was one of many thriving urban industrial centers that drew European immigrants from many nations and a small but growing number of Black Americans.

River City's Black population increased with the broader regional influx of African American migrants from the South. Between 1910 and 1970, millions left to escape a stagnating economy and the violence of Jim Crow. In the aftermath of the Civil War and the demise of Reconstruction, southern states developed new legal, economic, and social systems to maintain rigid racial hierarchies. The sharecropping system reproduced plantation relations, as African Americans were tied through tenantry to land owned by whites. The social and legal codes of Jim Crow also ensured continued white dominance by confining Black people to underserved public facilities, suppressing political participation, and criminalizing intimate interracial relations. Those who violated the rigid etiquette of this system risked vigilante attacks. Given the brutalities and degradations of the Jim Crow regime, many Black people left the South for the promise of new social and economic opportunities.[7]

Northern industrial centers were a prime destination. The world wars increased demands for labor in the Fordist manufacturing economy, opening doors that had been closed due to race. Prior to World War I, the small Black population in River City had been relegated to domestic and common labor through racial discrimination and the steady arrival of European immigrants. After the war, Black workers gradually gained tenuous footholds in the city's industrial economy. Though the Great Depression reversed collective economic gains, demands for labor following World War II cemented access to industrial positions with an upward shift in status and wages, even as Black workers were forced into the most precarious positions in factory hierarchies. Through labor organizing and cross-class solidarities, River City's growing Black population carved out new economic and political opportunities in the city.[8]

As in-migration continued, most Black residents settled in a concentrated district, home to many community institutions.[9] The core of River City's Black belt encompassed approximately ten by ten blocks near the downtown. This neighborhood saw the development of a lively commercial corridor and nightlife scene and was home to Black businesses and professionals, from restaurants and hotels to lawyers and physicians. It also included several prominent churches, new financial institutions, and local chapters of the Urban League and the NAACP. Neighborhood accounts fondly recall its self-sufficiency and tight-knit sense of community.[10] Like other Black belts in cities throughout the region, the community offered opportunities for class mobility, political mobilization, and cultural production.[11]

But Black neighborhoods in industrial cities were also socially and spatially shaped by racial discrimination.[12] Nativist and racist ideas still circulated widely in the North, even if they were not a formal Jim Crow system. The segregation of Black-belt areas served to maintain racial boundaries and hierarchies within diversifying urban spaces.[13] It also confined Black residents to neighborhoods characterized by dilapidated housing and limited urban services and infrastructure. Governments, real estate agents, and white residents used multiple tools to enforce spatial separation. In many cities, acts of violence—including attacks of Black residents and the bombing of Black-owned homes and businesses—sought to terrorize African Americans out of white neighborhoods.[14] Beyond overt racial brutality, a variety of discriminatory practices in government policy, urban planning, and real estate ghettoized Black urbanites and laid the groundwork for enduring racial segregation patterns.[15]

Though many actors participated in constructing segregation in River City, the federal government played an essential role through policies that enabled scores of middle-class white families to become home owners while systematically undermining investments in Black neighborhoods. One such policy was redlining. New Deal–era programs established the Home Owners' Loan Corporation (HOLC) to assist families facing foreclosure by refinancing mortgages and facilitating home ownership. To assess the risk of default on a loan, the HOLC developed color-coded "residential security maps" designating risk based on neighborhood characteristics like the quality of housing stock, proximity to environmental hazards, and resident demographics. High-risk areas were marked red on these maps. Black neighborhoods were systematically redlined, driving huge racial gaps in home ownership, wealth accumulation, and overall neighborhood investment.[16] River City's residential security map clearly shows the redlining of the Black belt and adjacent areas.[17] Assessment notes described these neighborhoods as slum areas and as old and ragged; they also explicitly cited status as a "Negro" area as a factor relevant to risk.[18] Such federal guidelines contributed to the economic marginalization of the Black belt and its residents.

Meanwhile, government policies facilitated the growth of the suburbs and white flight. The Federal Housing Administration (FHA), established in 1934, insured bank-issued loans for first-time homebuyers. The FHA prioritized lending in newly built suburbs and subdivisions, and racial homogeneity factored into its evaluations of risk. The FHA's *Underwriting Manual* instructed assessors to give higher ratings to neighborhoods protected against "adverse influences," including "lower class occupancy, and inharmonious racial groups."[19] Following World War II, the GI Bill and the newly established department of Veterans Affairs (VA) offered guaranteed mortgages for returning veterans. However, VA appraisers relied on the same FHA *Underwriting Manual* in making loan determinations, largely excluding Black service members from these benefits. Federal policies contributed to the growth of white suburban neighborhoods in metro areas around the country. In River City, a ring of such communities grew around the outskirts of the city center. Rather than face annexation into River City, these communities incorporated into their own municipalities, establishing independent local governments and creating new forms of segregation boundaries.[20]

Indeed, racial exclusion was a defining feature of burgeoning white neighborhoods and towns, facilitated by private agreements among developers, real estate agents, and home owners. By 1940, racially restrictive covenants covered the vast majority of suburbs surrounding River City.[21] Restrictive covenants in deeds outlined home buyers' obligations to preserve neighborhood property values. While requirements could address permissible uses of the property, paint colors, and landscaping, some explicitly forbid selling or leasing property to anyone not of the white race.[22] These private agreements intersected with public investments shaped by federal lending guidelines. One of the first subdivisions in the River City metro area to include a clause limiting the sale or lease of property to people of "white race" alone in its property deed was given an "A" rating by the HOLC. The area was marked in green on a residential security map on the basis of its exclusive status, designating it as low-risk and encouraging lending.[23] Public and private discrimination converged to produce new landscapes of inequality, with emergent divisions between developing suburbs and declining urban cores.

Though housing discrimination was formally outlawed by the Fair Housing Act in 1968, urban planning practices continued to amplify segregation patterns in the River City metro area. Many suburban communities turned to exclusionary zoning. Land-use regulations outlining lot sizes, housing density, and other requirements prioritized single-family over multifamily housing, restricting residential access for low- and middle-income residents.[24] As suburban residents fought to retain the exclusivity of their neighborhoods, residents in River City's urban core faced new threats. Across the country, local governments labeled neighborhoods as "blighted" and targeted them for projects of urban renewal and highway construction.[25] Thousands of houses in River City—a majority in the Black belt—were torn down in the 1960s.[26] With support from federal programs, the city built an interstate highway through the heart of the community, displacing many of its Black residents.[27] Moreover, the city's public housing, which had once served working-class families in predominantly white neighborhoods, shifted to concentrate low-income housing in marginalized, predominantly Black areas.[28] Collectively, the many institutional projects that built River City's racial segregation paved the way for additional divisions to arise with subsequent political-economic shifts.

Deindustrialization, State Retraction, and the Rise of Mass Incarceration

Profound transformations accompanying deindustrialization reconfigured urban landscapes beginning in the late 1960s. To lower costs of production, corporations began to relocate from traditional manufacturing centers to rural and suburban areas and, as the economy globalized through neoliberalization, to other countries. Changes in technology produced new jobs and made others obsolete. The manufacturing sector declined, and the service sector expanded. These developments reshaped labor-market opportunities.[29] Fordist mass production had offered blue-collar employment and job ladders that could provide stable earnings for low-skilled workers. By contrast, service-sector jobs tended to stratify. New technologies and advanced services in finance, computing, health services, and the like required workers with higher levels of education and training. Meanwhile, low-wage service-industry work in hospitality, retail, and other sectors lacked the protections of unionization, which had declined along with manufacturing, leaving workers in more economically precarious positions.[30] Deindustrialization was felt acutely in the River City area, which lost over three-quarters of its industrial jobs. This had profound economic effects: between 1980 and 2010, median household income decreased by over 25 percent, and the percentage of the city's population living below the federal poverty line nearly doubled.[31]

As in many other postindustrial cities, these effects were experienced unevenly. As the sociologist William Julius Wilson explains, predominantly Black inner-city communities were particularly hard hit. Many working-class African Americans had relied on factory work and found themselves shut out of emerging sectors that required advanced education and technical training. As a consequence, joblessness rates rose. Middle-class Black residents began to leave the city for the suburbs, concentrating problems of divestment, unemployment, and poverty in the central city.[32] In alignment with these regional trends, River City's

Black male population experienced plummeting employment, and Black communities saw accompanying social challenges following the decline of manufacturing. The employment rate for Black men of working age in the metro area fell continuously from around 85 percent in 1970 to around 50 percent four decades later. By 2010, the Black poverty rate in the River City metro area was over four times that of the white poverty rate. More than one-third of Black residents lived in neighborhoods with a poverty rate greater than 40 percent.[33] River City became the epitome of the widening racial and spatial divides of cities in decline.

Alongside these global economic transformations, national political shifts triggered a concerted rollback of federal aid to cities. From the New Deal through the postwar period and the War on Poverty, federal-government policies and programs had actively emphasized social welfare provision (though, as the previous subsection makes clear, benefits were not equitably distributed along racial lines). Interventions viewed a robust and redistributive welfare state as central to economic growth, drawing on Keynesian principles to regulate markets and maintain consumer demand.[34] The rise of neoliberalism and its ideological penetration into governments at all levels during the 1970s and 1980s dismantled key pillars of Keynesian welfarism. In contrast to the interventionist state, neoliberalism rested on "the belief that open, competitive and unregulated markets, liberated from state interference and the actions of social collectivities, represent the optimal mechanism for socioeconomic development."[35] Beginning with the Nixon presidency, the federal government scaled back many social programs that had aided city residents. In the 1980s, the Reagan administration eliminated commitments for subsidized housing construction, restricted eligibility for means-tested programs like Aid to Families with Dependent Children and Food Stamps, and otherwise attacked social expenditures. Welfare-state retrenchment was legitimized amid the federal government's push to promote free-market enterprise through reduced domestic spending and deregulation.[36]

In other areas, however, the federal government expanded its role in cities. During these same decades, political projects reframed problems associated with concentrating urban poverty as best addressed by the criminal justice system.[37] The new logics of carceral governance had an overtly racial character. In the aftermath of the civil rights movement, elected officials in the South characterized civil-disobedience tactics as "criminal" and laid the groundwork for a racially coded "law and order" rhetoric that would motivate punitive policies for decades to follow.[38] Beginning in the 1960s, urban unrest across the country gave conservatives further opportunity to crystallize linkages between race, place, and crime. The presidential campaigns of Barry Goldwater, Richard Nixon, and Ronald Reagan constructed these discourses nationally, translating into policies that greatly expanded law enforcement funding.[39] Political accounts framed crime and poverty as rooted in the cultural shortcoming of the poor rather than in structural conditions and legacies of racial discrimination. This explanation of inner-city dynamics found widespread popular support. Following the election of Reagan and the initiation of the War on Drugs, politicians and the media focused on crack cocaine as emblematic of urban pathologies. By the 1990s, public concern about crime and drugs was pervasive, and politicians across the political spectrum embraced punitive policies: more investments in policing, three-strikes and habitual-offender provisions, truth-in-sentencing laws, and many others. These post-civil-rights-era developments ultimately reconfigured US crime control and gave rise to mass incarceration.[40]

Between 1980 and 2016, the US prison population increased by nearly 500 percent.[41] The United States surpassed all other nations in both its absolute scope and rate of incarceration. Studies showed that, in the twenty-first century, the United States accounted for 20 to 25 percent of the world's prisoners and incarcerated at rates of between 600 and 750 per 100,000 people.[42] The total number of individuals under correctional-system control—either in prison, jail, or community supervision—grew from approximately 1.8 million individuals in 1980 to over 6.6 million in 2016.[43] Within these stark trends, even starker patterns of racial disparity emerged. By 2018, over 60 percent of those who were incarcerated were people of color. The rate of incarceration for Black men was nearly six times that of white men, and the rate for Latino men was more than two and a half times that of whites. Black men born in 2001 had a one-in-three lifetime likelihood of imprisonment.[44] Incarceration became a common feature of the life course for many young men in race- and class-subjugated communities.[45]

Racial patterns in policing and incarceration reflected practices that were unevenly distributed across urban space. For instance, despite no evidence of significant racial differences in rates of drug use, drug enforcement concentrated on open-air drug markets in disadvantaged minority neighborhoods instead of the trafficking occurring behind closed doors in middle-class white communities.[46] Large-scale criminalization produced spatial consequences by further eroding the social and economic foundations of marginalized neighborhoods. Imprisonment corresponded to an array of collateral consequences: weakened labor-market outcomes, disrupted family life, depressed political and civic participation, and even greater community instability.[47] The political constructions of criminal threat and the structural inequalities attendant to inner-city life increased the likelihood of incarceration, and incarceration, in turn, compounded neighborhood disadvantage. Beyond the material consequences of these coconstitutive dynamics, they bolstered long-standing symbolic associations, particularly those that linked predominantly Black neighborhoods to crime and disorder.[48] In short, the impacts of racial residential segregation and racialized mass incarceration found mutual reinforcement: the ghetto and the prison acted as two poles of a "carceral continuum" between which residents of marginalized Black neighborhoods circulated.[49]

River City exemplified these broader trends playing out across the country. Bolstered by the rise of tough-on-crime policies, county-level incarceration levels for Black men increased fourfold between 1990 and the early 2000s. Drug enforcement drove much of this growth; Black men were over 80 percent of those who were sentenced for drug crimes. Some estimates held that over half of working-age Black men were or had been incarcerated between 1990 and 2010.[50] The impacts of the carceral state were also felt by the area's burgeoning Latinx population, which tripled in size over the same decades, even as it continued to constitute a small fraction of River City's total population. Hispanic-white segregation levels in the city remained high, and predominantly Latinx neighborhoods also experienced lagging household incomes and high levels of poverty. While the rate of incarceration of Black men in the state dwarfed others, the rate of incarceration for Latino men was nearly eight times that of the white male incarceration rate in 1990 and remained over double the rate for whites by 2010.[51] The expansion of the punitive arm of the state, combined with the federal government's retraction of redistributive social programs and the economic devastations of deindustrialization, solidified social inequalities between River City's segregated neighborhoods.

Neoliberal Urbanism, State Dis-Integration, and the Rise of Urban Revitalization

As postindustrial decline wreaked havoc across the Rust Belt, cities grappled with how to remain viable. Their fortunes had been seriously destabilized by rising unemployment and concentrated poverty, the exodus of a middle-class tax base, and the devolution of social spending from federal to state and local levels. The dis-integration of urban governance at the national level left cities to essentially fend for themselves. Local governments became a primary locus of public services; democratic mayors across the country continued to support social programs, which their constituents needed more than ever.[52] However, political-economic shifts had undermined the resources cities had to offer these services and rendered them increasingly vulnerable to fiscal crises. As one response to such crises, municipal governments pursued austerity measures by cutting public services.[53] But cities also turned to entrepreneurial development as a means of salvaging their economic prospects.[54] In the context of deregulation and reliance on free-market enterprise, a system of "subnational mercantilism" emerged, with state and local governments competing to attract investments and jobs.[55] Just as cities were the primary loci of Fordist-Keynesian systems of production, they became the "institutional and geographic forefront of neoliberal rollout programs."[56]

The transition to neoliberal urbanism invited emergent inequalities between cities. Industrial centers in the Northeast and Midwest were particularly hard hit by the decline of manufacturing. The ten largest cities in 1950—almost all in the Rust Belt—experienced dramatic population loss, shrinking per capita income, and plummeting housing values as a consequence. However, while these cities declined, a handful of major cities emerged as central to the new economic landscape.[57] The rise of globalized markets for finance and specialized services required sites to manage flows of information and capital. The sociologist Saskia Sassen describes these places as "global cities": key nodes within a networked world economy that serve as both marketplaces for high-end services and production sites for information and technology innovations.[58] Cities like New York, Los Angeles, and Boston experienced growth throughout the 1980s and 1990s.[59] The success of global cities ignited a vision of urban development that saw globalization as a reality to which cities needed to adapt.[60] As intracity inequalities grew, leaders in the Rust Belt adopted this model of urban growth and began fighting for a place in a globally networked economy.

Urban-revitalization efforts were spearheaded by growth coalitions, or "growth machines" that were "interlocking progrowth associations and government units," including the mayor's office, City Council, real estate developers, urban planners, and business leaders, among others.[61] Growth coalitions sought to enhance the exchange value of place by constructing and transforming the built and social environment.[62] Redevelopment projects focused on attracting entrepreneurial developers and, as prescribed by the urban scholar Richard Florida's influential work,[63] appealing to the "creative class" at the heart of knowledge-based and technology industries. To court this ultramobile population, growth coalitions emphasized the development of high-end urban amenities. The city was to become an "entertainment machine" that catered to a consumer class.[64] Growth discourse singularly emphasized "the establishment of posh neighborhoods, high technology growth nodes, elite culture districts, and conspicuous consumption retail zones."[65] Many Rust Belt cities pursued this growth model, and the proliferation of downtown redevelopment, high-end housing, and historic-preservation projects attest to this trend.

While efforts to recover from economic and social decline aimed to lessen the divides between cities, they depended on widening divides *within* cities.[66] Local governments, urban planners, and developers in Rust Belt cities faced resource constraints and turned to strategies of urban triage or uneven development. Strategic uneven development channeled investments toward more robust areas, marking declining neighborhoods as unsalvageable and relegating them to further neglect.[67] Municipal-government officials and private developers framed such triage as necessary and, ultimately, good for the entire city—the entrepreneurial growth spurred by the revitalization of targeted areas could renew the city's tax base and resources, eventually providing for widespread economic recovery.[68] Discursively, stakeholders framed investment as the inverse of "blight": it could spread from one neighborhood to surrounding areas, to the benefit of all.

However, in practice, strategies of uneven investment and growth left marginalized neighborhoods to deteriorate further.[69] Urban triage exacerbated inequalities wrought by broader economic transformations. The decline of manufacturing and the rise of the service sector, with its high-end and low-wage structure, concentrated opportunities at the top and bottom of the economic hierarchy.[70] Rising wage inequality drove income segregation, poverty further concentrated in inner-city neighborhoods, and new affluent enclaves emerged.[71] The fate of inner-city Black neighborhoods appeared bleak. As the geographer David Wilson notes, these areas served as foils to the downtowns, entertainment districts, and high-end residential neighborhoods. While growth coalitions framed the latter as sites of exchange value and potential, media portrayals and investment patterns positioned the former as economically unproductive and civically problematic. This discourse positioned Black neighborhoods as in need of containment and control rather than reinvestment and revitalization.[72] Hence, neoliberal growth strategies reinscribed foundational associations between Blackness, poverty, and crime, versus whiteness, productivity, and value.[73]

River City's specific trajectory in the aftermath of deindustrialization followed these regional patterns. Urban redevelopment strategies initially focused on stabilizing neighborhoods. In the mid-1970s, the city was consumed by concerns about urban divestment. Local media reports warned that blight could spread to stable neighborhoods and threaten the fate of the entire city. Amid these fears, city leaders and urban planners adopted a tool for determining the state of neighborhood decline on the basis of indicators such as average assessed property values, proportions of multifamily units, and rates of vacant units. The resultant map overlaid the city's segregated landscape and classified an area including many of the city's predominantly Black neighborhoods as "barely functioning." Rather than invest in the lowest-rated neighborhoods, public officials used the map to funnel resources into middle- and working-class white neighborhoods that were seen as requiring stabilization. They also prioritized maintaining high-quality public services in the city's "better" neighborhoods. Per city planners, these projects would ensure that River City retained its tax base and did not lose additional residents to the surrounding suburbs.[74]

In the decades that followed, River City's urban growth coalition turned from preservation toward growth. By the early 2000s, key stakeholders had fully embraced a strategy that depended on entrepreneurial development. The city's major business coalition, the River City Business Association (RCBA), invited Richard Florida to visit and adopted his recommendations that the city rebrand as a playground for the creative class. The RCBA formed an association for young professionals to lure this population. Another collective of downtown interest groups created marketing materials that framed the city as a regional cultural hub, with a burgeoning tech industry, several universities, and a lively arts and music scene. City officials joined in this effort to court mobile creatives and young professionals. The city's downtown "master plan" initiated pedestrianization and infrastructure redevelopment projects, which, in turn, sparked housing development. Municipal expenditures reinforced the emphasis on downtown amenities, with a substantial majority of the city's economic-development budget devoted to real estate and physical projects in the area. Public and private investments focused on upscale condominiums and offices, retail developments, and streetscape improvements.[75]

The emphasis on downtown revitalization has continued since. Billions of dollars poured into commercial and residential development projects. This targeted focus had the support of public officials. River City's mayor, Mark Taylor, continued the legacy of his predecessor by emphasizing that downtown revitalization was the lynchpin of the city's economic recovery.[76] A plan put forth by the mayor, the City Council, and the government's city development office in 2014 emphasized the importance of fostering entrepreneurship, innovation, and quality of life in River City, specifically noting the importance of drawing young professionals and millennials to the city. Public officials justified the focus on the downtown as a means of "raising all boats," as the president of the City Council put it during a public forum. While the council president represented a predominantly Black district on the edge of the city, he described the downtown as "accessible and available to everyone"—a shared set of resources and amenities that could benefit all residents.[77]

But decades of focus on the city's predominantly white residential neighborhoods and the downtown had increased spatial and racial inequalities in River City. On the one hand, the city saw the positive economic effects of its growth strategies. After years of population decline, the population began to rise, and the median income increased in the early 2000s. Officials projected additional employment opportunities in many sectors, particularly education and health services, information and other professional services, leisure and hospitality, financial activities, and construction.[78] On the other hand, these benefits were distributed unevenly. By 2012, the zip code with the highest average annual income in the county reported an average twelve times greater than that of the city's poorest zip code.[79] While official reports highlighted new opportunities, other studies concluded that outcomes were worsening for the poor. Ongoing systematic investments into better-off areas portended even deeper economic and racial divides.

In sum, River City's development shows how contemporary urban governance in cities intersects with the historical construction of racially and economically segregated landscapes. Decades of government policies, private investments, and collective decisions marginalized the city's predominantly Black neighborhoods while advancing opportunities in predominantly white areas. In this context, the challenges of urban governance have fallen increasingly to cities themselves. While federal initiatives laid the foundation for local actors to construct racial segregation and build carceral power in cities, the retrenchment and dis-integration of the role of the federal state in urban life left local governments to secure their own economic fates. As River City's political leaders and business elites fought to elevate the city within the globalized economy, they targeted their efforts toward highly specific geographies, defining some places as valuable and worthy of further investment and others as criminally threatening or inevitably declining. This neighborhood-based approach to urban revitalization intersects with trends in the field of policing, inviting the police to regulate space in alignment with the goals of growth.

The Evolving Role of the Police

Endowed with the state's capacity for the legitimate use of coercive force and tasked with territorial control, the police are uniquely empowered to regulate space.[80] As the geographer Steve Herbert explains, the police accomplish internal pacification through their ability "to mark and enact meaningful boundaries, to restrict people's capacity to act by regulating their movements in space."[81] Spatial practices in policing depend on neighborhood context.[82] These practices can take varied and divergent forms, whether aggressively stopping and searching people in specific places, banishing particular people or behaviors from designated areas, or scrutinizing those who appear to be "out-of-place."[83] No matter the specific project, police work engages with and reproduces ideas of "what *should* typically occur in an area and *who belongs*, as well as *where they belong*."[84] Policing consistently operates in relation to distinct interpretations of space, even as the specific ends and means of spatial regulation have changed over time. The power of the police to control the activities and people in a given area can further define the character of neighborhoods and reinforce their social and spatial boundaries.

The ends to which the police put their powers of spatial regulation have transformed over time and in relation to two tendencies: retrenchment and reform. Regarding the former, the police have historically maintained the status quo and its attendant inequalities. As the "front line agents in the reproduction of social order,"[85] the police enforce legal and normative systems that have often served dominant groups' interests. For example, early police formations in the South emerged from slave patrols and institutionalized practices rooted in racial violence.[86] The police subsequently enforced the Black codes and Jim Crow laws that proliferated following the Civil War and Reconstruction.[87] Many scholars and organizers argue that the ties between policing and racial exclusion have persisted.[88] Indeed, the police have both triggered and violently suppressed racial uprisings throughout history; they have contributed to racialized mass incarceration through the implementation of the War on Drugs; and they continue to kill Black and brown people in high-profile events at the center of debates around racism in US society. Popular perspectives, like those offered by the Black Lives Matter movement, argue that these dynamics reflect the ongoing link between state-sanctioned violence and anti-Black racism.[89] Insofar as the police maintain the structures and norms of a white-supremacist society, they will continue to play a role in reproducing racial hierarchies and upholding the spatial forms they take.

At the same time, policing has also experienced major reform efforts and paradigm shifts. Influential scholars, political bodies, activists, and police leaders have pushed to institutionalize novel approaches to pressing challenges, often precipitated by acute crises of legitimacy.[90] For instance, the rampant corruption and inefficiency of nineteenth-century policing resulted in efforts to professionalize and bureaucratize police forces. By the 1970s, mounting public fear and fraught relations with communities of color motivated a host of innovations focused on community relations.[91] More recently, in response to high-profile police killings, departments have adopted body cameras, implemented implicit-bias trainings, and revised their use-of-force policies.[92] These reforms reflect an important reality: the police respond to an institutional field of diverse government stakeholders, private entities, and citizen groups. Policing changes along with shifts in the social landscape, and police reformers throughout history have seen the possibility of more equitable outcomes with the turn toward new accountability structures and strategic innovations.[93]

The case of River City illustrates how the retrenchment of racial inequality can occur despite—and even through—police reform. Given the centrality of spatial regulation in policing, reform efforts often focus on reconfiguring spatial arrangements. As every major reform era aimed to remedy previous shortcomings, policing strategies have swung between two poles: decentralized, neighborhood-based approaches and centralized, citywide approaches. However, reforming spatial practices invites new hazards. The history of US policing highlights the endurance of racial discrimination and disparity, despite evolving police goals and tactics. This risk persists in the current era, which has shifted to focus on the local level. Advocates of strategies like community policing view tailored approaches to neighborhood-level issues as a means of democratizing policing and redressing the past mistreatment of racialized communities. But place-based strategies have also given rise to harsh tactics like stop-and-frisk, continuing and even exacerbating racial inequities. Indeed, scholars note that police reforms, including community policing, can coexist alongside and be implicated in expanding police power and punitive social control.[94] The River City case illuminates a particular set of hazards that emerge at the intersection of local policing and urban growth politics.

From Neighborhood-Based Policing to Centralization

The early history of the River City Police Department closely followed that of many departments in the Northeast.[95] During this initial "political era," policing was closely integrated with local politics. Ward politicians and precinct-level leaders often managed districts like small-scale departments, making relatively autonomous decisions about organization and activities. The police provided wide-ranging services at the neighborhood level. Officers patrolled on foot and dealt with issues of crime and disorder as they arose, enjoying discretion within their individual beats. Thus, early policing began as a decentralized and highly local enterprise. This approach had clear benefits (for the politically and socially dominant): officers were integrated into neighborhood life and could draw on knowledge of the communities they policed to solve problems. But close ties to ward politicians and a lack of centralized supervision gave rise to widespread corruption and inefficiency. By the first decades of the twentieth century, police departments across the country began to implement reforms to insulate the police from political influence.[96]

These efforts were spearheaded by people within the field of policing, including Berkeley Police Chief August Vollmer, his protégé O. W. Wilson, and FBI Director J. Edgar Hoover. Reformers saw law, rather than politics, as the basis of police legitimacy, and they sought to professionalize the police through more rigorous selection criteria, training, and supervision. They situated the patrol officer as a bureaucrat with a narrow mandate of law enforcement and a distinct skill set based on qualifications. This "reform era" led to a professional model of policing that reigned from the 1930s through the 1970s. Departments centralized police administration, moving away from local approaches and toward standardized activities across the city. They also routinized tactics of preventive patrol, rapid response to citizens' 911 calls, and criminal investigations. In theory, these activities could be uniformly applied throughout a jurisdiction. The model of incident-based response—officers responding as quickly as possible to incoming calls—could be assessed with standard metrics like response times, while investigations could be evaluated through clearance rates.[97] In the midst of national policing changes, River City was at the forefront of reform-era efforts. The police department became a model of efficiency and professionalism during the early half of the twentieth century. The state legislature established a nonpartisan body, the Civilian Review Board, to oversee police personnel appointments. The department introduced a centralized command-and-control system, a training academy, entrance examinations, and employment standards, all common attributes of professionalized police organizations.

However, by the 1970s, challenges to the professional model had surfaced. Research began to demonstrate that tactics of preventive patrol and incident-based response had little effect on crime.[98] These failures of the reform era's core technologies were just one facet of a broader crisis of legitimacy. Public fear of crime rose. Patrol officers experienced problems of morale in the midst of technocratic administration. Moreover, race relations reached a crisis point. The promise of standardized police response proved to be a myth as communities of color experienced ongoing mistreatment and neglect. High-profile cases of police brutality and the suppression of urban unrest drew widespread condemnation. As professional policing was called into question, federal commissions and scholarly research began recommending more attention to police-community relations. Studies noted that information-sharing and collaborative problem-solving could meaningfully impact problems of order, quality of life, and fear.[99]

Contemporary Strategies and a Return to the Local

In light of these dynamics, police departments began incorporating innovations like community-based and problem-oriented policing.[100] These new strategies shared an emphasis on tailoring policing to highly local dynamics, often focusing on the neighborhood. They also encouraged a proliferation of tactics in service of enhancing police responsiveness to distinct issues. For instance, early community policing initiatives included deploying officers on foot patrols, canvassing neighborhoods door-to-door to identify problems, conducting drug-education projects, collaborating with other city services, and publishing newsletters.[101] As a strategy, community policing does not mandate these tactics, but rather, it encourages tactical flexibility under a broader "organizational strategy that leaves setting priorities and the means of achieving them largely to residents and the police who serve in their neighborhoods."[102] Given this ethos, advocates believed community policing could help build trust. Theoretically, citizen participation and public deliberation could become the locus of police decision-making, giving local residents a say in what the police did in their communities. In addressing residents' concerns in marginalized neighborhoods, community-based policing had the potential to enhance procedural justice and mitigate racial tensions.[103] Collectively, strategic innovations expanded the array of recognized interests, problems, and functions that the police could address. The rise of community-based policing reflected a shift away from standardized and centralized practices and back toward differentiated, local approaches within specific neighborhoods.

While many departments embraced the turn toward community policing, the River City Police Department was slow to respond to these developments. In the 1960s and 1970s, fraught relations between the police and River City's Black community solidified. Despite civil rights mobilization and protests against police brutality and racism, the River City Police Department's chief encouraged the "blue wall of silence" and explicitly and implicitly associated crime with the city's Black population. The department also remained committed to incident based response and continued to rely on response times and clearance rates as indicators of success. Status and power concentrated within the detective bureau, undervaluing patrol work just as the national field of policing was recognizing the importance of the work of patrol officers and their potential to facilitate community collaborations. Though the RCPD made small inroads toward community policing as its leadership changed, it did not experience fundamental shifts in its strategic or organizational approach. In short, many people described the River City Police Department as "trapped in the 1970s" well into the twenty-first century.

When the department prepared to hire a new police chief in the early 2000s, stakeholders across the city and many within the ranks felt the need for change. In this context, the search focused on Brian Lancaster, a charismatic police executive with extensive credentials and a growing reputation as an innovative leader in the national field. Though Lancaster came from a pool of external candidates, he was appointed to head the River City Police Department with strong public support from Mayor Taylor and a unanimous vote by the Civilian Review Board. Soon thereafter, Chief Lancaster began by reworking the department's mission statement: the police would shift away from the reactive mentality of the incident-based response model toward proactive, neighborhood-based policing. Lancaster enshrined crime *prevention* in the mission statement; this would be accomplished through popular strategic innovations, including community-based policing and problem-oriented policing. River City seemed to have found the leader it needed to modernize its police.

Indeed, Chief Lancaster rapidly implemented initiatives and organizational changes to align the activities and structures of the department with its new goals. He began by asking district commanders to develop a problem-solving initiative. Each had to identify a specific problem in their district, design an intervention, collaborate with local stakeholders and community groups, and assess progress after implementation. In one district, the police recovered jewelry from pawnshops, citing stores that sold stolen jewelry and displaying the recovered property at the district station so that citizens who had reported a burglary could reclaim their items. Another district hosted a neighborhood celebration in an area historically marked as "crime-ridden." In collaboration with area residents, businesses, and churches, district leaders organized an event that included a neighborhood cleanup, job fair, and cookout.[104] These initiatives served the dual purpose of kicking off community-based problem-solving efforts and pushing greater decision-making authority down to district leadership.

During the first year of Chief Lancaster's tenure, he also initiated major changes to the police department's organizational structures. Many modifications further emphasized district-level policing. The chief aggregated specialty activities that traditionally operated as autonomous entities, such as those focusing on drug crimes, prostitution, and gang issues, into a single unit whose deployments would be determined in collaboration with district captains. He also confronted the insular investigations bureau by incorporating detectives into local problem-solving efforts, assigning them to neighborhoods instead of crime types. These changes dissolved functional divisions between patrol and investigations and instead emphasized geographic divisions. Reforms concentrated on tailoring police response to neighborhood-level problems. The chief's new model appeared to work as violent crime in the city began to drop. Support and enthusiasm for the chief and his new methods of place-based, proactive policing climbed in the early days of his administration.

The redistricting proposal emerged during the second year of Chief Lancaster's term as part and parcel of his overarching organizational reforms. While just one of many changes, the redistricting was central to the chief's vision of problem-solving policing. Chapter 2 describes how the reform flowed from the overarching logic of the River City Police Department's new, neighborhood-based approach. It shows how the redistricting drew on the language of community policing, even as it embraced growth imperatives and eventually widened gaps in service provision and social control. Police reform and the retrenchment of racial inequality ended up going hand in hand.

Conclusion

River City police executives implemented reforms that were often focused on enhancing democratic voice and equitable policing outcomes in historically marginalized neighborhoods. Yet, in this case, strategic innovations would end up serving the interests of the city's economically and racially dominant places and people. As the city government and the police department both homed in on the idea of localism—and the distinctions between specific places within the city—new affinities between policing and growth politics emerged. In some respects, River City's place-based policing reflected a swing back toward the decentralized, neighborhood-based spatial arrangements of early police formations in northern cities. Local policing even invited renewed ties between police administration and the city's political-economic apparatus. But this all unfolded through a new rhetoric of community problem-solving.

While community-based and problem-oriented policing promise more inclusive, fair, and equitable policing through collaboration and community voice, democratic and racially just outcomes are not foregone conclusions of local policing. An emphasis on spatial differentiation has also given rise to strategies with the potential to exacerbate racial tensions. One set of practices, including hotspots policing and proactive policing, targets law enforcement to highly local geographies where crime concentrates.[105] This often involves deploying officers to specific block clusters to intervene in suspicious activities through investigatory traffic stops or stop-and-frisk. Some studies find that hotspots policing effectively reduces crime.[106] But aggressive stop practices targeted to minoritized communities also overgeneralize a presumption of criminality, driving racial disproportionality and undermining trust in the police.[107] Other strategies like order maintenance and broken windows policing facilitate the spatial exclusion of marginalized populations by homing in on "disorder" in public areas.[108] These strategies emerged during the same decades as community policing, and River City police executives folded in such tactics as they turned to a place-based approach. Thus, localism also opened the door to practices that uphold social boundaries and inequalities.

As chapter 2 shows, whether local policing moves toward democratic inclusion or the reinforcement of social hierarchies depends on how places and their problems are defined. Addressing "place-based issues" requires the police to mark boundaries between areas that are thought to be different, to articulate that difference, and to identify what constitutes policing concerns. Such processes are laden with subjective determinations because definitions of place are varied and contested. For instance, a developer may see little opportunity to enhance exchange value in a marginalized neighborhood, while grassroots organizations and neighborhood residents may emphasize the collective efficacy and use-value found there. These competing understandings contain different blueprints for action: the developer might choose to build in a different area, while residents might advocate for investments in public goods like fair housing, educational opportunities, and city services. Actions, in turn, further articulate the boundaries and inequalities between places. In short, stakeholders with varying degrees of social, economic, and political power vie to realize their vision of the city.[109] The police are players in these processes of defining place, as they interpolate and create particular sets of meanings among contested options.

The police department is particularly susceptible to the interests of the urban growth coalition in the current community policing era.

Organizationally, the move toward greater responsiveness to the surrounding environment invites closer ties between the police, the local political apparatus, and place-based interest groups. While ideal-typical community policing may envision resident associations in communities of color as the target of these ties, many other parties can seek to leverage the police for their own purposes. With mayors across the country spearheading urban-revitalization projects and elected officials, developers, corporations, and affluent residents advocating for the creation and preservation of particular kinds of urban spaces, the police are often called on to participate in spatial-regulation projects. Police executives may find that using their place-making power in service of the city's most capital-rich and influential entities has benefits. As an organization, the police agency depends on its surrounding institutional field for legitimacy and resources.[110] Political and economic interests related to uneven urban development can penetrate into policing priorities due to the relative power of growth-coalition members. This is precisely what occurred in River City. As chapter 2 shows, the police department's redistricting reform was a key site where the ties between the city's growth interests and its policing strategies converged.

2

The Promises and Perils of the River City Redistricting

When the River City Police Department redrew several police districts' boundaries to align with the city's stark racial residential segregation boundaries, few people seemed to bat an eye. Local newspapers mentioned the coming changes in passing, and elected officials and community groups appeared unaware or unconcerned. Perhaps the reform slipped under the radar as a purely administrative change. Compared to debates around the use of force or racial profiling, rearranging police districts is unlikely to pique the public interest. However, as I argue in this chapter, redistricting has far-reaching and deep consequences. Redrawing police-district boundaries requires decision-makers to negotiate and clarify the nature of police work and the functions of the police in the city. Their options as they do so are shaped by practices in the national field of policing and pressures stemming from the local political-economic environment. Moreover, decisions about district boundaries shape officers' work environments in ways that determine how policing unfolds on the ground.

Many police departments redistrict to address the uneven distribution of calls for service between districts. This focus on balancing workload, represented by calls, reveals an enduring commitment to incident-based response. However, during the River City redistricting, the police department intentionally created districts with a higher volume of calls and districts with a lower volume. Police officials explained that district boundaries followed neighborhood lines and crime patterns. Departing from a focus on incident-based policing, decision-makers framed the redistricting as part of the department's transition to neighborhood-level, issue-based strategies. They positioned the redistricting as a logical—even uniquely innovative—extension of community policing. Drawing district boundaries around "coherent neighborhoods" would allow the police to develop local approaches that could enhance the safety and livability of all communities. Ultimately, the police department asserted an ability to further *construct* neighborhoods by addressing their specific challenges. Elected officials from across the city saw great potential in local policing, which seemed to hold the promise of a more equitable city.

Yet, in practice, the redistricting institutionalized a crude binary between spaces that experienced quality-of-life issues and those characterized by violence. This distinction masked the heterogeneity within the new districts. It laid the groundwork for practices that would focus on crime suppression in predominantly Black neighborhoods, at the expense of efforts to enhance commercial and community strength. And it prioritized order maintenance and service activities in predominantly white districts, glossing over potential criminal activity within them. Beyond marking these distinctions, police executives elevated the importance of the city's new "low-crime" districts. Presentations of the redistricting emphasized that the boundary changes would facilitate better police service in middle-class and affluent neighborhoods and in prominent commercial areas like the downtown. It became apparent that the police department's innovative strategies were poised to benefit the city's better-off places and people.

This unfolded as the police department aligned its priorities with those of River City's urban growth coalition. Police executives explained that middle-class neighborhoods and downtown areas were vital to the city's economic fate. They argued that protecting and serving better-off communities was a means of uplifting the entire city. As one police official described,

> Viable cities that are going to serve the needs of the poor have to have, *have* to have, prosperous commercial districts and a middle class. You cannot serve the needs of your poor without that. And so our challenge is that we, the police, are the social agency of first resort for the poor, we're not going to do a good job if we lose our middle class or if our commercial corridors become a wasteland.

Police leaders argued that redistricting would facilitate tailored policing within these critical areas. Such an approach would allow the police to provide responsive and specialized services for middle-class residents, businesses, tourists, and other visitors.

As I interviewed City Council members, representatives of business improvement districts, leaders of neighborhood associations, and community organizers, manifold explanations emerged as to how policing strategies and growth politics ended up aligning. Interviews revealed a close and mutually beneficial relationship between the chief of police and the mayor, who had long emphasized downtown development as a growth strategy. Respondents also described empowered residents and stakeholders in white communities advocating for policing as though it were an urban amenity. Some noted that this same kind of advocacy was rarer in Black neighborhoods, where histories of police neglect, abuse, and exclusion left little confidence in the police. City officials and police executives also hinted at resource constraints within the police department, which required a degree of triage. Whatever the confluence of factors, the police privileged the interests of powerful political and economic entities.

By embracing a role in the city's growth regime, police executives' attentiveness to space reinforced long-standing racial tropes and inequities. Racialized constructions of place emerged in a reform that many elected officials and community groups saw as aligned with progressive policing principles. Ultimately, the possibility of more democratic and equitable policing was compromised as the police department drew on a binary that defined communities primarily in terms of their economic value or their violence. This chapter traces the promises and pitfalls of the redistricting, beginning with an account of why underexplored police redistricting processes are actually so fundamental to shaping policing strategy and on-the-ground police work.

The Significance of Police Redistricting Reforms

It is surprising that redistricting processes in policing have received relatively little analytical attention from social scientists, given their racial, economic, and political implications.

Redistricting has been extensively studied in arenas like electoral politics and education. For instance, scholars, jurists, elected officials, and advocacy groups have debated how various boundary configurations enhance descriptive and substantive representation of minority voters.[1] Gerrymandering along racial or party lines has intentionally diluted political influence by "cracking" voting blocs across districts or "packing" blocs into particular districts to minimize their influence elsewhere. In politics, redistricting is understood to be a means of political inclusion and exclusion.[2] School districts have also received similar attention. Because school district boundaries can reinforce segregation and disparate opportunity structures,[3] ameliorative proposals home in on the district as a point of intervention. Some proposals argue for periodic redistricting to break up "concentrations of wealth, poverty, or racial disadvantage," while other reforms, like school choice, aim to lessen the salience of geographic boundaries.[4] In both electoral politics and education, key stakeholders analyze redistricting processes as central mediators of access to public goods and the rights of citizenship, with particular attention to racial consequences.

Like the electoral district and the school district, the police district is a consequential administrative unit. Many large urban police agencies, including the River City Police Department, have incorporated a military-style bureaucratic structure to distribute their work and services across space.[5] This structure depends on formal subdivisions and hierarchies. Police agencies often subdivide by function, through bureaus for patrol, investigation, and administration, as well as by geography, into districts, sectors, and beats. The chain of command translates priorities and resources across these subunits. River City offers an example of a common organizational hierarchy: at the executive level, the chief of police oversees the entire department, in collaboration with assistant chiefs and inspectors who, in turn, supervise a collection of geographically defined patrol districts or functionally defined divisions (for instance, internal affairs, sensitive crimes, and technical communications). Below this level, each district is headed by a captain responsible for all activities within their territorial subdivision. Several lieutenants report to the captain, each overseeing a shift. Several sergeants report to each lieutenant and supervise a group of officers. In the context of this paramilitary organizational structure, the district is a foundational unit: it is where strategic priorities and resource allocations originating at the top of the chain of command are translated and distributed into the police services that city residents receive.

Beyond the administrative significance of police districts, they also contribute to the normative dimensions of policing. Districts define unique work environments, and the conditions within a district can produce distinct practices and expectations among officers.[6] As outlined by the criminologist David Klinger, districts are an important analytical unit because officers cross the boundaries of beats or sectors within a district, but they rarely cross district boundaries. Within a district, officers share many responsibilities and activities. They use the same radio channel, attend roll call and briefings together, and serve as backup on assignments. They become familiar with specific criminal patterns and neighborhood conditions found within the district. They also develop work-group rules—around workload, "normal" crimes, the deservingness of victims, and levels of cynicism—that determine levels of formal law enforcement. Given the uneven distribution of criminal and social problems across the city, district boundaries define divergent environments that can produce "distinct systems of policing."[7] For instance, Klinger predicts that deviant acts must be more serious to receive a vigorous police response in high-crime districts compared to low-crime districts because officers in the former face resource constraints, experience more cynicism, and may see deviant acts as normal and victims as less deserving. Hence, district work environments play a central role in shaping how particular neighborhoods are policed.

Despite the significance of the police district as an organizational unit, there is little professional guidance on the best way to determine appropriate district boundaries. In a professional publication, the former president of the International Association of Crime Analysts Christopher Bruce joked about the "'Bud-Shell Method' of creating police districts," which describes "a police administrator who sits down one night with a 'six-pack of Budweiser and a Shell station road map' and uses a magic marker to draw lines down major streets."[8] Though an exaggeration, the idea reflects the reality that redistricting and resource-allocation procedures remain somewhat arbitrary. As Bruce explains, "when analysts have set out to create allocation plans, they generally have invented their own formulas and processes, with varying degrees of success."[9]

To the extent that a consensus exists around technical recommendations and implemented reforms, it coalesces around the goal of evenly distributing calls for service across districts.[10] A review of publicly available information on twenty-first-century police department redistricting reforms in thirty-four major cities found pervasive references to balancing calls for service, equitably distributing workload, improving efficiency and response times, and enhancing service delivery.[11] Like other kinds of redistricting reforms, police redistricting processes also aim to distribute resources and services across space. But they often employ a dated idea of what those services entail by orienting around the incident-based response model and its central goal of reducing response times to citizens' calls for service.

As described in chapter 1, ideas surrounding the function and corresponding spatial arrangements of the police have undergone dramatic shifts in recent decades. During the reform era, police departments embraced a narrow crime control mandate and relied on rapid response as one of their core technologies.[12] But innovations like community policing, problem-solving policing, hotspots policing, and broken windows policing enshrine new roles and tactics.[13] Many contemporary strategies expand the official purview of policing beyond crime control. They emphasize order-maintenance functions and the "proactive" role police can play in preventing crime, reducing fear, and enhancing perceptions of safety. These strategies also rely on many different tactics, from foot patrols and police-community advisory boards to saturation patrols and investigatory stops.[14] In addition to this expanding array of activities, new strategies can produce intentional divergence across space. For instance, community policing encourages territorial decentralization: it holds that district captains should have more autonomy to develop novel solutions to locally defined problems.[15] With distinct priorities and initiatives implemented at the neighborhood level, it is even more likely that policing styles will vary between districts.

As strategic approaches in policing proliferate, redistricting reforms implicate two important conceptual issues about the nature of police work and its distribution. The first involves questions of resource allocations and deployment. The seemingly straightforward goal of balancing workload between districts raises questions about defining and measuring "work" and "balance." Should the police measure work as response times to calls for service, or do they capture proactive or community-based work like liaising with neighborhood groups, walking foot patrols, or conducting investigatory stops? How do they ensure sufficient and proportionate personnel allocations when activities may differ intentionally?

The second set of decisions involves determining "logical" boundaries. In practical terms, the size and shape of a district must be easily navigable for officers, and its boundaries must be clear and memorable.[16] But should such boundaries be drawn by arterial streets, natural boundaries like rivers, crime patterns, or other administrative units like census tracts and local political districts? The current focus on neighborhoods suggests that recognized social divisions may emerge as salient boundaries, though ideas of social divisions can be varied and contested. How these conceptual ambiguities are resolved is contingent on the police department's overarching strategic goals.

Because police redistricting reforms are centrally concerned with allocating public resources across the city, they are also shaped by broader municipal financial imperatives, both public and private. Though police departments develop their strategies on the basis of practices in their professional field, they are also embedded in and constrained by specific urban contexts. The police are part of municipal governments, and their goals and means evolve in relation to the local political environment.[17] The emergence of neoliberal urban governance has impacted policing in many ways. Like other city agencies, police departments face budget cuts in times of economic crisis, but cities also rely on the police to respond to an array of social problems as urban austerity measures cut spending on housing, health care, jobs programs, and other social services.[18] In addition, the police have been shown to participate in growth politics through the securitization of downtowns and gentrifying neighborhoods.[19] Policing strategies are thus also rooted in the politics of local governance and administration.

Hence, police redistricting reforms are an underexplored site where interests from the surrounding political-economic field enter into policing priorities and organizational structures. Through redistricting, stakeholders negotiate strategic priorities in policing, at a time when options have simultaneously expanded in the national field of policing and been constrained by municipal government needs. In this context, redistricting reforms institutionalize contingent ideas of what the police do in the city, and in the process, they actively *construct* the roles and functions of the police. For instance, the continued reliance on measures like call volume and response times across many redistricting projects further enshrines the incident-based response model and defines the primary function of the police as responding to calls for service. The endurance of incident-based response—in spite of the model's datedness in the national field of policing—reflects, in part, how urban governments rely on the police as emergency service providers.

The redistricting in River City represented a rare departure from a focus on incident-based response. Instead, police executives crafted a role for the police in further *creating neighborhoods*. Drawing on a framework of localism, officials highlighted the power of the police to shape place by suppressing crime in neighborhoods defined as violent and by enhancing perceptions of safety in areas that were already comparatively safe. The police deployed this constitutive power in service of the broader political-economic project of urban revitalization. The redistricting ultimately reinscribed boundaries and meanings that amplified the salience of the city's racial segregation, augmenting inequalities in police service and social control. Yet, when the redistricting was first proposed, it seemed to contain the promise of a more equitable future for all of the city's neighborhoods and residents. The rhetoric of neighborhood-based problem-solving masked how local policing would end up serving the interests of powerful places and people, whether through intentional decisions or unexpected consequences. These tensions and contradictions of the redistricting emerged at the complex intersection of strategic policing innovations and local governance imperatives.

Redistricting in River City

In many regards, the redistricting in River City appeared to be a uniquely innovative and progressive reform. When it was implemented, few other police departments had used redistricting to institutionalize issue-based policing at a citywide level.[20] The project of redrawing police-district boundaries clearly stemmed from the new police chief's project of reform. The redistricting emerged as an immediate and central change that the department could make to align its administrative structures with its new neighborhood-based approaches.

Goals of the Reform

Chief Lancaster offered an eloquent and convincing overview of the reform during a public meeting before the Safety Committee of the City Council. Video footage of the meeting captured a thorough account of the motivations behind the redistricting, as well as the efforts of police executives to assure stakeholders of its benefits.[21] Sitting before five city-council members representing varied parts of the city, Lancaster began by framing the proposed district boundary changes as integral to his broader vision:

> The beat and district redesign is based on our mission, quite frankly. We've worked hard to create a mission statement that says that we're going to work closely with the community. Our goal is to create neighborhoods that can sustain civic life. . . . And our strategy is community-based, problem-oriented, and data-driven.

By citing these three popular strategic innovations and a commitment to community, the chief firmly situated the redistricting within the department's modernization efforts. He went on to explain existing district boundaries:

> Our current boundaries were based on a very work-intensive effort; a lot of people worked very hard to draw the current district boundaries using classical formulas. And the classic formula for dividing up districts was, historically, let's equalize the workload so every district has roughly the same number of calls for service.

He then characterized the trouble with this model:

> The problem with that is that sometimes resulted in district lines being drawn right through the middle of neighborhoods and separating them from each other. It didn't take into consideration geography or topography—where the railroad tracks are, where the rivers are, where the bluffs are. And it didn't always take into consideration crime trends and patterns. We have some district lines right now that quite literally run right in the middle of a [crime] hotspot, so that half of that hotspot is one district commander's responsibility and half is the other's.

Finally, Lancaster introduced the logic of the planned changes:

> Our new proposed boundaries are entirely built on the notion of keeping coherent neighborhoods with similar problems together for a stable policing presence and single accountability from the beat to the district commander. That's the entire reason we did this. We're doing our best to see that common concerns are dealt with by one district at a time.

In this explicit contrast between typical reforms based on equalizing workload and the new proposal, the chief clearly demarcated the links between the redistricting and the department's strategic transformation. The redistricting was one aspect of the department's shift away from incident-based response and toward proactive place-based interventions.

The redistricting would make a key administrative unit consistent with the goal of community policing. It would streamline problem-solving efforts by giving district commanders additional autonomy to develop solutions to local problems. To illustrate the purpose of the change, Chief Lancaster used the example of two of the districts that would undergo substantial modifications. Each old district had a northern area that experienced violent crime and a southern end that experienced property crime and quality-of-life issues. Lancaster explained this as he pointed to a map:

> Every time I had a garage-burglary problem down here, I needed a North District–South District task force to deal with garage burglaries. And every time I had a gang-related issue up here, I needed a North District–South District task force to deal with the gang issue. Nobody could own the entire gang issue; nobody could own the entire burglary issue. And so the challenge for us was, How do we give you the coherent, stable policing presence that owns the problems common to that neighborhood?

Lancaster presented the redistricting as an answer to this question. The reform would enable tailored responses to discrete problems: leadership in the North District could focus on gang issues, while the South District could focus on garage burglaries.

Police officials explained that the major changes would realign district boundaries with neighborhood lines and crime patterns, primarily impacting four districts. The adjacent North District and the South District originally covered an area bifurcated by a boundary running north to south. The redistricting designated railroad tracks running east to west as the new boundary. Under the new plan, crime hotspots in the northern part of the former districts would all fall within the North District, while the South District would include lower-crime neighborhoods to the south. The East District and the West District would also undergo substantial changes. The area shared by these districts included the city's downtown and the neighborhoods radiating from it to the north. The challenges were similar—both districts contained neighborhoods to the west that experienced more calls for service and violent crime, while those in the east rarely experienced problems of violent crime. The new north-to-south district boundary of the river separated crime hotspots into the West District, while the low-crime neighborhoods to the east would be in the East District.

Rather than balancing workload across districts, the redistricting would create some districts characterized by a higher volume of criminal incidents and calls for service and other districts that experienced a lower volume. Chief Lancaster assured stakeholders and the Safety Committee that the separation of high-crime and low-crime districts would result in better service in both:

> The thing that seems to detract from the service level is the sense in some districts that their squads spend all their time in the high-crime area of the district. Our belief is that if we draw the district lines in a way to more naturally reflect neighborhood lines and crime patterns, that people who live in a fairly quiet area aren't going to lose their officers inside the district.

While residents in the new low-crime districts would experience a more stable patrol presence, the police would continue their crime-reduction efforts in high-crime districts. Chief Lancaster pointed to a heat map of crime hotspots, saying, "We've redrawn the lines so that those hotspots that currently exist, which are the darker areas, are inside one district." He noted, "We're making progress," as the areas were even darker in the prior year's map: "We stabilize those neighborhoods by reducing crime there. Even if it's dispersed, we can keep track of those smaller numbers in different neighborhoods. And that's part of the evolution of our policing style, which is to follow the crime where it goes and to have an impact on it." Lancaster then summarized their strategy: "Our underlying goal: stable neighborhoods, common problems, in the same district, with one accountable commander and officers who are familiar with their problem."

With regard to resource allocation, the chief explained that districts would have personnel proportional to their needs. A lieutenant from the police department's research office who accompanied Lancaster to the Safety Committee meeting noted several factors the department considered when making staffing decisions. Citing a captain involved in determining district-level personnel allocations, the lieutenant said, "He used nationally recognized modeling for looking at police staffing, modeling that Northwestern University [School of] Police Staff and Command utilizes." The lieutenant explained how this model used weighted averages to consider calls for service, crime type and volume, geographic size, and supplemental staff—including officers assigned to specialty units, administrative positions, and community-based work. While calls for service remained a workload metric, the department incorporated an array of other considerations in operationalizing district-level needs. The lieutenant also noted that many officers would retain their original squad areas, even if the squad area fell within a new district. This would ensure continuity, as officers could continue to patrol neighborhoods with which they were familiar. Chief Lancaster then quipped, "Though some of our baseball teams will be smaller, the same number of people will be on the field."

The redistricting was well received by the members of the Safety Committee. They represented areas including some of the designated "high-crime" and "low-crime" neighborhoods in the changing districts. During the hearing, council members from districts that included "quieter" residential neighborhoods expressed service concerns similar to those of the chief. Early in the hearing, council member Raymond White, who represented an area in the proposed South District, described these concerns:

> I did a ride-along probably two years ago in one squad area in my district, and we spent about two hours in that squad area and the rest of it a lot

further north, pretty much out of my district totally. So I'm hoping that residents in my area will get speedier service than what they got in the past and won't be losing protection here.

After Lancaster had explained that one goal of the reform was precisely to maintain a stable policing presence in these neighborhoods, this same council member concluded, "Chief, I just want to say thank you for bringing this change forward. I will begin with my neighborhood association meeting tonight to tell people about it and the positive things it can bring to River City. So thank you for this plan." Another council member who represented a district with low-crime residential neighborhoods similarly complimented the chief: "This makes all the sense in the world. . . . Now, with the way you have the districts redrawn, they're similar neighborhoods." He continued, "I support this one hundred percent; this is a much better way to tailor policing in these respective neighborhoods than how we were doing it in the past. Thank you for that."

Representatives of political districts that included crime hotspots also endorsed the proposal. Council member Arthur Gomez, who had himself been a police officer, asked the chief about the risk of burnout for officers working in high-crime areas. Lancaster surveyed the processes in place for identifying and transferring officers between districts, noting that this was always an option for those looking for a change. Nevertheless, he also said some officers preferred work in busier areas: "The officers I've encountered in our highest crime districts have very high morale and feel like they're doing a very important mission. . . . They feel an obligation to the people that live in those neighborhoods and are performing at an extraordinary level." Ultimately, Gomez enthusiastically supported the change, telling the chief, "I understand resource allocation, and I think you're doing an excellent job with it finally. I think this is long overdue for this city." Council member Roger Franklin, who represented a predominantly Black district, asked Lancaster about monitoring crime diffusion and measuring the effectiveness of the new boundaries. The chief responded,

We'll be guided by the data. We want to see continued crime decreases. We want to see responsiveness to neighborhoods. Obviously, some of the data will be objective data—the numbers—and some of it will be feedback from community associations and, I suspect, concerned councilmen. And so we will monitor all the feedback we get, for the long term, to see how this works out. But we're confident that it will provide benefits for your constituents.

Franklin also supported the changes, telling the chief, "You've got a lot of folks who believe in you. They really understand that you're trying to use data—it's a data-driven department now." By the end of the hearing, Chief Lancaster had effectively addressed council members' concerns. The goal of tailoring policing to reduce crime in some districts and provide a stable patrol presence in others appealed to representatives from across the city.

Approval of the Reform

While Chief Lancaster's efforts to garner the Safety Committee's support were successful, there was no mandate from the council for the police department to engage in a public process before undertaking the redistricting reform. From a procedural standpoint, only the Civilian Review Board could approve or deny the police department's administrative proposals. Nevertheless, police executives worked to inform community stakeholders and the local political establishment of the coming changes. By displaying a list of agencies that had been consulted through "informal communications," Lancaster described to the Safety Committee the balance between internal decision-making and public participation: "We weren't doing a public process, but we were trying to make sure that the folks that would be affected by this change understood the rationale and felt comfortable that we were doing it in a way that would render a better community service." He noted that community-based officers and district captains had been meeting with community stakeholders—including business associations, neighborhood groups, schools, and churches—"so they would get a sense of what was motivating this adjustment." He also reminded the committee that the department would continue to work with groups at the neighborhood level to evaluate the reform.

My interview with Paul Daniels, one of the police department's assistant chiefs, clarified other aspects of the redistricting logic and behind-the-scenes processes of the reform's approval. Unlike the chief, who had come to River City from elsewhere, Assistant Chief Daniels had spent his entire career with the department. After completing an apprentice-style civilian program that tracked toward admission into the police academy, he moved from patrol officer to sergeant, then lieutenant, then captain, working in several different districts and divisions in the process. Daniels had skipped two ranks when he was promoted by Chief Lancaster to his current position of overseeing all patrol and detective operations in one of the city's three geographic command areas. He framed his rise through the ranks as a reflection of a commitment to the chief's new way of doing things: "Part of being promoted to a command position is that you believe in [the chief's] vision. And if you don't believe in his vision, which is problem-solving, intelligence-led, data-driven, well, you're not going to be promoted."

Assistant Chief Daniels had been an integral part of the redistricting. He described some of the behind-the-scenes processes that the police undertook to work toward the success of the reform. Daniels explained how information-sharing ensured that stakeholders were familiar with and convinced by the logic of the redistricting:

> One of the things the chief was very cognizant of is that there would be potential pushback. So he wanted to make sure that the political establishment was well aware of what we were going to do. . . . He presented what we wanted to do to the City Council, to the mayor's staff. He did what's called "accountability of management" meetings with the mayor, and the information on redistricting was also presented in that format as well.

Indeed, as with the City Council, the proposal encountered no resistance from the mayor's office. This was consistent with the general perception of Mayor Taylor's role in police policy development, which Daniels characterized as follows:

> We're in a city where we have a supportive mayor who lets the police chief be the police chief, and who doesn't try to interfere with policing. This may not have flown under a different mayor. The mayor didn't resist. The mayor put faith in this man's long tenure as a police chief and agreed to let him do what he wanted to do, and it's been effective.

Mayor Taylor's confidence in the chief reflected the mutually beneficial relationship between the two men. Chief Lancaster had been brought to River City with Taylor's support. Moreover, as described on a city-government webpage, the mayor's budgets consistently ensured resources for the police department.[22] These investments paid off in the successes of the chief. For instance, in a local news article that described declining homicides the year after Chief Lancaster's appointment, Mayor Taylor took credit for making public safety a priority for the city.[23] The mayor and the police chief had a symbiotic relationship that coalesced in their overlapping agendas.

Other elected officials shared a confidence in Chief Lancaster's professional expertise. Therefore, they saw the redistricting as an administrative change requiring neither significant oversight nor input. My interview with Sam Ward, a City Council member who had not served on the Safety Committee, revealed his perspective on the process of redistricting: "I would not say it's the kind of process where the public needs to weigh in early on. . . . I generally think that's the kind of thing where you hire a good manager—a good chief—and then expect efficiencies and tactical results." Council member Ward shared that though the reform had unfolded with little public involvement, Lancaster "did it right," adding, "the chief came in with a lot of national best practices." With the strength of his reputation and the early successes of his tenure behind him, Lancaster easily acquired buy-in for this new reform.

The redistricting was ultimately approved easily by the Civilian Review Board. Per detailed minutes of the hearing,[24] Chief Lancaster gave a presentation similar to the one he had made for the Safety Committee. He outlined the department's new strategic orientation, the departure from past redistricting efforts, key changes to the four affected districts, staffing considerations, and consultations with other stakeholders. The minutes concisely summarized the key distinction emphasized by police executives: "the goal is to concentrate on violence and quality-of-life policing." When one commissioner asked about possible negative effects of the redistricting, the chief noted residents' concerns about losing officers and district commanders. He clarified again that officers and commanders would not necessarily change their geographic jurisdiction, even if their administrative district changed. The director of the Civilian Review Board told the chief that the proposed redistricting went "above and beyond" by including input from the community. When a commissioner moved to approve the district boundary changes, the motion carried unanimously among the five commissioners present.

The Promise of Local Policing

The redistricting drew on the language of community policing. Indeed, Chief Lancaster appeared to be on the cutting edge of efforts to modify police districts in relation to evolving ideas of the police function. Traditional redistricting reforms based on balancing calls for service relied on the most common measure of police workload, but in doing so, they signaled an ongoing commitment to incident-based response. By contrast, the River City redistricting disrupted the assumption that responding to calls was the primary role of the police. The chief recognized that greater district-level decision-making authority could facilitate the goal of tailoring policing to community problem-solving. Under the new plan, semiautonomous police districts could pursue innovative strategies, each sharing an end goal enshrined in the department's mission statement of *creating neighborhoods* that could sustain civic life.

By claiming the capacity to "create" the character of neighborhoods, the police department actively embraced a role in shaping River City's landscape. Such place-making aspirations seemed to contain the seeds of policing's democratic potential. If the police could ameliorate specific problems afflicting varied communities, then residents could all enjoy the benefits of urban life: connection and belonging, meaningful participation in the public sphere, and a host of other communal and individual opportunities. Working with communities on their own terms and devoting additional resources to neighborhoods on the basis of need could serve to redress the past abuses and indignities of segregation. The general logic of the redistricting suggested an outcome of greater equity between neighborhoods, where residents across the city would receive the services needed to enjoy safe, livable, and healthy urban spaces.

Could Separate Be Equitable?

In laying the foundations for neighborhood-level, issue-based policing, the River City Police Department pursued boundaries aligned with the

"coherent neighborhoods" supposedly characterized by distinct problems. In practice, the redistricting resulted in the de facto alignment
between police-district boundaries and racial-segregation boundaries.
The new West District included the highest proportion of Black residents of any district in the city, while the new East District included the
highest proportion of white residents. A majority of the city's Latinx
residents lived in the neighborhoods north of the railroad tracks separating the new North District from the South District, which included
predominantly white neighborhoods.

The easy success of the redistricting stemmed, in part, from a widespread perception among city leaders, residents, and civic groups that
segregated areas were, indeed, different. For instance, when I interviewed council member Sam Ward, who represented a district near the
downtown, he reflected on the police department's new boundaries. He
began by noting, "Frankly, the river is a big enough geographical boundary that for tactical reasons, that probably makes a lot of sense." He continued, addressing me, "Now, you probably want to start talking about
some socioeconomic factors too." Ward went on:

> The reason it made sense to combine the east side with the downtown dis-
> trict is all these things go together: poverty, race, economics, educational
> achievement, number of people in the prison system. . . . The poverty being
> as separated as where it is, you're going to have certain crime patterns in
> rich versus poor neighborhoods. It's inevitable. And I would say that the
> crime patterns on the east side and the crime patterns downtown match:
> almost no murders, almost no rapes, not very much domestic violence, at
> least not reported, but lots of muggings, lots of car break-ins, lots of bur-
> glaries, property crimes—because that's where the property is more valu-
> able. Once you go into poor neighborhoods, you've got shootings, murders,
> domestic violence, those kinds of issues. So it makes some sense.

Ward recognized that there was "a possible moral hazard" in apply-
ing different policing modalities across segregated districts. Yet he
concluded that this was not what was happening in River City. Ward
explained, "You want different models—but not different levels of service—in different neighborhoods. That's what community policing is
all about."

Augmenting Difference: Value and Violence

In reality, the characterizations of social difference that emerged in Ward's description and in police executives' accounts of the redistricting collapsed different kinds of places into homogenizing categories and eventually opened the door for different levels of service. The neighborhoods in the new East District and the new West District were varied. The East District included the campus of a large university, the city's downtown, several entertainment corridors, and many residential neighborhoods, some home to the city's most affluent residents and others to student renters. The interests and problems in these areas could differ, but police executives and other city stakeholders defined them as similar based on their "quality-of-life" concerns. Moreover, the focus on quality-of-life issues glossed over potential criminal activities like drug dealing, sexual violence, and white-collar offenses. This laid the foundations for policing approaches rooted in service and order maintenance. The neighborhoods in the new West District also included heterogeneity that was lost in the preeminent focus on violent crime. While Assistant Chief Daniels had described the West District as the "epicenter" of violence, it was also home to quiet residential neighborhoods, commercial corridors, and entertainment establishments. Yet the emphasis on criminality encouraged a reliance on formal law enforcement, rather than activities aimed at cultivating the area's commercial potential or community strength.

Ultimately, officials relied on a central racialized dualism that amplified contrasts between crime-ridden and violent inner cities and orderly, secure, and deserving white neighborhoods. By acting on these ideas, the police would further reinforce segregated spaces in ways consistent with these representations. Moreover, resource constraints within the police department and across the institutional landscape of the city laid the groundwork for inequities in routine policing practices. Though promising on the surface, the redistricting reified a vision of the city tied to legacies of racial exclusion and uneven development.

Indeed, the logic of the redistricting did more than just identify a distinction between places characterized by violence and quality-of-life issues. Police executives made it a dominant priority to preserve resources in the latter. The rationale aligned with River City's urban-revitalization efforts, which positioned middle-class residential neighborhoods and the downtown as vital to the city's economic prospects. The police took up a role in trying to avoid the flight of capital to the suburbs by ensuring that middle-class neighborhoods received adequate public services. The police also sought to cultivate the downtown as an attractive site for tourists, developers, businesses, new residents, and other visitors by enhancing perceptions of safety. Police executives saw this work as essential to the overall viability of the city, which, in turn, shaped the resources the police had to serve poor neighborhoods. Department officials positioned the police as an urban amenity that could be deployed to maintain or cultivate the city's economic standing. Police executives did not conjure this sense of their significance to the political economy of the city out of thin air; these ideas found frequent reinforcement from elected officials, citizens' groups, business coalitions, and other members of River City's growth coalition.

Elected officials and representatives from neighborhood associations and business districts in middle-class residential areas stressed the importance of their communities to the city's tax base. They compelled urban service providers, including the police, to be responsive to local needs, threatening to leave the city and withdraw their financial resources otherwise. Indeed, police service in the suburbs was an attractive lure away from the city. In an interview with me, Janice Sanders, a neighborhood group leader in the East District, described a nearby suburb as a "nice, quiet town where, if you called the police, you got somebody on your doorstep in five minutes. It doesn't matter how minor it is." Political pressures to offer comparable responses were on display during the Safety Committee meeting. Council member Raymond White noted that his constituents resided in "the third-highest-taxed area in the city," adjacent to several suburbs. White explained that residents "look at services that are a block away, and they look at services that are in their neighborhood." He continued, "If people here develop fear and believe that crime is moving into their area and we lose tax base here, then we don't have the finances to support crime efforts. It just goes down in total."[25] When I interviewed White, he elaborated: "I did talk to this chief about the fact that it's important to keep healthy areas healthy, that it's not all about fighting crime where it is; it's preventing it also where it isn't."

The River City Police Department seemed receptive to this argument. The goal of providing a stable policing presence in low-crime neighborhoods was central to the narrative of the redistricting. As Chief Lancaster had explained during the Safety Committee hearing, separating high-crime areas from low-crime areas via new district boundaries would ensure that the police in low-crime neighborhoods would not be pulled to the other side of the district. Assistant Chief Daniels reiterated this problem's existence in the former East and West Districts:

> What would happen regularly is squad cars that were deployed and assigned to east of the river would be pulled to take calls west of the river. And you could literally have long, extended periods of time where the police were void from the public spaces of the east side.

The redistricting would allow officers to remain in quiet neighborhoods where residents wanted a visible patrol presence. A police official illuminated the economic motives for this shift: "The people that are paying enormous property taxes, they need to know that when they call the police about their problem, that there is, in fact, a police response for them."

Attention also focused on River City's downtown. As described in chapter 1, public and private growth interests coalesced around protecting and further cultivating the economic resources of the area. This strategy relied on attracting visitors and investors through entertainment, tourism, conventions, and corporate growth opportunities. Stakeholders suggested that the police should have a role in facilitating these projects. Martha Hines, the executive director of a downtown business improvement district, explained in our interview,

> Downtown is extremely visible. And in terms of our police leadership and city leadership, we have the ear of those leaders because we represent so much of the city's tax base. We represent very powerful corporate entities. . . . It's really important to the city's tax base that downtown is a great place to do business and live.

Police executives recognized the economic significance of the downtown when considering strategies in the area. Assistant Chief Daniels described the importance of policing to perceptions of safety:

One of the things you really want to maintain in a big city is a police presence downtown, even though downtown is safe—it's got one of the lowest crime rates of any neighborhood in the city. But the bulk of all tourism occurs in the downtown area, and the perception that people have when they travel to a big city is that downtown isn't safe.

Daniels explained that this perception stemmed from the blight of downtowns decades ago but that, since then, "many cities have really focused on a kind of rebirth effort of their downtown areas, not just River City." Curtis Hartman, the former police captain of the East District, also noted the economic importance of the downtown during a public hearing when describing the origins of the department's approach to policing the entertainment corridors: "We needed to develop a policing model that would effectively police the nighttime economy, knowing its connection to the daytime economy."[26] Police officials embraced their role in furthering investments in the downtown, a project they viewed as vital to River City.

The distinctions institutionalized during the redistricting emphasized service and order maintenance in low-crime districts and crime control and law enforcement in high-crime districts. This was particularly the case in the West District. Assistant Chief Daniels characterized the West District as distinctly violent in comparison to the new East District. Pointing to a map, he said, "Here's the river, and it's divided. It's like the Ukraine. This is Crimea, and this is the rest of Ukraine." He then indicated a small area within the new West District:

And the reason I say that is because the policing issues over here on this section—it was like two worlds, completely different districts. And this section over here had the most violent crime areas in the city, of the entire city. This little area right in here, that was the epicenter of crime.

Many people agreed that violent crime in the West District should be a preeminent priority for the police. City officials and media accounts focused on trends in homicides and nonfatal shootings. Moreover, interview respondents described the impacts of violence on residents and businesses in West District neighborhoods. The crime reductions early in Chief Lancaster's tenure suggested the promise of an approach focused on reducing violence. Assistant Chief Daniels explained that this attention was part of "evolving from a rapid response to a proactive, problem-solving type strategy." He went on, "We know that there are very small, locally very clustered areas of crime, and those became our focal point."

Yet the emphasis on violence glossed over other attributes of the West District's neighborhoods. Counternarratives emerged during interviews with community organizers, managers of business improvement districts, and representatives of neighborhood associations who worked and lived in the West District. They emphasized both the assets of these areas and the lack of trust between the police and Black communities. For instance, interviewees saw great development potential in their neighborhoods but indicated that little political will existed to realize it. Tyson Harrison, the director of a community development agency, said,

> The same kind of thing you see downtown, we'd like to see that kind of energy develop here. We have the footprint. What we need to do is garner the desire from government officials, folks who control the money and want to invest back over here on a larger scale.

Stakeholders also described problems of trust and legitimacy. Sydney Reese, a community organizer in several West District neighborhoods, explained, "People just don't trust the police. There are a lot of people that have been abused by police or have been told a narrative that police are wrong." Later, she continued, "[The work] is building the trust but also giving people the capacity to be able to voice things and be heard." These narratives suggested policing priorities that would extend beyond addressing violent crime to incorporate activities focused on building stronger police-community relationships, enhancing feelings of security, and cultivating the development potential of West District neighborhoods. In contrast to these priorities, police department presentations of the redistricting did not include an expansive array of activities beyond those focused on crime control.

Indeed, police executives preeminently focused on criminality when framing the predominantly Black neighborhoods of the West District. This contrasted to the way police executives described the predominantly Latinx neighborhoods in the North District. Police officials characterized both districts as sites of criminal hotspots and violent crime; Chief Lancaster referenced gang issues in the North District in his presentation to the Safety Committee, and Assistant Chief Daniels noted that "violent crime was much more problematic and more prolific" in the North District area that was separated from the South District through the redistricting. But Daniels also described the redistricting as responsive to commercial and community interests in the North District. He had met with some of the city's Hispanic leaders before the redistricting, and he listened to their complaints about different levels of police response because the community was split between two districts. The redistricting united the community. Daniels also described a commercial corridor in the area: "It's the heartbeat, I consider it, of the Hispanic community, and it's where a lot of Hispanic businesses have flourished." Daniels continued, "There's been a great sense of pride reestablished in that neighborhood, and I think the police department changing our boundaries and allowing us to work cohesively across [the corridor] has made a big impact in a positive way on our relations."

By contrast, I found an absence of such attention to community and commercial interests as police executives discussed the West District. Instead, narratives concentrated on violence and crime and the risks these issues posed for *East* District areas. Although Assistant Chief Daniels described a "haves and the have-nots" situation, he invoked it in reference to police service rather than to racial, social, and economic disparities between the two districts. When officers were "too busy over here policing gun violence" in west-side areas, white residents in middle-class neighborhoods on the east side could not receive the police service they desired. Police executives saw this as important to remedy, and the redistricting offered a means of doing so.

Differential Voice across a Segregated City

Police executives revealed affinities with and responsiveness to powerful political and economic stakeholders in the commitment to preserve policing resources for already-better-off areas in the city. Several interviewees described why this might be the case by citing different degrees of advocacy coming from various parts of the city. Martha Hines of the downtown business improvement district explained that "things that happen downtown are extremely high profile." She described how a potential criminal problem would be addressed:

> If there's this carjacking issue, it's going to get covered by the media. And those residents in downtown and in [other neighborhoods] which are part of our district are extremely vocal. They're going to complain to the leadership, and more so than many other residents that don't understand the structure or aren't as invested in the city. There's just a different level of accountability to those residents, to those stakeholders.

Joe McKnight, a former City Council member who went on to direct a different business improvement district in the East District, reflected on how such responsiveness to the community could occur in the East District and not in other parts of the city. He began by musing, "A cynic might say that these lines were drawn along racial borders and that white people have their own district." After noting that some City Council members had been insistent on community policing, he continued,

> I'm not sure I saw that insistence from my African American colleagues— that they were as involved or that they were demanding the same kind of policing strategies. And so is it a function of the police department not do- ing it, or is it a function of the police department not being asked to do it?

Stakeholders in the West District speculated that some differences in priorities between districts resulted from the city's legacies of racial exclusion. Sydney Reese, the community organizer quoted earlier, ex- panded on her perception of the differential capacities for voice in the city:

> It definitely feels like the focus is downtown. It's like, the loudest wheel always gets the oil, right? So that's the saying. And when you are work- ing with a population that has been so disengaged for so long and feels so disempowered, they often don't ever make a noise. People that have had privilege or people that know if they speak up for something, it can change, then they're going to make a lot of noise, and they're going to make a lot of hustle, and then all eyes are going to be toward that area. And typically, that's white neighborhoods.

Her comments captured the pervasive sense that city entities, including the police, responded to dominant individuals and entities in setting their priorities. In overlooking the full array of local interests in the West District and instead adopting a narrow focus on crime control, the logic of the redistricting foreshadowed tactical choices rooted in racialized presumptions of criminality, violence, and threat. By contrast, across an urban landscape of differentially empowered stakeholders, those in the East District wielded particular leverage in shaping relations with the police department. The police responded in kind by prioritizing service in the district.

The Reality of Resource Constraints

The emphasis on enhancing service in low-crime districts hinted at another reality that would come to define policing in the East and West Districts: that of resource constraints. Though Chief Lancaster cited the lofty goal of creating neighborhoods that could sustain civic life, police ability to do so was limited from the start. Many problems confronting the city's marginalized areas were far outside the jurisdictional capacity of the police. As described in chapter 1, they stemmed from a long history of compounding inequalities in housing, employment, education, health care, and public services.[27] Just as the police were not solely responsible for shaping the segregated landscape of the city, they could not remedy its ailments alone. Even under ideal conditions, democratic policing could not repair the social fabric of institutionally neglected neighborhoods or connect residents to extralegal resources that did not exist. Truly transforming neighborhoods would require addressing the structural underpinnings of the city's inequality. However, River City leadership had not embraced this approach, opting instead for a vision of growth that emphasized the continued enhancement of "salvageable" areas, thereby insinuating the decline of others. Police executives aligned themselves with this project by linking policing priorities in the downtown and middle-class neighborhoods to a narrative about the economic and social fate of the city.

In taking up these priorities, the police department hinted at its own resource constraints. The redistricting intentionally created disparities in call volume between districts. It was clear in Chief Lancaster's presentation that a primary goal of separating high-crime and low-crime areas was to ensure that officers in low-crime neighborhoods would not leave those areas to respond to calls in high-crime areas. This logic suggested that the existing personnel allocations in high-crime neighborhoods were insufficient in relation to the volume of work there, as officers from other areas needed to be pulled from preventive patrol to take assignments. Redrawing the district boundaries to keep officers in quieter neighborhoods raised the question of who would be available to respond to citizens' calls for service if officers in busy districts were already assigned elsewhere.

While the redistricting emphasized crime control in the newly created high-crime districts, residents in these neighborhoods also had needs in relation to service and order maintenance. They wanted the same visible police presence that was promised in the East District and a reliable response when they called the police about issues of disorder. Equitable police service would also require meeting West District residents' needs around response to calls and quality-of-life issues. The account of the redistricting, which prioritized police presence and response in low-crime districts, foreshadowed divergences in strategies and resources that would play out in the years to come.

Conclusion

In the process of marking distinctions between areas of value and those of violence, the police department reified long-standing racial and spatial boundaries. The police did not create the deep structural divides between the city's predominantly white, better-off neighborhoods and its more marginal Black and Latinx areas. In many ways, they responded to the exigencies of real differences when considering how to transform their organizational arrangements. But police executives also claimed a constitutive power over place, and their institutional definitions and activities did have the capacity to augment salient divides. By drawing district boundaries around "coherent" neighborhoods, police executives elevated particular understandings of place, lumping some areas together as similar and separating others as distinct. This erased the heterogeneity within districts and emphasized the differences between them.

The preeminent distinction that police executives and other stakeholders drew between "low-crime" areas of value and "high-crime" areas
was itself more constructed than inherent. A long line of scholarship
on the deviance of the powerful recognizes that dominant individuals
and groups frequently engage in criminal activities—like insider trading, corporate malfeasance, illicit drug use, driving under the influence,
intimate-partner violence, and sexual assault, among others. But crimes
of the powerful are less visible and often go unpunished by the justice
system, despite causing economic and social harms.[28] The East District
was considered a "low-crime" area on the basis of common measures
that focused on street crime rather than crimes of the powerful. The
police further fostered the idea that the East District mainly experienced
quality-of-life issues by defining activities that could be construed as
criminal violations—for instance, underage drinking or drug use on the
college campus in the East District—as nuisance problems. Beyond the
general societal biases that favor the powerful and obscure their wrong-
doing, the police were likely to take a conciliatory rather than punitive
approach to East District residents and businesses on the basis of their
economic standing within the city.

Meanwhile, crime statistics painted a picture of the West District as
objectively criminal rather than historically *criminalized*. Research has
shown that while homicide statistics tend to be relatively reliable, other
measures of crime are heavily influenced by reporting patterns and
police-initiated activities.[29] As a classic example, choices over how to
enforce drug laws fueled the disproportionate incarceration of African
Americans and Latinos for drug crimes, despite similar reported rates
of drug use across racial groups.[30] Crime rates in the West District were
partially produced by discretionary police activities, including those that
had historically contributed to the hyperincarceration of the city's Black
male population. Narratives during the redistricting doubled down on
ideas of criminal threat and resulted in strategies focused on separation,
containment, and suppression. In short, police officials relied on racialized definitions of criminality that would shape how officers engaged
subsequently with residents in predominantly Black versus predominantly white neighborhoods.

The tensions and outcomes that emerged through the redistricting
reflected several institutional realities for the River City Police Depart-

ment. In responding to the national field of policing, Chief Lancaster and other executives adopted administrative reforms aligned with innovative strategies. Organizational changes to facilitate community policing were widely seen as progressive, and stakeholders generally supported this vision. However, it is likely that it was precisely the flexibility of goals and tactics embedded in popular strategic innovations that paved the way for the police department's participation in growth politics. As community-based policing and problem-oriented policing, among other strategies, promote an expanding array of activities, police departments adopt new functions, such as reducing fear, enhancing perceptions of safety, and linking communities to extralegal resources. In doing so, they claim new capacities to transform neighborhoods. This raises questions about how these capacities are put to use and who influences decisions around the functions of the police.

The police in River City responded to differentially empowered and vocal stakeholders—elected officials, business coalitions, community organizers, and residents—and they ultimately aligned their strategic priorities with the economic-development agenda put forward by Mayor Taylor and other members of the city's growth coalition. This agenda was underpinned by the assumption that all residents will eventually benefit from targeted growth. However, the racial implications of uneven development strategies raise important moral hazards, and the consequences of devoting additional policing resources to serving and protecting predominantly white communities have yet to be fully explored. The following chapters document the district-level policing practices that followed the redistricting in River City. In redefining discrete work environments and identifying overarching priorities, the police department set goals and crafted constraints that laid the foundations for divergent policing styles. Ultimately, differences in policing consolidated deeply entrenched facets of River City's racial segregation and neighborhood inequality.

3

Policing the East District

Officer Albert Ramirez, a middle-aged Latino man and twenty-five-year veteran of the police department, had been on the scene of an apartment-complex burglary near River City's downtown for two hours. During this time, Ramirez had worked continuously on varied tasks, interviewing the building manager and a maintenance technician, gathering evidence—including photos of the scene and swabs of blood presumably from the suspect prying a television off the wall—reviewing security footage, and providing additional precautionary advice for the building manager. After returning to the squad, I asked about the way Ramirez handled this assignment. He drew a sharp contrast between his response in this case and his experience working in the West District, where he had been for a year prior to his transfer to the East District. He suggested that a burglary investigation in the West District would require less time—maybe forty minutes—because the police would be unlikely to solve the crime. In the West District, a cop would run around "like a chicken with its head cut off," taking assignments all day long. In many cases, officers could respond to a scene, write the report, then "file it and forget it." In the East District, however, the police might take fewer assignments, but those assignments required more thorough investigation, follow-up, and report-writing because residents demanded and expected more.

Like Officer Alport in the book's introduction, Ramirez did not think the East District had less work than the West District—the districts just presented "a different set of headaches." Ramirez talked about past assignments where he had interacted with powerful downtown stakeholders. Once, a supervisor had accompanied him to "make sure he did everything right" when he responded to a break-in at the building of a large corporate philanthropic organization. Ramirez mused, "The law supposedly treats everyone equally, but money talks." I was surprised by such an overt admission. Even though scholars have demonstrated that equal treatment under the law is more myth than reality,[1] hearing an agent of law enforcement recognize as much unsettled a core premise of the justice system.

Ramirez was not alone in the idea that police service varied based on the social standing of citizens. I found this notion to be widespread among officers. After observing and hearing about work in the East District, I understood how officers' experiences could sustain such a perception. The East District police encountered politically connected citizens unafraid to wield their influence. Several officers made comments along the lines of "people here are one phone call away from the chief [of police]." Officers indicated that even the university students in the area attempted to leverage their status. An officer mocked the claims that drunken students made when confronting the police: "My dad is this; my dad is that." But, as another officer asserted on a separate occasion, "If they say their dad is a lawyer, he's probably a lawyer." Good work could receive unexpected recognition: one officer said his efforts to reduce speeding along a thoroughfare had been reported to Mayor Taylor because the owner of one of the condo buildings along the street happened to be Taylor's "walking buddy." But missteps or inadequacies might also be relayed to police higher-ups or city officials. These pressures cultivated a sense that the stakes of handling assignments in the East District were high, even if the incidents themselves were less serious.

To interact with the district's empowered residents, officers felt that they needed a distinct skill set that they likened to "public relations" or "people skills." Officer Kevin Hickey—a middle-aged white man— thought this accounted for his assignment to the East District. During a ride-along, Officer Hickey called to summon a tow truck while we were sitting at the scene of a car accident. He spoke to the woman on the line clearly and playfully, calling her "dear" and thanking her profusely before hanging up. Then he turned to me and explained that he tried to be warm toward people working such jobs—it could make someone's day, and people in these bureaucratic positions wielded a lot of power. Hickey noted that he had been directed to positions that required people skills throughout his career, including his time with smaller law enforcement agencies in the region. Hickey had requested assignment to the East District after field training, though he had been surprised to receive it given the needs of other districts. He suggested that this reflected his personability. This quality did indeed seem to be recognized by his colleagues: during roll call later that week, a sergeant tapped Hickey as a potential recruiter for new officers. Many officers shared Hickey's sense that work in the East District required special skills. Even supervisors noted that talking to people in the East District was often "a different kind of interaction," as one sergeant put it.

The police drew on moral judgments when making sense of their work in the East District. Officers, many from working- or middle-class backgrounds, resented occasionally demeaning treatment by wealthy and entitled citizens. For instance, Officer Alport recounted with indignation an incident in which a prominent local attorney asked Alport to remove his boots before entering his home. Despite these headaches, the police generally understood East District residents as "good people." Officer Ramirez suggested that about 80 percent of the city's revenue was generated in East District. He further speculated that residents' demands were fair, as these people were taxpayers. Indeed, many officers invoked this idea of the deserving taxpayer: the citizen who directly contributed to the city's economic health and its ability to fund public services, including those provided by the police. In this regard, officers' perceptions of East District residents aligned with police executives' narratives about the economic importance of the area. While attitudes favoring this segment of the city's geography and population could have easily preceded the redistricting, the reform created new opportunities to act on such ideas.

Strategic Coherence and the Community-Service Ethos

This chapter elaborates on the connections between the police department's strategic priorities and the on-the-ground work of officers in the East District. During the redistricting, police executives articulated a vision of the police role in the East District tied to urban development. Stakeholders in the growth coalition framed police service as an amenity desired by middle-class residents, patrons of the downtown, and potential developers. In order to retain and court these important contributors to River City's economic prospects, the police sought to shape the appeal of the East District's geography through activities focused on service, order maintenance, and collaborative problem-solving. The redistricting facilitated these goals by creating a work environment around quality-of-life issues. With a lighter workload and few serious criminal incidents, patrol officers had ample time to respond quickly to calls for service, to follow up and provide justice for victims, and to focus on crime prevention instead of merely reacting to individual incidents. Moreover, district leaders instituted novel problem-solving initiatives that offered tailored solutions to issues experienced by residents and downtown stakeholders. Many perceived improved policing and changes in the downtown based on the strategic initiatives that followed the redistricting.

Much of the work in the East District coalesced around a *community-service* ethos. Even as the downtown experienced different kinds of problems than residential neighborhoods, the police treated these areas as similar through a consistent emphasis on service provision and community policing. Each district in the city had a community policing unit, which included officers who liaised with local stakeholders. The East District had two community-based officers whose primary responsibility involved working with business leaders, neighborhood associations, community organizations, and other groups. Unlike other districts, community policing in the East District transcended the work of these officers. The paradigm's mandate—to use community partnerships and proactive problem-solving to address local concerns[2]—was taken up by district leaders as they developed special initiatives. Patrol officers' responsiveness in the East District also reflected this approach. A pervasive and cohesive community-service ethos could take hold in the East District because best practices in the national field of policing aligned neatly with urban-governance imperatives that prioritized collaborative, responsive, and preventive police service for the area's residents and visitors.

However, it bears noting that the community-service ethos was not uniformly applied within the East District. The police scrutinized those who did not "belong" in the downtown. Officers drew on racialized ideas that marked Black people as potential criminal threats, and institutional practices targeted subtler indicators of race and class. Chapter 5 describes in detail this phenomenon of policing "race out of place." It shows that the police were implicated in maintaining segregation boundaries and defining the East District as a white space. But before exploring the contours of police attention to Black people, I outline the policing modalities that applied to predominantly white places and people. This chapter focuses on the practices characterizing the community service ethos and the connections between East District policing and the project of urban revitalization.

The chapter also examines how East District officers made sense of their work. The community-service ethos entailed activities that diverged from common imaginings of policing. Even as decades of research have recognized that the police perform a wide array of activities, many members of the police and the public continue to view aggressive crime fighting as "real" police work.[3] Officers place great emphasis on the dangerous and potentially violent nature of their jobs, and their role as crime fighters is valued and rewarded institutionally.[4] The associations between catching criminals, danger, and valor are part of what make policing a hypermasculine occupation.[5] Yet, in the East District, the police primarily engaged in service provision and order maintenance. This kind of work is often undervalued, if not outright disdained, by officers.[6] East District police made sense of performing traditionalized feminized activities by emphasizing the unique challenges of the work environment and the exceptional skills they required to navigate it. For instance, they focused on the finesse needed to handle the city's most powerful residents and stakeholders. Ultimately, East District officers elevated their work by elevating the importance of the district. Like police executives, city officials, and business leaders, they framed their activities as serving and protecting the places and people thought to represent the heart of River City's economic, political, and social life. This narrative reinforced the centrality of the East District work environment, which had been crafted intentionally through the process of redistricting.

The New East District

Prior to redistricting, the East District had included an east end with fewer criminal issues and a west end with higher rates of recorded criminal incidents and calls for service. With the reform, the west end was excised from the district, and the quieter residential areas to the east were incorporated along with the city's downtown into the new East District. This area was home to two major types of places of interest to the police. The first was the district's residential neighborhoods. Eighty percent of the land use in the district was residential, and the neighborhoods in the East District were middle class or wealthy. The average assessed residential value of homes in the East District was more than three times greater than the city's overall average. Residents were a mix of long-term home owners and young adults, drawn by the university, professional opportunities, or urban amenities of the area. Approximately 80 percent of the district's residents were white—the highest proportion of white residents of any police district in the city.[7]

The second area of interest was the downtown. While nearly fifty thousand people lived in the district, thousands more entered it on a routine basis. The central business district drew a weekday influx of commuters from other parts of the city and the surrounding metro area. Nightlife and shopping corridors, cultural institutions, and entertainment venues attracted evening and weekend visitors. High-profile concerts, sporting events, and festivals could draw tens of thousands of people into the district. Though residential neighborhoods and the downtown presented different dynamics, the police department grouped these areas together as similar based on their economic contributions to the city. Police executives defined primary policing problems in the East District as those relating to quality-of-life and nuisance issues. They had sought to separate these from the "high-crime" areas now in the West District and had thus created a district characterized by a lower volume of crime and calls for service.

Indeed, East District could be characterized as a "lower crime" part of the city on the basis of reported and recorded criminal incidents, particularly in comparison to the West District. In data that examined major index crimes over a year-long period,[8] the East District reported fewer than half the number of incidents as the West District: 3,162 compared to 6,439. Moreover, a smaller proportion of those incidents involved violent crimes of homicide, assault, sex offenses, and burglary. Such incidents constituted 17 percent of the incidents in the East District and 40 percent of those in the West District. Only one of the city's 122 homicides had occurred in the East District. The district's crime problems were driven by higher-than-average rates of locked-vehicle entry and theft—events commonly reported in urban downtown areas. The rate of car break-ins in the East District was double the citywide rate at 15.3 per 1,000, compared to 6.4. Together, thefts and locked-vehicle entries constituted over 50 percent of all reported crimes in the district.

Disparities in calls for police service also reflected the differences between districts. Calls better reflect the workload handled by patrol officers because they capture a host of neighborhood disturbances and noncriminal emergencies that never result in an arrest or crime report. The year after the district boundary changes, approximately 16,400 calls came into the East District, while just over 45,000 came into the West District.[9] Beyond these differences in volume, the districts had different kinds of calls. Only 12 percent of East District calls were designated "priority one,"[10] indicating that they involved life-threatening conditions. During ride-alongs, I commonly observed officers sent to assignments like traffic accidents, noise complaints, calls for "trouble with a subject," checks on an individual's welfare, burglaries, and thefts. Occasionally, officers responded to calls for battery, fights, or other violent incidents, but this was rare compared to calls for property crimes and nuisance issues. By contrast, over six times as many calls involving life-threatening situations came into the West District, and these calls constituted about one-quarter of the total call volume. In short, the East District had a significantly lower volume of calls and a smaller proportion of serious calls compared to the West District. Furthermore, disparities in call volume had widened since the redistricting: in comparison to the year before the reform, the East District reported approximately 5,000 fewer calls the year after the reform, and the West District experienced about 4,400 more calls.[11]

The new East District work environment reflected the redistricting's goals: to aggregate problems defined as similar within particular districts and to separate the quiet neighborhoods of the East District from the busier neighborhoods of the West District. The police could now develop strategies that addressed the distinct concerns of East District residents and stakeholders in the downtown. Police officials identified two preeminent priorities tied to the redistricting. First, patrol officers could provide prompt response and a stable presence because they would no longer be pulled to busier areas. As Assistant Chief Daniels explained in our interview, "Having the downtown and [other East District neighborhoods] together in a district, . . . it made sure that the police were equally patrolling [within the district]." East District neighborhoods would no longer experience a lack of police presence that had occurred when squad cars had to respond to calls in the district's former west end. Second, district leaders could address the downtown's unique issues, exemplified by a policing initiative in the district's entertainment corridors. Daniels explained the initiative: "Now we've got almost all of our major entertainment zones contained within one police district." He continued, citing an innovative model for policing these areas, "We've been able to apply that type of strategy across the entire East District." By labeling East District neighborhoods as similar, the police could offer a consistent style of policing—one rooted in an ethos of community service.

Service Provision and Community Problem-Solving

When police executives presented the redistricting, they emphasized the goal of increasing their visible presence and providing responsive service in middle-class neighborhoods that were seen as an essential tax base for the city. Many recognized that these residents might leave River City if services, including policing, were better in the suburbs. East District residents were also unafraid to express their concerns and desires. These dynamics converged to produce a culture of responsiveness among the police. This culture was evinced in the attitudes and everyday practices of patrol officers, as they handled citizens' calls for service and engaged in preventive patrol. It also found more systematic institutionalization in problem-solving initiatives to address ongoing concerns in residential neighborhoods.

Responsiveness to Calls for Service and Preventive Patrol

As the opening of this chapter highlights, pressures from the department and citizens, along with officers' sense of residents' deservingness, encouraged line officers to provide exceptional police service in the East District. Their ability to do so was facilitated by the district's lower call volume. Patrol officers said it was not unusual for a shift to involve just a few assignments. Indeed, on the basis of my ethnographic observations, officers in the East District responded to an average of three assign-ments as the primary squad during a shift, while officers in the West District responded to six. Officers often pulled up a list of pending calls to which a squad had yet to be dispatched. In the East District, the list could be empty. Officer Alan Callahan, a white man in his forties who had started his career in the West District, noted that some nights in the East District, he would take a single call. This allowed him to be more involved with the people he encountered during the assignment, and interactions were smoothed by citizens' attitudes toward the police. Cal-lahan explained that "99 percent of people here want the cops here." For many police, this was a relief. Officer Tammy Hall, a white woman who had been with the department for over twenty years, suggested, "We're all lucky to be in the East District."

Given the lower volume of calls, it was generally easy to find an unas-signed unit to send to an incoming call, and officers drove promptly to the scene of an assignment. At the scene, the police were thorough in their preliminary investigations and responsive to citizens they encoun-tered. During one ride-along, Officer Hall was dispatched to a traffic accident at a downtown arterial street. She arrived within minutes of receiving the assignment. A teenage girl had run a red light and hit a car entering the intersection. Her car had spun out, ripping off the bumper and scattering debris along the curb. As all parties at the scene had only minor injuries, Officer Hall began her investigation.

Hall interviewed both drivers and a witness who had initially called in the accident. She conferred with the paramedics to document their response. A bystander told Hall that he happened to capture footage of the accident on his dashcam, and Hall reviewed it several times. She requested the video and listed the man as a witness. Then Hall docu-mented the damage to the vehicles and began compiling the accident report. She shared the incident number with both parties and noted that she did not plan to give the girl a citation, as her day had been bad enough. Hall conferred with the other driver and offered to call a city tow truck if his insurance company could not arrange to tow the car. She then said that she would clean up a bit so that a hotel next to the curb would not be upset. She retrieved a broom from the trunk of the car and swept the debris from the accident into a neat pile. The second driver struggled for some time to find a tow truck for the car, and Hall continued to work on the accident report while waiting. Eventually, a tow truck arrived, and as the scene was clearing, Hall offered to take the driver to the train station. She radioed in with a "citizen conveyance" to indicate that she was giving him a ride, and she wished the man well as he departed. In total, Hall worked on the scene for around three hours.

The time and effort Hall spent on this assignment reflected, in part, the requisites of handling such an accident. However, her concern for the parties involved and affected—including the downtown hotel—seemed beyond the demands of conventional police response. Hall's interactions with the drivers typified many of the police-citizen encounters I observed in the East District: officers were often reassuring and helpful, and they maintained this demeanor even when the issues appeared to be minor. For instance, Officer Todd Geiger responded to a call for property damage in the university area. A landlord reported that his porch railing had been "smashed to bits," potentially by the former student tenants. When Geiger arrived, the landlord apologized and asserted several times that the police probably had more important things to do. Nevertheless, Geiger gathered the man's information and provided an incident number, assuring him that a police report for the property damage would be completed.

The police generally offered collaborative assistance when working with victims. For instance, Officer Ramirez asked a hardware-store manager if he would prefer a municipal citation or a state charge for an employee caught stealing several hundred dollars from the company's safe. The manager said he was leaning toward state charges in order to enforce restitution. This kind of inclusive decision-making ensured that police response matched the interests of callers. It also gave victims control over the outcomes of a criminal incident in ways that many never experience.

Patrol officers' work in the East District extended beyond their response to calls. With fewer assignments, East District officers spent a smaller proportion of each shift tied up on a scene, compared to those in the West District. During their unassigned time, officers could respond as backup to one another's assignments or engage in an array of preventive activities. During all but two patrol ride-alongs in the East District, officers sought out additional work. Indeed, on particularly slow shifts, like Alport's shift described in the introduction, most work was officer-initiated. Common activities included conducting traffic stops, checking in with businesses, and patrolling on foot in areas with pedestrian flow.

Traffic safety stops seemed to be a particularly popular activity in the East District. The department incentivized traffic stops by including them as a measure of officers' performance. While there was no quota for stops, officers within a district were compared to one another and risked eventual sanctioning for poor performance. Many officers would seek stops by idling at a favorite intersection where moving violations were likely to occur or where equipment violations were easy to spot. Notably, most traffic stops in the East District dealt with traffic enforcement; they were used rarely as a pretext for criminal investigation. Officers pulled over drivers for expired registration, illegal turns, burnt-out headlights, and similar infractions. In most cases, officers let drivers go with a warning. Traffic-stop practices exemplified preventive work in the East District, which was collectively oriented toward maintaining order and public safety. This trend stood in stark contrast to the proactive work in the West District, which focused on ferreting out crime. Compared to traffic safety stops in the East District, West District officers were encouraged to make investigatory stops. The implications of this difference are discussed further in chapter 4.

Ample downtime in the East District also facilitated visible patrol, consistent with Chief Lancaster's vision of stabilizing police presence in East District neighborhoods. Officers spent much of their unassigned time driving through the residential areas of their sectors. Sometimes, they targeted their patrol to particular times and places. One officer routinely drove through the university area during peak foot-traffic times. Another noted a region in the downtown where car break-ins had been common. Officers understood not only that preventive patrol could deter crime but also that it was important to residents, who wanted to see a visible police presence in their neighborhoods.

For instance, on one sunny afternoon, Officer Geiger drove to the far end of the district to patrol along an avenue lined with some of the city's most expensive and opulent homes. When I asked if the neighborhood had many crime issues, he said no, but residents liked to see the police driving through. Geiger mentioned a spate of incidents a while ago involving stolen copper drainpipes from the houses. As many were historic homes, the home owners had to replace the drains, sometimes for thousands of dollars. Like other officers, part of Geiger's account was tied to perceptions of residents' deservingness. Geiger suggested that some home owners in the area paid $35,000 a year in property taxes. He went on: "People say they shouldn't get better police service, but that's how my salary is paid." Again, Geiger's comment explicitly suggested that wealthy residents both sustained and deserved better policing on the basis of their contributions to the city's coffers.

Community Policing and Neighborhood Problem-Solving

Beyond the thorough and responsive service that patrol officers provided, police in the East District undertook special efforts to address the concerns of residents. This was most apparent in the work of the district's two community-based officers. During my fieldwork period, Officer David Petty had recently been assigned to one of these positions. His primary tasks involved liaising and information-sharing with stakeholders across the district, including networks of business owners, neighborhood associations, and civic organizations. Petty, a white man in his early forties, was well suited for this role. Before taking the position, he had a downtown walking beat where he interacted with dozens of people on a daily basis. Petty was talkative and friendly, with a penchant for offering his cellphone number and encouraging people to call if they needed anything. After over a decade with the River City Police Department, including five years of work in the West District, he said he liked the change offered by the East District. Petty suggested that it was easier to see the results of his work and that he appreciated how the East District residents were generally happy to see the police. His personability equipped him to respond to the concerns and demands of the district's vocal and empowered residents.

The depths of police efforts to accommodate the interests of East District citizens were on full display when I accompanied Officer Petty to a winter-evening meeting of the Larkwood Neighborhood Association. Larkwood was a scenic residential area characterized by wide tree-lined streets and inviting single-family homes. The neighborhood was populated by both long-term residents and students at the nearby university. It appeared to be long-term residents who participated in the neighborhood association and attended this meeting.

As people filtered in, some approached Petty, who had arrived in uniform and taken a seat near the back of the room. Two women—both middle-aged and white—had taken a seat behind us. Once Petty seemed available, one declared emphatically, "We need more cops!" She asked if Petty had met with the mayor yet. He replied tactfully that there were crime problems throughout the city and that he did not directly meet with the mayor. The woman went on to describe the college students as the neighborhood's biggest problem. She noted that turnover made relationships difficult—just when residents got a set of students to respect the neighbors finally, they moved out, and new ones moved in. She concluded by describing the neighborhood as "the college ghetto." Her application of this racialized term to the majority-white student population carried a pejorative connotation of disorder. Petty shared that the police were excited to give a presentation at the university's student orientation for the first time in several years. The woman's companion then jumped in to mention problems at a busy intersection in the heart of the neighborhood. She declared that she would *pay* to have a squad sit at the intersection between 11 p.m. and 3 a.m. I was shocked by such an unabashed proposal to buy city policing as if it were a private service for sale. Yet this idea was not so different from officers' assertion that those who paid higher taxes deserved more police service.

The room was soon full. Approximately thirty people had arrived, all of them white and ranging from their late twenties into their seventies. The president of the association, who had introduced herself as Cynthia, called the meeting to order. She referenced a PowerPoint with an agenda, including updates from the university, the River City Police Department, and a task force focused on the bars along a central commercial corridor. As the meeting unfolded, much attention was devoted to "the Call Log," an ongoing initiative established by Captain Curtis Hartman, the East District's previous leader, in collaboration with representatives of the neighborhood association. The program gave Larkwood neighborhood residents the phone number to the East District lieutenant's office, which provided access to the supervising commander during night shifts. Residents were encouraged to call this number when nuisance issues arose—usually loud parties or other student-related noise complaints. The lieutenant would then bypass dispatch and send an officer to the scene directly. The complaint would also be logged; after multiple incidents, the landlord could be cited under the city's nuisance-property ordinance. Cynthia encouraged people to use the system and to keep calling the number to the lieutenant's office if their issues were not addressed promptly.

Cynthia then invited Officer Petty to introduce himself and give an update. He began by asking if people had questions about the Call Log. One woman said she had a compliment rather than a question: she had used the system, and it worked well. A man raised his hand and relayed that he had used the Call Log months ago; but he had been transferred to a dispatcher, and it took forever. Another man asked if there were a database of the calls, and a woman noted that sometimes no one answered the phone. Petty responded in turn to the praise, questions, and complaints. He said he felt for residents and understood that these noise issues were very frustrating. He announced that representatives from the police department would be presenting at the university orientation this year, which elicited applause from the group.

Petty then asked, "What could we do better?" People raised several related issues: large roving groups of drunk students who would wake residents, the risks of underage drinking, and the possibility that students would be victims of crime if they were unaware of their surroundings. They also made several recommendations: additional patrols on weekend nights, more reporting to the university, threats of sanctions during the university orientation. Petty affirmed these comments. He agreed that a greater uniformed police presence would be helpful and said he would bring these issues to the district captain. He concluded by reporting recent criminal incidents in the area, which included five burglaries, six armed robberies, and four motor-vehicle thefts over the past several weeks.

The meeting then broke into smaller brainstorming clusters for workgroups around an array of neighborhood issues. While the groups convened, individuals continued to approach Petty. One woman asked if she could speak to him privately, so they stepped into the hall. Cynthia came over and thanked Petty for his presentation. An older couple chatted with him for a few minutes. Finally, a tall, middle-aged man approached and introduced himself. Earlier, he had commented to the group that residents should keep their own records of nuisance incidents in case they needed to testify in municipal court. Now he chatted with Petty about police deployment in the university area. He said the increased heavy police presence in the fall really seemed to act as a good deterrent. He also noted that things had been "so good since the redistricting." While Larkwood had been in the former West District, it was now in the East District after the boundary change. Petty explained that the biggest problem had been that the former West District police had been pulled over constantly to the other side of the district to respond to violent crime in the inner city, leaving Larkwood with no police presence. Petty and this Larkwood resident concurred that policing had improved after the reform.

The Larkwood Neighborhood Association meeting distilled several dynamics of community policing in the East District. It highlighted prototypical neighborhood conditions in better-off areas: with few serious criminal incidents reported, stakeholders focused on quality-of-life issues, like noise complaints. The often-savvy residents felt empowered to request—or demand—that the issues of their neighborhood be addressed. Officer Petty's role involved validating residents' individual and collective concerns. He also communicated existing and planned police interventions. This was more than lip service. Police leaders in the East District had developed multiple long-term initiatives to deal with the nuisance activities of the student population. The university provided a grant to the police department to deploy additional officers in the neighborhood on weekends. The Call Log also emerged as a collaboratively developed response to address short-term problems like parties and underlying causes of nuisance problems like poorly managed properties. Even if such problem-solving initiatives emerged independently of the redistricting, they nevertheless reflected the same overarching goal of institutionalizing innovative, neighborhood-based policing approaches.

Between problem-solving initiatives and the responsiveness of patrol officers, district stakeholders felt that the redistricting had made policing better. Janice Sanders, a neighborhood group representative, characterized police response in her area prior to the redistricting, when officers were routinely pulled to the other side of the district to handle calls: "You could call them, and somebody might eventually show up after a couple of hours, about a loud party or something. And I swear, I believe one officer actually said, 'Look, lady, you don't have anything going on over here; we've got problems, and you don't.'" Janice went on to note the change since then:

[The redistricting] was just something that the police department did, and I'm so glad they did. Somebody figured out that this was a better arrangement. I have no idea how they figured that out. . . . But it's been better ever since. They actually gave us the number of the desk captain to call if we need to at night.

A director of a business improvement district similarly described his perceptions of policing in East District: "Responsiveness has improved, and there are more officers out of the car now and in the street. And I think that the emphasis on community policing, with the community-based officers, has made them more responsive." Consistent with the police department's goals, East District stakeholders perceived increasing investments of public-safety resources intended to make their neighborhoods more livable, orderly, and safe. This outcome was integral to the growth coalition's project of devoting public services to middle-class neighborhoods to try and keep these residents—and their economic resources—within the city limits.

Order Maintenance and Downtown Development

In addition to efforts to appease existing district residents and stakeholders through responsive service provision, the police embraced an active role in the project of further cultivating the city's resources. River City's mayor concentrated on downtown development as key to citywide revitalization, and downtown projects aimed to attract tourists, conventions, entrepreneurs, and developers to burgeoning professional and cultural districts. As Assistant Chief Daniels described earlier, the police had a role to play in enhancing perceptions of safety, even though the downtown was already comparatively safe. Police executives embraced the capacity to reassure and encourage visitors to the downtown, and they understood it as integral to protecting and attracting businesses and their patrons. One of the most prominent initiatives related to this goal developed a few years into Chief Lancaster's term. This initiative—the Entertainment Corridor Deployment (ECD)—populated the downtown nightlife districts with additional officers on foot patrol. Police executives framed the safety of the city's nightlife scene as central to the downtown's appeal. The ECD showcased the police department's commitment to collaborative, problem-oriented approaches in service of protecting and attracting capital.

The Goals and Strategies of the ECD

Captain Curtis Hartman spearheaded the creation of the ECD when he stewarded the East District. He had since been promoted to an executive position. The connection between the ECD and the goal of downtown growth was clear from the start of the deployment. When a local newspaper article announced the initiative, both Chief Lancaster and Captain Hartman described it as important to the city's economy. Hartman emphasized the significance of tourism and conventions, while a quote from the chief explained the interest of potential developers in the safety of their employees.[12] In a public hearing related to tavern license renewals, Captain Hartman elaborated on the ties between the ECD and the broader economic health of the downtown: "We've learned that the number-one reason young entrepreneurs come into a city is what nightlife offerings that are there. I also know from law enforcement that the probabilities of something bad happening would happen at night." Hartman continued, explaining that his greatest concern was a shooting during the weekend that could deter tourism activities like conventions: "Knowing what the media does with that, knowing that they tend to proliferate this—'it's not safe downtown'—that's my fear. . . . And that perception proliferates through, and we don't get the conventions." Hartman described a recent week-long influx of conventioneers that had generated an estimated $10–$11 million in local spending. He concluded, "We need to have these conventions come here. We need to give them safe alternatives to do at night."[13] The captain's comments highlighted that the ECD was ultimately a preventive initiative. It aimed at ensuring things *did not* happen in order to preserve and bolster the attraction of the city's revitalizing downtown.

To accomplish the preventive aims of the ECD, the police strategically positioned a highly visible presence throughout the nightlife districts. The police department budgeted overtime pay for additional officers during peak weekend hours throughout the summer and other busy times. While many officers who worked the deployment were assigned to the East District, the work was also available to officers across the city. Most officers were deployed on foot rather than in squad cars. They gathered on some of the downtown's busiest blocks and intersections, where they acted as a deterrent to crime and performed an array of order-maintenance activities.

The downtown area attracted weekend revelers from across the metro area, and the influx of thousands of people—many of whom were eventually drunk—gave the police plenty to do. As I observed during ride-alongs, officers regulated large crowds, checked on taverns, intervened in disputes, and managed people who seemed unruly, excessively intoxicated, or otherwise unsafe. The deployment could entail formal law enforcement. Officers might cite or arrest disorderly individuals, and they could fine bars for serving minors or operating over capacity. However, punishing taverns and their patrons was not the main objective of the initiative. As a newspaper article reported, the deployment's strategy encouraged officers to cultivate collaborative working relationships with bar and restaurant owners.[14] If establishment owners were less concerned that the police would take a punitive approach, they would be more likely to communicate about chronic and emergent problems. Collectively, ECD activities sought to maintain order and enhance perceptions of safety rather than to arrest people or punish bars, though these goals were not uniformly applied. As chapter 5 describes, the EDC was also implicated in racial regulation and contributed to the disproportionate policing of Black people in the downtown.

On the Ground during the ECD

A Saturday-night ride-along with Sergeant Jeff Crawford offered a glimpse into ECD work. Crawford, a white man in his thirties, was one of the supervisors who routinely oversaw the deployment. After seven years in the police department, Crawford had recently been promoted to sergeant and transferred to the East District. Before the transfer, Crawford worked on an antiviolence unit focused on intervening in gang-related crimes in one of the city's busier districts, which he characterized as "real police work." I took this to refer to the crime-fighting role that officers often elevated as the essence of their profession. Crawford said he had been unenthusiastic initially about his transfer to the East District, though he had grown to like it. Nevertheless, he insinuated that his work now involved incidents that departed from his standard of real policing. Over the course of the shift, Crawford turned to me periodically and labeled a situation an "East District problem," which seemed to signal some degree of absurdity. Despite this eye-rolling, Crawford saw the work of the ECD as important to protecting the downtown economy. He explained that a shooting would be terrible for the downtown; it would really impact the city by frightening people away from the entertainment districts. Crawford, like many others, saw the police as vital in preventing such an incident.

Crawford began his oversight of the ECD shortly after 10 p.m. when he drove to the deployment's epicenter on Main Street. This intersection of two wide thoroughfares offered a vantage point over several blocks of clubs and bars. The ECD had closed down vehicular traffic on Main Street, and officers congregated on the road's median to watch the pedestrian flow and crowds on the sidewalk. Crawford parked the squad in the street and walked over to talk to the vendor at a hot-dog cart. As he was standing there, the bouncer from a nearby bar flagged him over. The bouncer pointed to a white man in his twenties and told Crawford that he had kicked out the man from the bar for sleeping, prompting the man to threaten a fight. Crawford escorted the man over to a parking lot adjacent to the bar. A small group of exceptionally drunk young men followed, continuously trying to talk to Crawford until he forcefully told them to go stand behind a car several feet away. Crawford summoned additional officers via radio. When they arrived, one officer checked the man's license, and another stayed with him as Crawford left to speak with the bouncer, who confirmed that the group had become loud and aggressive after being told to leave. Crawford returned to the group and informed them that they should stay away from the bar for the rest of the night. Despite mild protest, the group eventually acquiesced and debated where to go next. The officers released the man to the care of his friends, and the group shuffled down the street. Throughout the interaction, I stood a short distance away, trying to avoid the drunk crew on the sidewalk. At one point, Crawford made eye contact with me and knowingly declared, "East District problem."

Crawford continued to patrol on foot. He stopped by a newer bar with a small line of people waiting to enter. The owner, a middle-aged white man, stood at the door with a bouncer. Crawford and the owner had a friendly conversation, with Crawford telling him that the bar was doing a great job of crowd control on the sidewalk. Crawford signaled to the posts and chain put out to contain the line, and the owner said it would allow eight people to queue. Crawford again affirmed that the owner was doing a great job. We walked around the block toward another set of bars, where Crawford had another friendly exchange with the managers of "The Irish Pub," one of the nightlife district's largest establishments. Crawford complimented the manager on the pub's effective crowd control. As we walked away, Crawford told me that the owners had several establishments, including a club across the street, and they were very good at hiring enough security to regulate the crowd inside and on the sidewalks. Crawford returned to the squad and drove several blocks to another ECD site. He checked in with the small group of officers outside "The Edge," a large nightclub catering to "the hip-hop crowd," as Crawford described it. Crawford maintained that the owner was "one of the best bar owners in the city." He cited the owner's ample staffing, security, crowd management, and cooperation with the police.

By midnight, the ECD police presence had grown: two wagons, a large police truck, four squad cars, and the horse unit were all stationed at the Main Street intersection. Crawford and I circulated among the officers, observing and discussing the scene. At one point, two young white women approached one of the horse-unit officers, saying they were locked out of their car. The officers retrieved a set of tools and left to assist. Crawford pointed out a seasoned officer whom he described as a "food-cart expert," explaining that the officer was familiar with the ordinances governing food-cart placement; this had allowed the police to intervene in the location of the food carts and, therefore, the sidewalk crowds. Crawford labeled the food-cart issue an "East District problem."

Later, Crawford patrolled in the squad for a while, rushing to a call for a fight at one point but leaving upon seeing that several officers had the situation under control. He then checked in on two officers investigating three underage girls trying to enter a bar. The girls, who protested that several bars had let them in already, seemed to come to terms with their night ending when the officers threatened citations. At one point, back in the squad, Crawford muttered "Christ" with exasperation and abruptly pulled over at the sight of a white woman curled on her side on the sidewalk. Two other women were approaching, and Crawford asked if everything was all right or if the woman on the ground needed to go to the hospital. The group's designated driver explained that she would take the woman home, and they helped her up.

These myriad interactions highlighted important facets of the Entertainment Corridor Deployment: collaborative relations with bar owners and managers, an emphasis on order maintenance, and interactions with citizens that addressed potential nuisance or public-safety concerns, often without resorting to formal law enforcement. Officers' engagements with the downtown establishments and their patrons were consistent with the collaborative, problem-solving orientation of the ECD. Officers also understood the deployment's ties to the broader economic interests of the city. Even as Crawford subtly derided some incidents he encountered during the EDC, he saw the deployment as important to preventing incidents that would frighten away visitors to the downtown. Police work to protect businesses and their clientele was part of the project of ongoing and future economic growth. Notably, these efforts served a predominantly white population.

Perceived Impacts of Policing in the Downtown

In many regards, the Entertainment Corridor Deployment proved to be another successful East District initiative. Downtown stakeholders described the deployment's positive contributions. In a newspaper article, a bar owner noted that he was happy with the program and described it as "truly, unbelievably proactive." The executive director of a downtown business improvement district framed the ECD as part of a larger effort to support downtown nightlife.[15] During my interview with council member Sam Ward, who represented an East District area with a prominent entertainment corridor, he explained,

> You could just come in and crack down and just come in force in [the entertainment corridor] and ruin everybody's good time. And you'd solve a problem, but you'd create a new one, which is now we've lost an entertainment district. So you need a kind of precision there or a different kind of focus. We've got that now.

Beyond appreciating the police department's goals, stakeholders attributed improvements in the downtown to the deployment. A local news article cited the example of loitering, saying that the police had worked with the bars to move loiterers off the sidewalks until the problem had diminished. In the article, Chief Lancaster also asserted marked crime reductions in the downtown area: aggravated assault, thefts of vehicles, and thefts from vehicles each dropped between 40 percent and 50 percent.[16] The deployment both shaped the character of the corridors and improved perceptions of the police by positioning officers as responsive and collaborative resources rather than punitive enforcers.

Moreover, the city saw economic development consistent with the growth coalition's aspirations. The downtown business improvement district reported over $3 billion of completed public and private projects, with another $2 billion of investment in ongoing projects, over a ten-year period. It also described over $3 billion in tourism sales and an estimated $240 million generated by the nightlife economy in a single year.[17] Though the contributions of the police could not be separated from other aspects of this broad push for investment, many people understood policing as important to growth. The executive director of a business improvement district in the downtown remarked that the area's "residential population is just exploding." She explained that much of this growth was driven by "young professionals that are new to River City" and condo owners, described as "more vocal because they're invested": "they're here to stay, and they have a lot to lose in terms of property value and such." She also noted that the deployment of beat officers in the downtown made an impact both on perceptions of safety and on relations with the police: "People feel like they matter—like they have someone to turn to when they're dealing with a problem."

Police executives also understood their work as contributing to growth. One police official, while clarifying that he could not claim causation but only correlation, said,

> Since we redistricted and since downtown and [East District neighborhoods] got their own real robust police presence—and it's not so much they got more cops; they just got intensive cops; they got a police district focused on their issues—there has been an explosion in the opening of restaurants and entertainment venues.

Even without isolating the specific contributions of policing to the overall trajectory of downtown development, the widely shared belief that the police had a role to play was important in its own right. It motivated the police department to prioritize the East District in its resource allocations. It also institutionalized a model of policing truly oriented toward protecting and serving. Both police leaders and officers understood the economic importance of the downtown, and they sought to maintain a safe and inviting environment for businesses, residents, and visitors. The police department's active participation in the project of downtown development channeled an important resource into a broader flow of public and private investments that targeted areas defined as valuable.

Conclusion

Policing in the East District represented a successful institutionalization of local, problem-oriented strategies. The police recognized the distinct interests and needs of middle-class neighborhoods and the downtown. Moreover, they addressed the concerns of residents, business owners, and political leaders by tailoring resources and initiatives to focus on service provision and order maintenance. Officers in the East District framed this work as central to the city—rather than marginal to the "real" work of crime fighting—and they noted distinct skills required of activities like responding to calls for service and engaging in preventive patrol. Patrol officers approached people courteously and were thorough in their investigations and follow-up. Residents and other stakeholders had the opportunity for input, and they felt the police to be increasingly responsive and community-based. These activities and attitudes collectively contributed to a community-service ethos in policing across the East District. Proponents of contemporary strategic innovations like community-based policing would advocate for just such an orientation. Yet many advocates of community policing also imagine historically marginalized communities as the beneficiaries of more democratic and collaborative relationships with the police.

In River City, the community-service ethos coalesced primarily in better-off, predominantly white neighborhoods, raising questions of how this occurred and with what consequences. As previous chapters indicate, the groundwork for this approach was laid through the affinities between local policing and growth politics. The police embraced an active role in crafting the meanings and experiences attached to place, and they did so in alignment with broader political-economic projects. Police executives recognized that enhanced perceptions of safety could draw in consumers and developers viewed as key to the city's revitalization. Furthermore, officers understood that thorough and helpful service played an important role in ensuring the satisfaction of taxpaying residents, who might otherwise leave for the suburbs, whisking away their capital with them. The mayor, elected officials, and business coalitions emphasized that attracting and retaining economic resources in the city was essential to its overall viability. Thus, they positioned police service as an urban amenity to be deployed in cultivating attractive arenas for further investment.

The sense of the East District's economic importance was not only a reflection of the municipal government's growth politics. The police experienced pressures directly from the district's residents and stakeholders. Officer Glen Conwell, a white man in his late forties, had worked as a community-based officer in the East District for several years as a primary point of contact of neighborhood associations, business executives, and other groups. He described the influence of residents in middle-class residential neighborhoods like Larkwood: "It smells a little of money. There's a higher tax base and a lot of educated people that have demands and will let you know what they pay in taxes and what they think they deserve." He also noted the importance of business interests in the downtown, rattling off a list of entities including universities, hotels, several banks, and a convention center: "There's a lot of big corporations down here. And when you're big like that, you want to know what your local police department is doing because anytime some incident occurs, somebody in some organization downtown is being affected." The police received feedback that East District stakeholders themselves were actively forging the links between police service and the economic benefits they brought to the city.

In grouping the downtown and middle-class neighborhoods together into a "low-crime" district, the redistricting ensured the police had ample opportunity to focus on the order-maintenance and quality-of-life issues in the East District. The community-service ethos was facilitated by objective workload conditions in the district, which had proportionally more patrol officers to respond to a lower call volume. But it also reflected discretionary strategic priorities. One could imagine the number of citations that the police could have written during the ECD for disorderly conduct, loitering, public intoxication, or a number of other offenses, had the deployment taken a punitive approach; or the offenses that might have been unveiled had the district developed a task force to investigate white-collar crime. But the police could not risk alienating middle-class taxpayers, corporate entities, tourists, and developers, given their central place in the city. It is unsurprising that the police generally approached East District residents and businesses as clients who needed to be served, rather than potential criminals in need of surveillance and regulation. These recipients of the community-service ethos were largely white. As will be described in chapter 5, the police distinguished between those who contributed to the city and those who represented criminal threats, and their distinctions fell along lines of race and class.

The emphasis on service in the East District had a ripple effect on other parts of the city, revealed by the contrasting activities and meanings that took hold in the West District, where local initiatives and organizational resource constraints resulted in a different style of policing. Ultimately, the police department reinforced the racial meanings and patterns of differential investment long characterizing the development of River City's segregated neighborhoods. This reinforcement happened overtly, as police executives and other stakeholders converged on a shared vision of the East District as valuable to the city and the West District as a violent place in need of surveillance and social control. But it also happened more subtly, as resources for service provision in the West District were stretched thin. Initiatives like the Call Log soon appeared to be particularly egregious cases of uneven resource distribution, as East District residents bypassed dispatch for an immediate response to their calls about noise complaints, while West District residents lamented the lack of a rapid response, even to more serious incidents.

As chapter 4 shows, policing in the West District was integrally and relationally tied to policing in the East District. West District leaders and officers had to juggle multiple imperatives, tied to the overarching emphasis on police service in "low-crime" districts. Whereas the police focused on cultivating the economic vitality of the East District, they were tasked with suppressing the crime and disorder that could threaten the city's revitalization in the West District. While the East District had ample patrol officers to ensure responsive and thorough service, scarce resources meant fewer for the West District. Even as the police in the West District pursued community policing and problem-solving through the work of their community policing unit, a community-service ethos could not coalesce in the West District, given the pressures to control crime and the constraints on service provision. Ultimately, the contrasting policing modalities that emerged in the East District and the West District reinforced enduring differences in the standing and treatment of Black and white neighborhoods.

4

Policing the West District

Officer Roger Stanley, a Black man in his thirties with over a decade in the police department, had begun his career in the West District and had recently returned. He said the West District used to be the best place to work for patrol officers like himself. People were always trying to be transferred there. Now the attitude seemed different. Stanley reflected that, before the redistricting, there was camaraderie, and very few people complained. He had only been back at the district for a few months, but it seemed like everyone was "crabby." Stanley attributed this to overwork, explaining that patrol officers never had a break from responding to calls. He was not alone in feeling that the redistricting had changed the work environment. Several line officers drew sharp distinctions between the current and old district: the old West District had a lot of variation between the busy west side—where the action was— and the slower east side, where officers could go to take a break. They lamented the loss of the latter, which had offered a respite from work with its scenic neighborhoods, residents who liked the cops, and, importantly, all the good places to eat. Now, like Officer Cory Snow in the introduction, many officers saw the West District as "all garbage." One officer described it as the "worst district ever created" and explained that, though there were pockets of decent areas, it was the most dangerous district by far. Another officer insinuated that the district was the least desirable area to work, describing it as the "red-headed stepchild" of the police department.

The West District's reputation as one of the busiest and most dangerous in the city created a shared sense that the police had to "do more with less," as several officers put it. Workload pressures could be exhausting. One officer sighed, "sometimes you just want five minutes after an assignment to breathe." The feeling of relentless pace suggested a higher risk of burnout. For instance, Officer Everett Dressler, a white man in his midforties, was assigned to the day shift in the West District. Dressler had grown up in one of the more racially diverse areas at the edge of the district, and he had wanted to return after years of working in other districts because he thought it would be neat to patrol his old neighborhood. Nevertheless, as our conversation unfolded, Dressler confided that he had recently requested a transfer to the East District. He wanted a slower pace as he approached retirement; he was tired of the potential dangers and the unexpected calls in the West District. Many officers shared the sentiment that the work was stressful and draining.

In contrast to this sentiment, some officers viewed the district's danger, pressure, and variation as a prime site for the "real" police work of fighting crime. During my ride-alongs, many officers identified Officer Bradley Hayes and Officer Gary Bachman as exemplary in this arena. Hayes and Bachman were assigned to a special unit devoted to intervening in violent crimes. Their primary goal was to recover illegal firearms. Instead of responding to calls for service, Hayes and Bachman proactively drove to the scene of calls involving gunshots when they came across the radio. Once in the area, they patrolled in search of suspicious vehicles or individuals and initiated investigatory traffic stops and pedestrian stops. Other officers described Hayes and Bachman as "runners and gunners." They were considered productive, effective, and action-oriented.

Hayes, a white man in his late thirties who had spent most of his nearly two-decade career on the third shift in the West District, had a well-known reputation as a crime fighter. Before I rode with him, two West District sergeants discussed how the observation might unfold. One quipped that Hayes could be back in the district station with a gun arrest within an hour. Another joked to me, "If Hayes gets out of the squad and starts running, don't follow him," hinting at the action and potential danger that Hayes's work entailed. Hayes's reputation even transcended the West District. During a ride-along in the East District, a sergeant said it was very rare for cops to come across crimes in progress but that Hayes was an exception who always seemed to be in the right place at the right time. Though Bachman was only in his late twenties, he had nearly a decade of experience and had also spent most of his career in the West District after being hand-selected from the police academy by the district's former captain.

The patrol work of Stanley and the proactive work of Hayes and Bachman shared an environment that officers saw as distinctly afflicted by crime and other social problems. In contrast to East District officers' narratives of the deserving citizen, relentless exposure to myriad conflicts tended to reinforce broadly circulating colorblind frameworks in the West District. Colorblind interpretations positioned ongoing racial inequalities as the product of nonracial dynamics.[1] Officers were immersed in the challenges of structural inequality and legacies of racial discrimination, but they often saw issues like poverty and violence as individual or cultural problems. They spoke of failures of personal or familial responsibility: bad choices, manipulative behaviors, and dysfunctional family structures.

Officers also suggested that victims were often suspects in their own right, such as callers reporting a robbery that actually was a drug deal gone awry or calling in about battery after losing a fight. These examples contributed to the perception that police service requests in the West District could misuse state resources. Officers expressed resentment that drew on the same logics of economic contribution to the city as East District officers did, only now, they did so to mark the noncontributory character of West District residents. One such officer said, "The police service goes to all the people who don't pay for it. The city bends over backward for the scrubbier side of town. If we don't do it, nobody else will." While attitudes that framed the West District and its residents as simultaneously criminal and undeserving reflected tropes that have been long applied to predominantly Black neighborhoods, these notions were reinscribed by the redistricting and the policing practices that subsequently unfolded across the district.

Strategic Fragmentation Reinforces Overpolicing and Underprotection

This chapter describes how policing in the West District took on a fragmented and layered approach in which several different policing modalities overlayed the same geography, subjecting district residents to many different kinds of potential encounters with the police. While police activities and orientations in the East District were made cohesive by a community-service ethos, those in the West District reflected multiple priorities, some divergent and even contradictory. First, as the police department pursued nationally recognized strategic innovations like community policing, it made space for this work within the West District. Officers in the district's community policing unit worked closely with representatives from neighborhood groups and strove to implement collaborative, problem-solving initiatives. Community groups and officers themselves noted the benefits of this work, though they also recognized its limitations.

A second set of district priorities largely focused on intervening in violent crime through a proactive approach.[2] Proactive policing in River City entailed the use of officer-initiated police stops to investigate suspicious activity. Proactive stops included investigatory traffic stops and pedestrian stops, also known as Terry stops or stop-and-frisk.[3] Technically, police executives framed proactive policing as part of the department's community-based approach. They emphasized that the police operated with community support and sought to make neighborhoods more livable and capable of sustaining civic life. But proactive policing also reflected the city's growth politics. Accounts of the redistricting emphasized separating criminal "hotspots" of the West District from the "quiet" neighborhoods of the East District; the police then used proactive stops to contain and control crime in the former.

Third, the police maintained their preeminent role as service providers. But the redistricting had created a distinctly busy work environment in the West District, and patrol officers experienced limitations on their ability to provide rapid and thorough response to emergency calls. Workload challenges were tied to the city's reliance on the police as first responders to varied social problems, and they also reflected resource constraints within the police department. Officers felt they had to triage among assignments, and residents of the West District described faltering police service.

The layered dynamics of community policing, crime control, and service provision came to amplify long-standing patters of overpolicing and underprotection in predominantly Black neighborhoods. Overpolicing was facilitated by defining and treating the West District as a prototypical "high-crime" district. The emphasis on controlling violence corresponded to strategies and tactics that extended a presumption of criminality across the district and its residents. Widespread use of investigatory traffic stops and stop-and-frisk subjected Black citizens to disproportionate surveillance and social control.

Meanwhile, the underprotection of the West District emerged through uneven resources for patrol. Though the chief had assured stakeholders that districts would have personnel allocations proportional to their call volume, gaps in police service expanded. This occurred, in part, due to unanticipated dynamics like personnel attrition. But it also reflected inter- and intradistrict resource allocations. Redrawing district boundaries sought to ensure that patrol officers could remain in quiet neighborhoods, prioritizing service in "low-crime" districts. Within "high-crime" districts, the assignment of officers to proactive patrol cut into the proportion of officers available to respond to calls for service. In my interviews, West District residents connected lagging response times to perceptions that the city government undervalued their neighborhoods. While the community policing unit made inroads in problem-solving and police-community relations, this work was confined to a small subset of officers; community service was certainly not a cohesive ethos in the West District.

Instead, different roles, functions, and pressures contributed to varied approaches among officers. Some, like officers in the East District, took pride in their ability to relate to people. Patrol officer Eva Irwin described working well with a former partner because they shared an approach that emphasized talking to people first and trying to deescalate situations. Indeed, during our ride-along, Irwin had friendly banter with people on the street, both as she patrolled and on the scene of assignments. But other officers approached people in a more aggressive or confrontational manner. Still others seemed to want to avoid work. Officer Philip Dean and Officer Ernest Moultrie, white men in their thirties, had worked the third shift in the West District for the entirety of their ten years on the job. When the sergeant announced that I would be working with them one night, Dean had openly joked, "We're not sure about working." Dean and Moultrie contrasted themselves to the "runners and gunners" like Hayes and Bachmann, explaining that they had never fallen in that category. Indeed, during their shift, two shootings came over the radio in short succession, and while several units radioed in to respond, Dean and Moultrie said they needed to return to the district station to fix a problem with their squad car. Given varied types of work and orientations among officers, West District citizens could experience many different kinds of interactions with the police.

These were structured by the exigencies and priorities of the district's work environment.

The New West District

Though some neighborhoods in the West District were adjacent to the downtown and middle-class residential areas of the East District, many residents of River City saw them as a world apart. While the East District included some of the city's most affluent neighborhoods, the West District included some of the city's poorest. As new luxury apartments and condos developed in the East District, vacant properties remained boarded up in the West District. A reflection of these differences, the average assessed residential value of properties in the West District was under $75,000, while it approached $400,000 in the East District.[4] In contrast to the concentration of commercial land use in the downtown, the West District had a handful of commercial corridors spread throughout. One primary cluster of businesses and restaurants sat on the district's east side. These neighborhoods adjacent to the river were home to many of the district's white residents, who constituted around 15 percent of the population. Over 75 percent of district residents were Black—the highest proportion of any police district.

As highlighted in chapter 3, crime and call patterns in the West District were quite different from those in the East District. Approximately one-third of the city's total homicides occurred in the West District, and the homicide rate per 1,000 residents was nearly three times the citywide average: 0.59 per 1,000 compared to 0.21. Rates were higher in the West District in every major crime category, and, in addition to homicide, differences were most pronounced for assault and robbery. For instance, the assault rate was about 25 per 1,000 residents in the West District, compared to a citywide rate of approximately 16 per 1,000. The overall crime rate in the district was around 95 per 1,000, compared to the city average of approximately 70 per 1,000.[5] Crime numbers contributed to the classification of the West District as a "high-crime" area, though it bears repeating that crime statistics are constructed by patterns in citizen reporting and by police enforcement activities that have long targeted marginalized Black neighborhoods like those in the West District. In any case, officers navigated an environment defined by more criminal incidents, and they dealt with an array of other issues, from family disputes to mental health crises to animals on the loose. Policing in the West District responded to and further shaped this landscape by layering it with multiple strategic priorities, some characterized by competing aims and outcomes.

The Inroads of Community Policing

When Chief Lancaster began his tenure, he explicitly incorporated community policing into the department's mission statement. In the East District, community policing easily took hold as the work environment had been designed to facilitate collaborative problem-solving, and the order-maintenance and quality-of-life issues in the district were responsive to police interventions like the Call Log and the Entertainment Corridor Deployment. Community policing also occurred in the West District, but it was largely confined to a handful of officers in the district's community policing unit. While citizens and officers both benefited from community-based work, their collaborative efforts came up against serious structural challenges and historically fraught relationships. Moreover, the unit's successes in forging better community relations risked being undermined by aggressive crime control and faltering police service. Such dynamics meant that community policing in the West District could not coalesce into an overarching approach, even as it made important inroads.

Officer Cassandra Vester, a white woman in her thirties, was the community-based officer in the West District during my fieldwork. Officer Vester indicated that she had sought out more community-oriented work after years of patrol. She had felt ineffective as a patrol officer because the police could not do anything but go from call to call and apply superficial band-aids. She felt that her current work had expanded her repertoire for problem-solving. Like Officers Petty and Conwell in chapter 3, Vester worked closely with community groups, regularly attending the meetings of block watches, neighborhood associations, and City Council members. During meetings, Vester provided information about recent crime patterns and specific criminal events: one night, she shared with a local group that a recent homicide was related to the activities of a drug crew, suggesting that violence was unlikely to affect people outside the drug trade. She also dispensed advice, for instance, by en-couraging residents to hide their cellphones to reduce street robberies and to record the phone's serial number and other information to help the police recover stolen phones. Vester also heard from residents about ongoing neighborhood problems, which she could relay back to district leadership. These activities fostered increased information-sharing and reassured stakeholders that the police were taking action to address their concerns.

An additional four officers in the community policing unit worked on quality-of-life issues, largely through nuisance-ordinance enforce-ment against problematic properties. For example, Vester might receive complaints from neighborhood residents about a potential drug house. Officers in the community policing unit would then collaborate with the city attorney, the district attorney, the city's neighborhood services de-partment, or other entities to take various enforcement actions against the landlord until they abated the nuisance at the address, often by evict-ing its tenants. Beyond this, the community policing unit did other work in police-community relations. Officer Robert McGraw, a white man in his late twenties, assigned to the unit, explained that officers' activities also included supporting youth programs, attending block parties, and reaching out to businesses. He noted, "The [community policing unit] is all about working with the community to make it a better place for them."

West District stakeholders spoke highly of the work of the com-munity policing unit and of Officer Vester, in particular. For instance, a neighborhood association representative described the impacts of Vester's work:

> [The police] have a really good community-based officer for the neigh-borhoods. . . . Having that advocate for our neighborhood and just being able to reach out and ask, 'What's going on here? What happened with this situation?' And then for her to pretty much be in regular attendance at our neighborhood meetings, being able to address citizen concerns right away, . . . that's helped a lot, I'd say.

A community organizer in a different neighborhood also lauded Officer Vester's efforts: "She is very hands-on in the community. I feel like I could ask her basically anything, and she would try to make it happen or connect me with somebody that did." The organizer then described the potential impacts of the unit's work. She noted how it was nice to have the police drop by in a friendly manner during neighborhood cleanups and block parties: "For the people that feel comfortable with the police, it's reengaging, like, 'Hey, we're around. We're here. We're doing things.' And for the people that feel uncomfortable with the police, if you're surrounded by enough people that feel comfortable, maybe that narrative can start to change."

Work in the community policing unit also appeared to have benefits for officers, who drew explicit contrasts between their activities and those of patrol officers. Officer McGraw described how residents' feedback reinforced his sense of efficacy:

> The unique thing about my position is that I'm out there being thanked by community people, the people that live in the neighborhoods. That is also not a side that a patrol officer normally gets to see. . . . I'm fortunate enough to go to the events with people who live in the neighborhoods, to know—"Yes, you guys are effective, appreciated. You're helping out on the block. We like you being here."

Whether through selection into these roles or socialization through the requirements of the position, community policing officers approached citizens with the goal of finding common ground. They were more likely to understand racial grievances and recognize the police's role in the lack of trust within Black neighborhoods. They viewed their work as integral to better relations, as McGraw explained: "We all know how important it is that someone trusts the police. . . . There hasn't been much of an emphasis [in the department] over the course of the years with community and police relationships. We're trying to work on that." Community policing initiatives in the West District appeared to benefit the officers and residents who engaged with them.

However, community engagement had to contend with legacies of mistrust and the challenges of resource constraints. Officer Vester's relationships with community groups were varied, as groups had different degrees of confidence in the police. One organizer who worked closely with both the police and several neighborhood associations described this contingent relationship: "The police do go to the Riverdale Group meeting—this Saturday, they'll be there reporting on crime. But the very next neighborhood association directly next to them, it's like, no, if you're going to bring a cop to the meeting, they won't come to the meeting." Officer Vester reflected that the reluctance to work with the police was valid because of the long-standing history between the police and the African American community. But this made information-sharing more piecemeal and undercut the reach of the community policing unit. In contrast to the East District, where groups called the police without hesitation, inroads in the West District were limited to those that were willing to work with the police.

Beyond barriers to robust collaborative engagement, community policing in the West District was also limited in its ability to meaningfully address residents' problems, ranging from homicides to nuisance issues. Many challenges had structural antecedents that police response could not fundamentally transform. Moreover, resource constraints meant that even basic services could be stretched thin. Officers did what they could to share information and engage in problem-solving, but they also sought to modify residents' expectations. These dynamics were on display one evening, as Officer Vester met in a storefront church with members of a neighborhood association in the heart of the district. Four people arrived, including the church pastor, a middle-aged Black man, and three Black women, one of whom appeared to be the primary organizer of the neighborhood association. Another introduced herself as a representative from a local community development corporation. The pastor explained that they had not distributed fliers for the meeting, so the sparse attendance was to be expected, though one of the women later insinuated that it was due to a lack of trust in the police when she quipped, "Call me a snitch. I don't care."

Despite being few in numbers, the group had plenty to discuss. Officer Vester began by describing several violent incidents, including a homicide earlier that morning, recent shots-fired incidents, and a few domestic assaults. She indicated that the police had people in custody for the assaults. The group then turned to several quality-of-life and nuisance concerns: a vacant property across the street from the church, a troublesome mobile-phone retailer, and fraudulent use of food stamps at convenience stores. One woman described the neighborhood as "the poverty areas that no one cares about." She wanted city services to write citations for nuisance issues, but she did not believe it would happen. She later suggested that social service agencies were trying to house too many kinds of people—like drug addicts and children—in the same building. She said she wanted the area's three City Council members to come together and "tell them to stop dumping stuff over here." Her discussion captured the vast array of structural challenges experienced in the area and the ties residents perceived between neighborhood conditions and patterns of neglect by city officials.

Eventually, the meeting also highlighted the limitations of the police. As we all stood to leave, the pastor asked Officer Vester if the police could increase patrol on a thoroughfare in front of the church. He explained that he rarely saw the police and people drove recklessly on the street. Vester explained that those deployment decisions were made at a level above her. She also noted how busy the police were in the district. She made a small circle with her hands, saying, "You have this many cops," and then expanded to make a large circle with her arms and continued, "for this many problems." The pastor said he understood. When we returned to the car, Vester admitted that the thoroughfare really could use additional patrol. In light of issues that were both deep-seated and wide-ranging, part of Officer Vester's job entailed accounting for why West District residents could not receive the police services they desired.

The limits of the community policing unit were exacerbated by intradistrict personnel allocations. Indeed, the number of officers devoted to community policing in the West District paled in comparison to the numbers devoted to proactive policing and patrol work. Proactive units and patrol officers did not incorporate core tenets of community policing in their work, precluding the possibility of a pervasive community-service ethos across the district. As described in the next section, proactive policing developed with little input from the community and eventually intensified racial tensions, even though Chief Lancaster framed the proactive strategy as consistent with the department's neighborhood-based, problem-oriented approach. Furthermore, patrol officers, burdened by the workload, did not have time to develop ongoing, collaborative relationships with residents. Though the chief sought to align the organization, strategies, and tactics of the River City Police

Department with the philosophy of community policing, proactive stops and response to calls for service in the West District departed from this goal and instead drove problems of overpolicing and underprotection.

Crime Control in Violent Hotspots

A particular tension emerged through the police department's proactive approach to crime control. When police executives presented the redistricting, it had been clear that they had intended to separate criminal hotspots from the city's spaces of economic value. Policing in the new "high-crime" districts subsequently concentrated on containing and confronting violence. Chief Lancaster promoted a strategy of proactive stops to accomplish this goal. Investigatory stops are controversial tactics, often at the heart of debates over racial profiling. Some studies find that proactive policing reduces crime.[6] But a great deal of scholarship draws attention to the role of investigatory stops in driving racial disproportionality in policing outcomes and in undermining trust in the police.[7] Investigatory stops occur when officers have a "reasonable suspicion" that criminal activity is afoot. This standard can be met based on activities as general as evasive movements in a crime-prone location.[8] Many studies have also shown that officers' perceptions of "symbolic assailants" focus on young Black men, consistent with broadly circulating tropes that link Blackness to notions of danger and threat.[9] As stops disproportionately accumulate in marginalized Black neighborhoods, they alienate citizens from the police and cultivate the perception that law enforcement is biased and exclusionary.[10] Unfortunately, this is just what unfolded in River City, as proactive stops reinforced overpolicing. The unexpected twist in the case of River City, however, was that police executives presented the proactive strategy as part of the department's community-based approach.

Chief Lancaster framed proactive policing as responsive to community needs and as a means of fulfilling the department's mission to create safe and livable neighborhoods. The chief outlined the proactive strategy in a video posted to the police department's YouTube page. Filmed as a presentation before a group of about two dozen stakeholders, most of whom were Black, the video appeared to be a public address of sorts.[11] In it, the chief began by describing the problem of violence in River

City communities and by reiterating the department's commitment to neighborhoods. He explained, "The reason a free people empowered democratic policing was so that they could use their neighborhoods for the purposes for which they were intended: to raise children and pursue the American dream." Lancaster continued, "In many of our central cities, including River City, there are neighborhoods where people are not enjoying the freedoms of free Americans. They are living in fear because people with guns, who are bullies and have their own agendas, hold neighborhoods hostage." This narrative positioned crime control as a requisite of crafting neighborhoods where citizens could experience full democratic inclusion and strive for upward mobility. But gaps between the accounts of police executives, the practices of officers, and the experiences of citizens would call into question whether the proactive approach could achieve this goal.

The Goals and Tactics of Proactive Patrol

Proactive policing in River City relied on saturating criminal hotspots with officers tasked with conducting stops. In order to intervene in crime, Chief Lancaster explained, the department needed to "create time for officers to investigate, to look into suspicious conditions, to occupy public space. . . . When there's no police in the public spaces, the community loses confidence. When the community loses confidence and abandons those spaces, then who do you think occupies them?" After identifying small areas where crime was concentrated, captains deployed police officers to initiate encounters with citizens in the form of investigatory traffic stops and pedestrian stops. Lancaster described the logic of this strategy: "That hotspot over there, I want you to stop cars and talk to people. I want you to disrupt the environment, 'cause the cops are here now." These efforts were part of the department's evolution away from a reactive approach and toward a proactive strategy aimed to prevent crime before it occurred. As the chief explained, "When I came here, I wanted to make sure that this police department went back on offense."

Nevertheless, Chief Lancaster qualified his statement by saying, "I wanted to make sure when we went on the offense that we did it in a way that connected to the neighborhood." He tied proactive stops to the department's community-based policing efforts. With enough time observing and talking to people in the neighborhood, officers would be able to make important distinctions between, say, the "guy over here who we know is a knucklehead" and "the guy who works at night," as Chief Lancaster had put it. Thus, stops should be targeted and specific—focused on factors like known offenders, the most frequently stolen cars in each district, and locations where crime was common. The chief summarized, "The cops get familiar with the comings and goings of the neighborhood and get to know who's who in the neighborhood, and even though we stay active, the key is to retain neighborhood support for those efforts." Officers were trained to engage professionally and respectfully during stops, and they were encouraged to often give verbal warnings rather than citations. Police executives explained that this proactive patrol method could even provide opportunities for positive police-citizen interactions.

Shortly after Chief Lancaster began his tenure, investigatory stop practices ballooned in River City. At first, stops seemed to correspond to reductions in crime. When the proactive strategy was in full swing a few years into the chief's first term, a police department report indicated that traffic stops had increased from approximately 50,000 per year to almost 190,000, and subject stops increased from 14,000 per year to over 60,000 citywide.[12] In the YouTube video, Chief Lancaster presented data correlating this rise in stops to a 24 percent reduction in violent crime and a 20 percent decrease in property crime during the same period. He noted, "Stolen cars are down almost 40 percent in some neighborhoods," and he later explained that research has shown that "active use of car-stop behavior by the police has a direct impact on stolen cars." The chief boasted of the strategy's success by comparing the current year to the year before he had started his term: "We want to show you the results of our work: eight thousand fewer victims in the first eleven months of this year compared to our baseline year."[13]

Chief Lancaster framed the stops as a trade-off for the safe neighborhoods that such tactics promoted. In a local news article, he said that communities, and innocent people, would accept the inconvenience of respectfully conducted stops for a safer environment.[14] Many stakeholders initially understood this logic. The city's NAACP chapter president issued a statement that the organization trusted the police department's intent to promote livable neighborhoods and accepted policing strategies in high-crime communities at face value.[15] To assuage concerns about stop practices, police executives cited a dramatic reduction in external complaints about the police since Chief Lancaster took office.[16] In his presentation, the chief noted that the department had increased traffic stops by 250 percent, but complaints had decreased by 44 percent. He concluded, "To me, that means we're operating with community approval and support."[17]

Proactive Policing in the West District

While the proactive strategy was technically citywide, it was geographically targeted to those areas where crime and violence posed a problem. As the West District's boundaries had been redrawn to contain some of the "highest crime, poorest neighborhoods in the city," per Assistant Chief Daniels, proactive policing was concentrated there. In an interview with me, Richard Williams, the captain of the West District, remarked on the district's distinct character: "Our geographic responsibility is much smaller than some other districts. But in relation to crime, we have pretty unique crime problems because it transcends the whole district geography." Williams noted that many other districts, even those with higher rates of violence, generally had hotspots confined to relatively small areas. By contrast, he felt that few places in the West District offered a reprieve. He described how an officer had recently confronted a man with a gun at the very café where we were having our interview. The café was a popular spot in a residential neighborhood just across the river from the East District. Captain Williams reflected, "You would think this was a relatively crime-free area, and it is. But there's still a high possibility that something's going to go to shit here." Thus, local priorities focused on crime control. As Williams explained, "My number-one long-term concern is reduction of violent crime within the district. . . . Everything that we do has to be geared towards, How can we have a positive effect on violent crime?"

West District leadership pursued several avenues to this end. Separate interviews with Captain Williams and Michael Gill, the lieutenant who oversaw the second shift, when most proactive activity occurred, outlined the district's primary crime control initiatives.[18] First, the district included a bicycle-patrol contingent. While these officers participated in some of the district's community policing efforts, they were tasked mostly with proactive work. Captain Williams explained that bike officers were deployed to high-crime areas to "go in that area and talk to people, find out who's causing the problems, and then take action against those people." Second, the district assigned several officers to an antiviolence unit (AVU).[19] Lieutenant Gill explained how in addition to investigatory stops, officers on the AVU conducted longer-term investigations:

> They're expected to be knowledgeable about the violent crime issues that we're having, whether it's robberies and shootings. They are also particularly tuned in to our drug-dealing problems and areas and individuals, so they do surveillance. Some of those guys have specialized abilities to work with confidential informants and do some undercover buys—things that we can do to intervene with individuals and houses to stabilize the whole neighborhood.

Of the seventy-two officers working the second shift in the West District, twenty-five were assigned to proactive work through bicycle patrol or the AVU.

Third, beyond these specialized assignments, patrol officers were also encouraged to conduct targeted traffic stops that focused on vehicle makes that were frequently stolen. Many officers noted that traffic stops were included in their performance evaluations. Like Officers Snow and Foster in the introduction, they tried to conduct stops when they had time between assignments.

While proactive patrol was a citywide strategy, targeting the approach to high-crime areas meant that stops were not evenly distributed. The West District had the highest average annual rate of traffic stops and pedestrian stops in the city: 71 traffic stops per 100 drivers and 3.4 pedestrian stops per 100 residents. By comparison, the East District rates were 31 traffic stops per 100 drivers and 2.8 pedestrian stops per 100 residents.[20] The differences in the absolute number of stops failed to capture the differences in type of stop; as stop practices in the East District were largely focused on traffic safety enforcement, the disparities in rates of investigatory stops, specifically, were probably even greater. With a sense that violence blanketed the district's geography and an imperative to use proactive patrol to address it, investigatory stops became a commonplace feature of police work in the West District.

On the Ground with a Proactive Squad

A shift with Hayes and Bachman showcased proactive policing in practice. Early on in my ride-along, I queried how the officers conducted their work. Hayes said their squad was rarely dispatched to calls for service; they might take one or two assignments on a particularly busy night. Instead, he explained that they began by driving to areas where guns or gunshots had been reported recently. For instance, because Hayes had been told early in his career that armed robbers were especially dangerous, he and Bachman always tried to go to those calls. Once in the area, Hayes characterized the work of identifying people and vehicles to stop as more intuitive. He and Bachman watched how people reacted when they saw the squad car. Hayes listed several behavioral criteria that would qualify as suspicious: if a person turned away quickly or if a group dispersed when the squad approached. He mentioned an indicator that several other officers also referenced: a person placing a hand in or over a pocket, which was taken as a reflexive "security check" performed when there was contraband to hide. Hayes said that this often indicated a person had a gun.

That night, the first call of interest over the radio was for a suspicious automobile. The dispatcher named an intersection and said a caller reported a person with a gun, driving a red station wagon around the area. Hayes sped over to the scene. Another squad had responded first and had already pulled over a wagon. Hayes and Bachman joined the two other officers as they approached the driver, a Black man in his twenties or early thirties. The officers asked him to get out of the car. One frisked him and asked him to take a seat on the curb while the others began searching the vehicle. They found nothing. Nor did any notifications of warrants or other violations arise when they input the man's driver's license information into the in-squad computer.

The man sat quietly on the curb. Hayes stood beside him and asked what he was doing in the area. The man said he was going to see his child's mother. Hayes inquired if there was anyone in the area who might have a problem with the man, explaining that they had a call about a red station wagon with a possible gun. The driver said that he did not have a problem in the area and did not know why anyone would have called the police. While waiting for the other officers to wrap up, Hayes began chatting more casually with the man, asking about his kids and then sharing that he was planning on taking his son to see fireworks over the weekend. As the stop concluded, Hayes told the man they were sorry to bother him and wished him a better night. He cautioned the man to stay away from the area if possible, to be on the safe side.

Hayes and Bachman continued on to check out specific blocks and conduct several stops during the shift. They drove to areas on the basis of reported or suspected gun activity. In two instances, the officers heard gunshots themselves. In three others, gunshots were reported by a caller or picked up by an automatic reporting system. Once in the reported area, Hayes and Bachman would investigate, interviewing people in the vicinity, searching for bullet casings, and occasionally conducting pat-downs or frisks for weapons. When they were not responding to a specific incident, Hayes drove the squad through the district, and they identified suspicious people or vehicles on the basis of the behavior criteria they had described earlier. At one point, three Black teenage boys abruptly cut through a parking lot upon seeing the squad. When Hayes pulled the squad car over, the boys began walking faster. Hayes called out and asked them to wait. One of the boys appeared prepared to run, but the others told him to stop. Hayes and Bachman frisked each boy, found nothing, and sent them off with an indication that it was past curfew and they should call it a night. In another instance, Hayes drove the squad toward a group of young Black people congregated on the sidewalk. The officers noted that there were both men and women in the group, and Bachman speculated that they were gathered to light fireworks. Hayes drove the squad past without engaging. Gender appeared to be a factor in decision-making. On a couple of occasions, the officers explicitly noted that a vehicle's driver was a woman, and this labeling seemed to disqualify the driver from suspicion.

Later, the officers noticed two cars parked along a dead-end street. Two men stood at the window of a gray sedan with an occupant in it. A red car with several people inside was stopped farther down the block. Hayes and Bachman initially drove past the vehicles, then stopped the squad and got out to approach the red car on foot. As they were nearly adjacent to it, the car suddenly pulled away and sped off. Hayes, who was soon leaving for vacation, called an officer on another proactive unit and suggested that they spend some time in the area while he was gone. Hayes explained that they would probably get some guns if they returned to check on the intersection.

Hayes and Bachman conducted about a dozen searches of pedestrians or vehicles throughout the shift. They found no contraband in any of them, though they routinely verbalized a rationale for the stops. While driving, Hayes or Bachman would identify people with a short comment: "his hand is in his pocket," "he seems leery of us, and he walked down the alley, and now he's back." Once the stop was made, Hayes generally communicated this same basis of suspicion to the person stopped. While patting down a middle-aged Black man who had been walking alone, Hayes explained that the way the man's hand was positioned in his pocket indicated he might have a gun. The man was indignant and said he did not have a gun. Hayes said they did not know him, so they would not know if he might or might not have a gun. While a few citizens expressed this kind of frustration, many complied with the officers; most interactions concluded in seconds. Hayes tended to wrap up each stop with an apologetic script, combining a few comments like "sorry to bother you," "have a good night," "stay safe," or "be careful." Overall, the stops that Hayes and Bachman made appeared to be sound procedurally. The officers were professional and efficient during the interactions that I witnessed that night (though my presence as an observer may have contributed to this, a dynamic I reflect on further in the methods appendix).

Hayes and Bachman's work was emblematic of the police department's approach to the problem of violence. The stops that they conducted were official duties associated with their organizational role—a role that existed in the West District but had no counterpart in the East District. The officers carried out their duties by the book, as far as I saw. They articulated a basis for stops, and they were not aggressive, rude, or antagonistic toward citizens. Their glowing reputations transcended the police department several years later when Mayor Taylor showcased their work in a press conference that simultaneously described the problem of illegal guns in River City and emphasized the progress of the RCPD. Officer Hayes was featured in the news, along with a table full

of recovered firearms.[21] But the officers' shift also revealed the consequences and risks of the proactive strategy: even under relatively optimal conditions—experienced officers, evidence of gun use in the area,
and specific and articulable suspicion—a dozen people, all Black, were
stopped by the police, and none of those stopped possessed a weapon.

The Consequences of Proactive Stops

Critiques of the police department's stop practices emerged over time.
While the goal of sustained crime reduction had motivated the proactive
strategy, crime control could not ultimately be achieved by the police
alone, and stop practices began to exacerbate spatial inequalities and
racial tensions. They did so, first, by failing to have long-term effects
on violence. Compared to a 2011 low, 2015 saw a 41 percent increase in
violent crime, with the absolute number of incidents rising above the
number from when Chief Lancaster had started his term.[22] The proactive strategy continued apace, justified on the basis of this increase in
violence. Whereas correlations between increased stops and decreasing
crime had previously been deployed to suggest that the proactive strategy was working, increasing crime rates soon became an indicator that
more stops were needed. Police executives drew on crime rates to legitimate the proactive strategy, regardless of whether crime was increasing
or decreasing.

In reality, the fluctuations in crime revealed the limitations of proactive patrol. Many stakeholders identified causes of crime that could not
be addressed through police stops. Police officers and executives, community representatives, and the media offered explanations for crime
that included shifts in the drug market and gun laws, problems of poverty and unemployment, gang conflicts, and environmental-design factors like street lighting. The complex array of causes cited as relevant to
crime patterns highlighted the "vast and unmanageable social domain"
to which the police had staked a claim.[23] Neither the police department
as a whole nor the individual officers tasked with making investigatory
stops had much power to impact the structural antecedents of crime.[24]
The proactive strategy also failed to address the geographically concentrated, relational, and networked nature of violence.[25] As crime rose in

River City and across the country, it continued to affect neighborhoods historically afflicted by violence, including those in the West District.

Moreover, targeted stop practices in "high-crime" districts subjected residents of the West District to the surveillance and social control characteristic of overpolicing. Even though many officers described the district as categorically violent, in reality, crime concentrated in specific hotspots, and the district had several quieter communities. However, I observed the investigatory stop practices of proactive units transcend the geography of hotspots and instead stretch to the district's boundaries. Proactive officers would often begin their shifts in designated hotspot areas, but eventually—en route to a new location or out of boredom or the desire for a change of scenery—they would drive away from these small areas to patrol other parts of the district. Consequently, drivers throughout the district were likely to be stopped. In my interview with Ed Brown, a community organizer in the West District, he described the overuse of proactive tactics: "[The police are] pulling right up with the mind frame of 'violence, drugs, guns—I'm coming ready.' And half the time, these people are just really hustling, trying to survive. . . . It looks like it could be something violent, but it really ain't." He captured the common sentiment that this manner of policing overgeneralized a presumption of criminality, extending it well beyond individuals actually engaged in violence.

Ultimately, the proactive strategy heightened long-standing racial tensions in policing. New outlets and external evaluations began documenting racial disparities in stops. A few years after the chief's term began, River City's major newspaper reported that Black drivers were seven times more likely to be stopped in River City than white drivers. Hispanic drivers were five times more likely to be stopped, based on an analysis of several months of stop data. The article also reported that Black drivers were twice as likely as white drivers to be searched after a stop, though the police found contraband items in searches of Black and white drivers at a similar rate of approximately one-in-five times.[26] A later report based on several years of stop data found that drugs constituted most contraband discoveries; only 3 percent of searches resulted in discovery of a weapon. The report also found that the rates of contraband discovery per search were slightly lower for Black and Latinx drivers than for white drivers. Indeed, some of the lowest contraband discovery rates in the city were in the West District and the predominantly Latinx North District: 26 percent in the former and 21 percent in the latter, compared to a citywide average of 27 percent and a high of 33 percent in the predominantly white South District.[27] This suggested that officers were more indiscriminate in their searches in Black and Latinx areas; it also highlighted the generally low "hit rate" of investigatory stops. Though stops did not always result in additional action, they could be a precursor to more formal law enforcement. During my fieldwork year, the department made three times as many arrests of Black people than arrests of white people, and the disparity was even greater for offenses like weapons possession, where 1,085 arrests of Black people were made, compared to 125 arrests of whites.[28]

Racial disparities in stop practices, in turn, informed racial differences in perceptions of the police. Surveys of city residents revealed a racial gap in satisfaction with the police, in addition to a relationship between experiencing a stop and having negative views of the police.[29] Concerns over racial discrimination eventually culminated in a class-action lawsuit alleging that stops in River City were unconstitutional— that the police subjected Black and Latinx residents to stops without any legal basis to do so.[30] This lawsuit reflected a mounting critique of the proactive strategy. For instance, the initial goodwill of the NAACP was replaced by calls for the police department to put a new strategy in place to address stop-and-frisk problems.[31] Coalitions of faith and advocacy groups developed and began pressing for police reform.[32] Assertions of racial profiling and bias circulated in the public sphere and further soured police-community relations.

Chief Lancaster defended the proactive strategy through the language of place and crime, explaining that the police targeted areas where residents were most victimized. He had initially raised this point in his community presentation, asserting, "The most disgraceful disparity we have in this city is victims of violent crime." He continued, "Our highest concentrations of poverty are our places where we have our highest concentrations of violent crime, our highest concentrations of citizens calling us, and therefore, our highest concentrations of proactive police activity."[33] As criticism increased, the chief continued to maintain that stops had been proven to reduce crime in several categories and linked the proactive strategy to the department's "moral duty" to address violence.[34] While few people denied the relationships between poverty, crime, and racial disparities in victimization, the growing resistance to the proactive approach revealed fissures in understandings of how to address them.

In short, the police department chose a controversial crime control strategy by relying primarily on investigatory stops. Furthermore, the redistricting helped structure the way stops were distributed across the city. With proactive work targeted at "high-crime" districts like the West District, predominantly Black and Latinx neighborhoods were disproportionately subjected to police stops. Stakeholders in River City increasingly recognized the tensions that proactive policing engendered. As council member Sam Ward told me in an interview, "[The chief] claims that these stops are done in a very friendly way, and it's true, proper community policing. Now, you know, one person's 'friendly' is another person's awkward, authoritative, passive-aggressive, hostile encounter." As such encounters multiplied, residents, the media, and civic organizations increasingly saw the proactive strategy as amplifying the overpolicing of Black neighborhoods.

Service Provision in West District Neighborhoods

The attention to violent crime had other rippling impacts in the West District. Namely, residents perceived flagging police response to calls for service. Though the chief had promised during the presentation of the redistricting that each district would have officers proportional to its workload, resources were impacted subsequently by many factors, including attrition across the department due to retirements, the reallocation of officers during busy summer months, and intradistrict personnel allocations—like the twenty-five officers assigned to proactive units in the West District. Indeed, the decision to prioritize resources for proactive patrol in high-crime districts directly affected the number of officers available to respond to calls for service. Lieutenant Gill, who oversaw much of the district's proactive work, described this tension, saying that the district had recently lost personnel to citywide specialty deployments for the summer, and this particularly impacted the squads available to take calls for service. Gill continued,

My specialty units—my bicycle, my AVU, and my community policing—
have remained stable. So when I lost all those officers, it came from officers that I would normally assign to my sector cars, my assignment team
cars. Because of that vacuum, instead of being able to put out two to three
cars a sector, I'm putting out one car a sector.

Chief Lancaster himself explained the trade-off between proactive units
and patrol in a news article published a few years into his term. The
chief defended devoting district-based resources to the proactive strategy rather than response to calls for service, asserting that he would
accept a small increase in response times for the decreasing crime associated with the proactive approach.[35] As proactive deployments were
concentrated in "high-crime" districts, these areas were the ones subject
to this trade-off.

   While stakeholders recognized the problem of violence in the West
District, most residents' daily concerns were actually similar to those of
East District residents: quality-of-life issues. West District residents also
wanted the police to provide thorough service, address nuisance issues,
and maintain order in their neighborhoods. As a former captain of the
West District explained in our interview,

> Your average citizen living in a challenged district is never going to be the
> victim of a homicide, never going to be a victim of a nonfatal shooting,
> never going to be a victim of a street robbery. So the most frequent com-
> plaints that you get are on issues of disorder, like loud music, disrespect-
> ful neighbors that aren't taking care of their property, that have teenagers
> that run amok and create disorder.

The police had to balance a violence-reduction priority with the need to
respond to other issues affecting citizens' well-being and quality of life.
In the West District, resource constraints raised the question of police
availability to attend to these concerns.

Pressure and Practices of Patrol

West District patrol officers had nearly constant reminders of their
workload. When they pulled up the list of pending calls, there were often

several on the board, indicating no available units, though callers were still awaiting a response. Officers would often use the list to anticipate the next call they would be assigned; in many cases, a dispatcher would give them a new assignment immediately after clearing their current assignment. Dispatchers would also check in on officers at the scene, asking how much time they needed. In some cases, officers would be pulled from an assignment and sent to a higher-priority call. During one ride-along, two fights appeared on the calls-pending board, one after the other. The dispatcher radioed to assign primary squads to each. She also requested backup squads—a requirement for a priority-one call. One set of officers volunteered to leave their current assignment to go to the first fight. The dispatcher did not receive a response to her second call for backup, so she followed up by requesting that a specific officer break away from his current call. Such moments highlighted strained patrol resources and a pace that could feel relentless.

Officers shared similar norms and practices given their distinctive work environment. The volume of calls meant that officers did, in fact, do a lot of work. Although griping could be common, many officers wanted to do their fair share. Most let dispatch manage the distribution of work, and they derided certain colleagues who would volunteer for "easy assignments" or always offer to back up others, thereby avoiding the more intensive work of the primary unit.

Officers tried to be ready to take calls by being efficient in report-writing and other tasks. One night, Officers Luke Mosby and Calvin Rhem, both white men in their twenties, returned to the district station to start a report for a domestic-violence battery. As Mosby worked, he kept an eye on the calls-pending board for possible assignments. Mosby had time to finish the report, but the shift commander was occupied when he brought her documents to review. She asked him to give her five minutes, and Mosby left the office, exasperated. He said, "We're waiting to get back out on the street, and she's in there gabbing with someone." Efforts to be available, like Mosby's, were particularly pronounced when it came to meals. In contrast to the East District, where officers might head to a full-service restaurant for lunch, many West District officers ate on the go. Officer Roy Allan, a white man in his forties, pulled into the district parking lot and went to heat up his lunch. He brought it back to the squad car and explained that cops often ate in their cars because they could not be sure if they would have time to eat. As if to prove the point, Allan was dispatched to a call a few minutes into his meal.

Though officers described the pressure to always be ready, they also felt they deserved a break. Their practices for taking a break introduced potential lags in call response time. It was common for officers to "lay in the weeds" or "draw out" an assignment, as they called it. In these cases, an officer would leave the scene—after completing the assignment interaction—without immediately notifying the dispatcher. This would usually create an additional ten to twenty minutes to drive around, interface with other cops, or eat. Laying in the weeds occurred in both the East District and the West District, but it found more broad-based and open support in the West District. A lieutenant described how he knew if an officer was drawing out an assignment: "I know that your particular investigation had these types of needs or these types of responsibilities, and why are you still out there? What is going on that is drawing this out?" He suggested that there was a balance to be struck when calling officers to account: "If I request a little bit more effort, I expect it." But he also recognized that "you can't ride people hard every day because they burn out. . . . You get to a point where there are going to be some consequences—calling in sick, work slows down—you don't want that." Tolerating officers' strategies for taking a break amid the high call volume preserved the district's existing resources, even if it meant that officers would be delayed in their ability to be sent to another call.

The Hierarchy of Assignments

Beyond the routine practices reflecting general norms about work volume, officers shared ideas about how specific kinds of assignments should be handled. Violent incidents reigned as both a badge of honor and a haunting specter in the district. When a serious call came over the radio, officers from across the district would drop what they were doing and rush to the area. I observed this response several times, including during my ride-along with Hayes and Bachman when a call came over for an armed robbery in progress and sent nearly every officer in the district station running to a car. During another shift, at least eight squads converged for a felony traffic stop after an officer radioed to announce that he had spotted a van connected to multiple armed bank robberies.

In another case, an officer responding to a fight involving many people called for additional police, and squads came over the radio one after another to say they were on their way. Officers felt that violent incidents could appear at any moment. The associated work could be dangerous, time-consuming, and resource-intensive. As a lieutenant explained, a shooting could tie up most of the district's patrol resources for hours on end, leaving few available to handle other calls.

Indeed, compared to the East District, I observed West District officers respond with more frequency to fights, batteries, and shots-fired calls. But even with this specter of violence, calls for service that did not involve violent crime constituted the bulk of officers' daily work in the West District. Officers responded to property crimes like burglaries and thefts, they went to assignments for nuisance complaints like noise and loitering, and they handled a wide array of calls regarding "welfare checks" (calls to check on a subject's well-being) and "trouble with subjects."

West District officers expressed two conflicting tendencies to this varied work. On the one hand, officers emphasized that they devoted the necessary time and effort to each assignment. Organizationally, they were encouraged to provide an appropriate and thorough police response. Officer Edward Sheldon explained this as he was wrapping up an assignment for a recovered stolen vehicle. The car's owner had found the vehicle parked in a neighborhood near the gas station from which it had been stolen. While on scene, Sheldon had advised the owner, a middle-aged Latino man, that he could drive the car home or the police could have it towed to a city lot, where the owner could later pick it up. Sheldon had waited on the scene while the owner went to his daughter's house to find the spare set of keys. When the man returned, Sheldon had made some administrative phone calls and gathered information to update the stolen-vehicle record. Around this time, the dispatcher radioed to request a status update, and Sheldon asked for another twenty minutes. He said that dispatchers would sometimes go so far as to call the sergeant to see if an officer really required additional time. Sheldon suggested that this was ridiculous because supervisors were always going to let the officers take the time needed to complete the assignments.

On the other hand, officers said they needed to prioritize certain calls. Officer Travis Foster explained that the police "couldn't take time on the stupid stuff because there are usually ten or so calls pending, and something serious might come up at any point." Many felt that district residents called the police to address problems that should be handled privately or in another venue. For instance, Officer Snow said that he hated "family trouble" assignments because they often involved people who had been drinking all day and then had become upset; there were no grounds for an arrest or other law enforcement action. When I queried how he resolved such cases, Snow said he would take one of the parties to another relative's house. After framing particular assignments as peripheral to the legitimate realm of police work, officers indicated that they could handle peripheral calls quickly. They noted that a higher proportion of calls in the West District could be labeled as "advised," indicating that the officers had given some counsel to the caller, or as "baseless," which indicated that a call was without grounds. When an assignment did require further response and investigation, officers noted that it could be done in a cursory manner. They explained that crimes reported during assignments could be difficult to solve due to unhelpful or uncooperative victims, and follow-up would probably prove fruitless. It was often possible to write a report and then "file it and forget it."

Officers' perception that some assignments were not "legitimate" came from multiple sources. In some cases, calls really were without grounds. During the shift I observed, Snow and Foster were dispatched to check on a person's welfare. A call had come in a day before in which the complainant—a woman suffering a mental health crisis—reported that she had shot two men in an apartment unit. Snow and Foster were sent to investigate the potential shooting. They interviewed neighbors, secured permission from the owner to enter the apartment unit, and searched for evidence of a shooting. Upon finding the unit unoccupied and empty, they classified this assignment as "baseless" with a note to the dispatcher indicating they conducted a search with consent from the owner and found no blood or other evidence of anyone being shot. Later that night, the officers were sent to a shots-fired call. After interviewing several people in the area who speculated that the sound had been fireworks, they also gave this assignment a "baseless" disposition. Certain assignments could, indeed, be addressed quickly when the police arrived on the scene and found no relevant activity.

But the perception that assignments were illegitimate was also ironically reinforced by the district's workload pressures: initially slow police response furthered officers' assumptions that an eventual response was potentially unnecessary. The longer lower-priority assignments sat on the calls-pending board, the *less* pressing they seemed to the police. Officer Sheldon explained that priority-three or priority-four calls could sit on the board for two hundred or three hundred minutes. In some cases, he would contact the original caller before responding, particularly for "trouble with subject" assignments. He figured that it was unlikely that someone would be having the same trouble with a subject three hundred minutes after the original call. Hence, people were often left to wait. If they tried to delay or cancel a call because they had to attend to something else—like putting a child to bed or going to work—it only added more fodder to officers' interpretation that a call was not urgent. This stood in sharp contrast to police response in the East District, where officers' ability to respond promptly to calls conveyed the assumptions that calls were founded and that the police took citizens' problems seriously.

The interaction of slow police response and officers' perceptions were illustrated by Officer Seth Howland's assignment to an apartment burglary. Before arriving on scene, Howland said that the assignment seemed "a bit bogus" because the incident had occurred on Thursday night and the caller was now reporting it on a Saturday morning. But the dispatch system revealed that the caller *had* reported the incident on Thursday; she had waited for a few hours and then called to cancel the assignment because she needed to put her kids to bed. A young Black woman and two young boys were out in their yard when Howland arrived on scene. He interviewed the woman, who took him through the house while giving him an account of everything that had been taken: a television, multiple video-game consoles, a Blu-ray player, several pieces of jewelry, and some random items like the scrubs she wore for work. Howland returned to the squad car to start an incident report. He explained that he planned to canvas the neighbors, but when he went to give the incident number to the woman, she said that she had already spoken to her neighbors and no one had seen anything. Howland concluded by telling the woman that she could use the incident report for insurance purposes and she could call him if she remembered anything else that had been taken. He did not suggest to the woman or to me that the police were likely to further investigate or solve the crime. Though Howland carried out his obligations on scene, his incredulity persisted, and, once back in the squad, he again expressed confusion over why the woman had canceled the first call.

While they waited on a police response, callers would have to handle whatever crisis they were reporting on their own. Snow and Foster were dispatched to a group home when a caregiver called in about a young man threatening suicide with a fork. When Snow and Foster arrived, the caregiver, a young Black man, said he had just called to cancel the assignment. He had placed the initial call over forty minutes earlier, and, in the meantime, he had calmed down the subject. Foster apologized for the slow response, explaining that it was a busy evening and encouraging the caregiver to call back if he had concerns later. The caregiver tried to ensure a more direct response by asking if he could have Snow's or Foster's cellphone number. Snow said that he would have to call through dispatch, but they would watch for the call and would return if they were still working.

Many assignments in the West District could be handled as "advised" because citizens had, by necessity, dealt with the situation while awaiting the police. In the process, they shouldered the associated dangers and uncertainties, and the emotional strain of doing so was often apparent. A sergeant recounted to Officer Eva Irwin that he had arrived at a strong-armed robbery call and received a "fuck you, you're late" response from the victim, who left the scene after refusing to provide his name or any information. This pattern of slow initial response, followed by a minimal response when it eventually arrived, was frustrating and endangering for callers, and it worked to sour police-community relations.

Residents of the West District saw flagging police service as a symptom of how their neighborhoods were devalued and deprioritized. They described a sense that police resources were stretched thin, and the pressing nature of violence overshadowed their other concerns. One representative of a neighborhood association explained,

> If it's not a shooting, you probably won't get anybody to come out. If they do come out, it's an hour to sometimes the next day. They're overwhelmed with what they've got right now. So that's our frustration. What

seems petty to them, a property crime, is something that we don't want to happen, but they see it as more of—it's just a property crime. They're not really that interested.

Moreover, stakeholders in the West District understood that the service they experienced was different from service in other parts of the city. As a director of a business improvement district in the area noted, "The people here get shitty response times, and yet you look at somebody out in [East District]: if their garage gets broken into, [the police] are probably there in twenty minutes. Why is that?"

Some people explicitly tied changes in police service to the redistricting. In our interview, a representative of a neighborhood association described her community, which had formerly been in the East District but was now in the West District: "After the redistricting, residents said it became the neighborhood that was the better ones of the West District, . . . so less resources were coming to our neighborhood. I'd say a common complaint was slow response times, a lack of police presence." These comments highlighted an unintended consequence of the redistricting and subsequent policing priorities. With the police agency focused on the East District and the West District leadership focused on violent crime, resources for service provision were strained. Neighborhood residents saw their everyday problems as overlooked. Ultimately, they felt that another long-standing feature of urban inequality—the underprotection of Black neighborhoods—had become more pronounced.

Conclusion

While finding that predominantly Black neighborhoods are simultaneously overpoliced and underprotected may, unfortunately, be neither new nor surprising, events in River City revealed how such trends could be furthered through seemingly progressive policing philosophies and reforms. Policing in the West District was neighborhood-based and problem-oriented, just as it was in the East District. But, unlike in the East District, policing in the West District did not coalesce around a set of consistent goals. Instead, the police approached West District communities in a layered way. Multiple definitions of problems resulted in different priorities that overlapped across the district's geography: to repair police-community relations, to control crime, and to provide emergency response. Each imperative was characterized by styles of police-citizen interaction that could work at cross-purposes. While the community police unit sought to build trust, slow service and intrusive stops alienated residents from the police. The redistricting—and the priorities and resource allocations that followed—had carved out and defined the discrete work environment of the West District. Competing pressures in the district produced strategic fragmentation.

Ultimately, local policing ended up amplifying inequalities in service provision and social control between the East District and the West District. The police department responded to a real challenge in its focus on violent crime. Residents of the West District wanted help in addressing the harms that affected their communities. But the proactive strategy ultimately thwarted the goal of making the West District neighborhoods more livable, orderly, and safe. Reliance on investigatory stops overgeneralized assumptions of criminality and disproportionately subjected the district's majority Black residents to intrusive policing. At the same time, patrol officers handled a large and stressful workload, and officers were not always available to respond to citizens' needs. Residents described being underserved, and officers drew on racially coded ideas of worthiness as they speculated about whether responsive service was deserved. Many stakeholders felt that the activities of the police relied on and reinforced stereotypes that saw Black neighborhoods as categorically dangerous and without value to the city. The few resources devoted to community policing could only make marginal gains in this context.

While policing in the West District reflected the discretionary strategic choices of police leaders, these choices were embedded in the broader context of River City's governance. The crime control strategy was related to the city's approach to economic development. Throughout the city's history, West District neighborhoods had been some of the most institutionally neglected and oppressed. These neighborhoods had been created through racial discrimination and were economically devastated by deindustrialization. Unemployment and poverty gave rise to social challenges that the state addressed through policing and mass incarceration, stamping West District neighborhoods with an enduring mark of criminality. Amid urban-revitalization projects that channeled public and private resources into spaces of productive value, the police—in alignment with the city's growth coalition—treated West District neighborhoods as sites that had to be segregated and controlled. The redistricting accomplished the separation between areas of economic value and those that threatened it, while the proactive strategy regulated a space defined as criminal.

Service provision in the West District also reflected urban governance strategies. A River City police executive described the police as the "social agency of first resort for the poor," and, indeed, they often were. Officers did the work of emergency responders, nurses, mental health practitioners, family counselors, and social workers as they responded to wide-ranging calls for service, which concentrated in areas like the West District due to structural inequalities like poverty and joblessness. The police were not always equipped with the training or the skills to handle the needs of people in such varied situations, and they had little ability to address underlying causes. For example, I heard many officers lament the inadequate infrastructure for mental health treatment in the city. They saw their interventions as limited to shuttling people through a revolving door between the county mental health facility and the community. As neoliberal governance and urban austerity measures eroded social services, the police were left to respond. But police activities alone could not address the root causes of the challenges that impacted poor Black communities in River City.

Truly transforming River City's unequal landscape would require many stakeholders to make concerted investments in neighborhoods that had long suffered systemic discrimination and neglect. Bonnie Rob erts, the director of a business improvement district that included areas in West District, described her vision for this transformation: "I would like a plan that would help our area and one that doesn't go on the shelf but one that actually is implemented to help with things like jobs, to help with poverty, to help with education, to help with mental health, alcohol, and other drug abuse." She elaborated, "It's not just law enforcement. It's going to take all hands on deck and a united effort, so the city could start coordinating that. They should get all the nonprofits, all the foundations, businesses, everybody signing on and throwing a lot of resources at fixing this problem with a sense of urgency." However, Roberts expressed doubts that such a plan could come to fruition: "I think this area is forgotten a lot of times because of the big racial-segregation issue in River

City. . . . We have a race-relations problem here. If this was white people up here starving and getting shot at, would we allow that?"

Indeed, segregation was a powerful material and symbolic structure in River City, and the police participated in maintaining it. As this chapter and chapter 3 have revealed, the police undertook efforts to further define and craft the character of River City's segregated neighborhoods. The redistricting drew on a widely circulating vision of social and economic differences that distinguished between ostensibly valuable areas and the violent inner city. The police positioned themselves as capable of serving and protecting the downtown and middle-class residential neighborhoods while containing and controlling areas that posed a criminal threat. The strategic priorities that followed eventually deepened the divides in the policing experienced by Black and white residents. Thus, policing configured the experiences and meanings that circulated *within* segregated neighborhoods, with the effect of reinscribing enduring race- and class-based inequalities. Yet, as chapter 5 shows, the police participated in another project central to maintaining segregation: regulating the boundaries *between* neighborhoods. Ultimately, spatial regulation in River City was also racial regulation, and the police played a role in defining where people "rightfully" belonged.

5

Policing Segregation Boundaries

West District patrol officer Lee Giles, a white man in his forties, was
chatting casually with me as he drove to the scene of a retail theft. We
had gotten on the topic of River City's segregation. Giles pulled the squad
car over for a moment and said he would draw me a map. He asked for
my notebook and proceeded to draw a series of blobs representing the
distribution of racial and ethnic groups in the city. He labeled one "H"
for Hispanic and he wrote "Black" above a line demarcating the highway.
Giles marked white areas, sometimes labeling specific European ethnic
groups, and he noted the presence of Asians in a few places. As he drew,
Giles explained that no one wanted a segregated city; it was simply the
result of when groups arrived initially. He noted that River City did not
have a very large Black population until the end of the Great Migration.
To elaborate, he observed that when he checked someone's identification, he often noticed that older African Americans were from southern
states. Giles speculated that the original European settlers established
their communities and then the Black population settled in the remaining areas.

I asked Giles if he thought that the city's segregation impacted policing currently, and he responded, "I don't really think it does." Giles
likened issues of race and policing to Jim Crow—the people who had directly experienced that system were from an older generation. While he
had heard about Jim Crow, he had never actually lived it. Giles said that
this was similar to policing. In the 1970s and 1980s, police departments
did engage in racist practices. But, Giles went on, these were over. Now,
when younger people claimed racial profiling, it was more based on the
lore of previous generations that actual lived experience.

Giles's narratives of River City's segregation and policing reflected
accounts I heard from many officers. They shared an insistence that racial discrimination was a thing of the past. Officers were particularly
adamant in maintaining that they did not use race inappropriately in

their work. The police asserted that they would behave similarly toward people of any race if they were engaged in similar behaviors. For example, they said that Black people could enjoy the downtown nightlife corridors if they were patronizing the taverns, and white people would be treated as criminals if they were linked to criminal incidents. They explained that their work reflected official duties, district-level work environments, legal standards, and department policies, rather than any kind of race-based decision-making.

Yet my observations suggested otherwise. On many occasions, I watched the police pay close attention to "race out of place"—moments when the race of a body did not match assumptions about the racial composition of an area.[1] This generally entailed police scrutiny of people who crossed segregation boundaries, but it could also apply to entities, like nightlife establishments or kinds of vehicles, that the police saw as catering to or signaling particular racial groups. The policing of race out of place occurred in both the East District and the West District. Chapter 6 describes how the police interacted with white people in the predominantly Black neighborhoods West District. This chapter focuses on the disproportionate policing of Black people in the East District.

The policing of race out of place in the downtown revealed that the community-service ethos of the East District was not applied uniformly across establishments and individuals. It became clear—as the police sought to regulate Black bodies—that the "rightful" clients of East District police service were assumed to be white. The policing of race out of place unfolded in several ways. First, during the Entertainment Corridor Deployment, the police collaborated with private establishments to exclude, contain, and control Black visitors to the downtown. Second, officers marked Black bodies entering predominantly white spaces as potential sources of criminal threat and disorder, subjecting them to additional scrutiny. Finally, racialized organizational practices in routine traffic enforcement targeted vehicles that signaled race and class, thereby contributing to within-district racial disparities in traffic stops. While these practices varied in how overtly they drew on stereotypes of Blackness, they collectively showed that policing was not only about spatial regulation but also about *racial* regulation.

Ideas of commercial viability, worth, and order, on the one hand, and those of threat, criminality, and disorder, on the other, mapped onto *people,* as well as places. As the police drew on these ideas to regulate where people "belonged," they actively maintained segregation boundaries. Disproportionate police attention to Black people in the East District defined it as a white space, conveying that the city's revitalization was not for everyone and upholding racialized hierarchies of urban citizenship. Yet officers did not view their practices as racial because their activities technically conformed to legal and departmental guidelines. A narrow, but common, understanding of discrimination enabled policing of race out of place. This chapter investigates how officers could offer race-neutral accounts of their work while engaging in the active maintenance of segregation boundaries.

Officers' Nonracial Accounts of Policing

As the previous chapters have shown, policing in the East and West Districts relied on raced and classed logics and produced raced and classed effects. Police executives created segregated districts and specialized units to treat neighborhoods in different ways. The redistricting institutionalized subjective distinctions between places of economic value and those that represented criminal threats, and it translated these ideas into administrative boundaries that shaped officers' routine activities. Police leaders subsequently developed deployments to facilitate service provision in some districts and crime control in others. Strategic priorities and district-level resources intersected with divergent work environments to produce vastly different experiences of patrol work for officers and experiences of policing for citizens. Race entered into these processes as long-standing structural inequalities, and symbolic associations—particularly those associating Black neighborhoods with crime and white neighborhoods with value—shaped organizational structures and strategic priorities. Policing practices further constructed racialized geographies by delivering service and social control unevenly across the city's segregated places and populations.

In an ironic twist, many of the same organizational dynamics that contributed to racialized policing citywide obscured officers' perceptions of racial inequities in policing. While subdivisions like police districts and specialized roles played a critical part in generating racial disparities, officers saw districts and roles as characterized by their own nonracial imperatives. For instance, officers interpreted racial patterns in their encounters with citizens as inevitable due to districts' racial homogeneity. One West District officer, an Asian American man in his fifties, explained that he did not intend to arrest people on the basis of race, but it happened that the district was 99 percent Black. Though this was an exaggeration, it captured a common sentiment that any racial patterning reflected whom the police routinely encountered in the neighborhoods they patrolled. A traffic officer in the West District similarly explained that any racial patterns in his stops were not about demographics but about the fact that he worked in a segregated district, quipping, "I don't pull over people. I pull over violations." Like Officer Giles, the police saw segregation as a natural phenomenon: a matter of people "choosing to stay with their own kind" or "go where they're most comfortable," as multiple officers put it. The police took for granted both the city's segregation and its subdivision into segregated police districts. This allowed them to view their discrete work environments as characterized by general, nonracial imperatives.

However, district environments intersected with the uneven distribution of specialized roles and units across the city. In some roles, officers experienced comparable imperatives, regardless of district. For example, the traffic officers I observed in the East and West Districts engaged in similar sets of practices: they had a favorite spot where equipment violations would be noticeable or traffic violations would be common. They checked for valid registration stickers and ran license plates to see if they were suspended. They talked about performance measures and tried to conduct a certain number of stops to feel productive. But some units *only* existed in certain districts. Hayes and Bachman and the other AVU officers in the West District implemented mandates defined by district captains and department policies, such as searching for illegal guns, conducting proactive traffic stops and subject stops, and investigating suspected drug houses. The concentration of proactive activities in predominantly Black districts was central to generating citywide racial disparities; however, they represented official duties from the officers' perspectives. The police had few incentives to consider whether stops were occurring in other districts or how they were distributed unevenly across the city.

When the police discussed decision-making in specific situations, their explanations relied on legal and organizational rules, including standards like reasonable suspicion and probable cause, procedures outlining the use of force, and policies on fair and impartial policing. Officers narrated their decision-making by fitting behavioral criteria to formal policies. For example, Officers Hayes and Bachman articulated grounds for traffic stops that were consistent with the standard of reasonable suspicion. In another instance, Officer Albert Ramirez explained the department's fair and impartial policing policy, which prohibited the consideration of race or other status characteristics, *except* when credible and local information linked people of specific characteristics to particular incidents or criminal patterns. Ramirez said a group of three to four Black males in a Dodge minivan had committed a recent string of armed robberies in a specific East District neighborhood. In this scenario, he explained that if the cops saw a Dodge Caravan with three to four Black males in the area, they would start to develop reasonable suspicion. He concluded that the same criteria of car type, location, and number of subjects would apply if a group of white males committed the robberies. Ramirez said that the police relied on far more than a presumption of criminality based on race; he offered a broader set of criteria that conformed with legal and technical standards.

I heard many police accounts of situational decisions that centered on legal standards, policies, and rules. Officer Dylan Erickson, a white man in his thirties who worked in the East District, gave the example of shooting a fleeing subject. He noted that people might think this was never appropriate but said that officers could use deadly force to prevent someone from escaping if the person displayed the intention to cause death or substantial bodily harm to the officer or others. His explanation closely followed the language in both the department's use-of-force protocol and *Tennessee v. Garner* (1985), the Supreme Court decision outlining this standard.[2] The police also described the permissible use of deadly force based on an officer's "objectively reasonable fear" of a threat of death or great bodily harm. Several officers rationalized killing a person and shooting them many times in the process by citing their training to stop a threat as quickly as possible. From officers' perspective, many situations involved a complex and specific set of factors that were bound to be more legible to them—based on their knowledge of procedures and rules—than to the public.

In sum, officers did not see themselves as racially discriminatory in their minds or in their actions. The racial logics and consequences of their work were obscured by bureaucratic structures like spatial and functional subdivisions and an abundance of legal rules and departmental policies. With their duties and territorial reach circumscribed by the police agency, it was difficult for officers to perceive and appreciate the broader racial patterns produced by their collective activities. Indeed, the police navigated a rule-saturated field; as the criminologists George Alpert and William Smith describe, "Virtually every aspect of policing is subject to some combination of law, policy, guideline, directive, rule or general order."[3] These bureaucratic arrangements allowed the police to assert the race neutrality of their work. After a year of fieldwork, I understood how officers could see themselves as merely executing official duties within an administratively circumscribed geography, all while conforming to the requirements of law and procedure. The pressures and imperatives of their work could indeed appear to be nonracial on the surface.

But I found that policing in River City *was* racial. Formal structures like district boundaries and specialized assignments obscured the ties between organizational routines, the racial attitudes of officers, and racial outcomes. They also transformed patterned events into discrete, stand-alone situations. Officers' explanations of situational encounters divorced a specific decision-making point from a chain of decisions laden with discretion.[4] For instance, many accounts took for granted the initial formation of reasonable suspicion, without recognizing the potential cognitive links between suspicion and racial stereotypes or the role of practices based on this legal standard in fueling racial disproportionality.[5] The remainder of this chapter turns to the power of deep-seated interpretive frameworks that linked race, place, class, and crime. While previous chapters have illustrated how these frameworks shaped the policing of segregated neighborhoods, they were also implicated in the policing of segregation *boundaries*.

Reinterpreting the Role of Race

Officers participated in the active maintenance of segregation boundaries through their attention to race out of place. I observed several examples of the policing of Black bodies "out of place" in the East

District. Practices ranged from racially coded place-based language as a signifier of criminal threat to organizational practices that disproportionately targeted vehicles carrying subtler markers of race and class. I describe these practices is more detail in the following section. For now, it suffices to note that the policing of race out of place appeared inconsistent with officers' assertions that their work was race neutral. The tension between racialized policing practices and officers' insistence that they did not racially profile reflected an understanding of discrimination that the sociologist and legal scholar Issa Kohler-Hausmann describes as the "counterfactual causal model." She explains that "discrimination, in this account, is detected by measuring the 'treatment effect of race,' where treatment is conceptualized as manipulating the raced status of *otherwise identical units* (e.g. a person, a neighborhood, a school)."[6] This understanding of discrimination has been institutionalized in arenas ranging from social scientific research to Supreme Court decisions. [7]

Officers often used this counterfactual causal mode in their explanations. For instance, Sergeant Crawford described robberies and loitering as problems in the downtown entertainment corridor, noting that loitering was particularly bad on one corner of the Main Street intersection. Without prompting, he mused that though the police department was often accused of being racist, they were just focusing on the problems: the people who came and grabbed women or were likely to start fights. He explained that plenty of Black people came from other neighborhoods to the entertainment district to patronize the taverns. Moreover, many Black residents living in the district would also visit the bars. The problem was other people who had no interest in supporting the businesses and started trouble. Crawford's account suggested that people engaged in the same behavior, under equal circumstances, would be treated similarly, regardless of race. Yet his comments also revealed the racial character of the distinctions between economic contribution and criminal threat by insinuating that most of the people engaging in troubling behaviors in the downtown were Black.

As Kohler-Hausmann explains, the counterfactual causal model of discrimination has, at its core, a misguided assumption about what race is and how it operates. The counterfactual causal model treats race as a superficial attribute reducible to skin color or phenotype. It assumes that two units *could* be the same except for their race. In reality, race is so integral to life chances—from the kinds of neighborhoods, schools, jobs, and health care people can access to the poverty they experience or wealth they inherit to the ways in which they are policed or protected— that disentangling the "effect" of race from other factors is impossible. Histories of colonial conquest, enslavement, immigration, and accompanying practices of racial domination and subordination have "created separate social and physical worlds for different groups" that preclude the assumption that units could be comparable, but for race.[8] This was certainly the case in River City, where segregation linked race, place, and a nexus of other experiences and meanings, allowing the police to attend to racial difference without always signifying it directly.

The policing of race out of place ultimately showed that the symbolic meanings attached to places also attached to bodies. The same constructs and dualities that emerged in official discourses about the East and West Districts emerged again in officers' efforts to distinguish between people engaged in legitimate, economically contributory activities and those who were potential criminal and civic threats. It became clear that the language of place often stood in for race. For example, officers in the East District used terms like "the ghetto" and "the hood" to signal the presence of Black people in the predominantly white nightlife corridor. Sometimes, they used labels corresponding to River City's distinctly segregated landscape, referencing "the west side," "the West District," or the other districts that covered predominantly Black neighborhoods. Broad designators like "the ghetto" suggested that all Black people were potential sources of disorder or criminal threats. They did not distinguish between the troublemakers and Black residents of the East District or Black patrons supporting the entertainment economy, as Crawford had suggested.

Officers' use of place-based language highlighted the entanglement of place, race, class, and criminality. While the redistricting had demarcated spatial boundaries and defined places in terms of economic value and the threat of violence, officers carried these associations into their actions toward racialized people. In some cases, it was clear that the policing of race out of place was part of the political-economic project of protecting areas of commercial viability from encroachments of crime and disorder, which were tied to constructs of Blackness. Other cases were more a reflection of organizational practices that compounded disproportionate law enforcement along lines of race and class. Despite these differences in motivating logics, all forms of policing race out of place in the East District served to strengthen the assumption that the city's sites of commercial and residential value overlapped with whiteness. As the police disproportionately surveilled and engaged with people "out of place," they conveyed messages about who belonged that ultimately reinforced segregation.

Policing Race Out of Place

The ties between the city's political economy and the policing of race out of place were most apparent during the Entertainment Corridor Deployment (ECD). As described in chapter 3, the ECD developed as a special initiative to serve the downtown's growth aspirations. Though the downtown was already relatively safe, police officials feared the economic consequences of a violent incident. Former East District captain Curtis Hartman, creator of the ECD, and Sergeant Crawford, who routinely oversaw it, noted that a shooting could frighten people away from the entertainment districts and potentially deter conventioneers and tourists from visiting River City. Thus, the police identified potential threats to the vitality of the downtown, relying on race-place associations that resulted in the enhanced police scrutiny of Black people. For instance, Crawford said that most problems downtown were caused by "people coming from other districts." Hence, some of the work of the ECD entailed policing the boundaries of where racialized bodies could be and what they could do in the downtown. The police focused on specific establishments that served predominantly Black clientele and on Black individuals in predominantly white spaces.

Policing Racialized Places

In collaboration with private establishments, the police sought to contain Black people to specific venues where they could be regulated and controlled. Their attention frequently focused on The Edge—the nightclub several blocks from the epicenter of Main Street catering to "the hip-hop crowd," as Sergeant Crawford described it. The Edge had a capacity for just under five hundred people. On the basis of my observations during several walk-throughs during ECD deployments, a vast majority of patrons were Black. The Edge did experience problems periodically. A year before my fieldwork, the club's tavern license was suspended temporarily after two shootings and a shots-fired incident in its vicinity. During the Licensing Committee hearing, Captain Hartman explained that his biggest fear was that the next victim would be a conventioneer and the city would lose convention and conference revenue. Hartman emphasized the impacts on tourism by noting that he had spoken to several out-of-towners: "these were guests to our city that were witnesses."[9] After the club reopened, there were still occasional incidents. During one of my observations, several officers discussed a large fight outside The Edge from the night before. During another, a report came in for shots fired from a vehicle a block away from the club. Such events contributed to the perception that The Edge was the primary source of potential violence in the downtown. Crawford pointed out a parking lot close to the club and said that if a shooting were to happen, it would be in the lot: people could not bring guns into the club, but they could have them in their cars.

While fights and shootings posed real risks for citizens and the police, information from specific incidents circulated along with stereotypes that assumed widespread criminality of The Edge's patrons. One night, I rode along with Sergeant Vincent Burkes, a white man in his thirties who, like Crawford, often oversaw the ECD. Around 11 p.m., Burkes suggested we do a walk-through of The Edge. It was still relatively early, so the club had few patrons; Burkes made a quick lap without taking note of anything in particular. Once we were back outside, Burkes speculated that there were at least twenty murderers in the club. Given the small crowd and Burkes's cursory pass-through, I read this comment as unlikely and hyperbolic. The emphasis on the criminality of the people in The Edge continued when we returned for another walk-through at around 1 a.m. Burkes and three officers climbed a flight of stairs to the "VIP" balcony overlooking a large open dance floor, now much more crowded. Peering down, one of the officers asked another, "How many murderers do you think are in here?" He said to me, "I would guess that 60 or 70—no, 75—percent of the guys in this club are felons." On a separate occasion, another officer placed the proportion as high as 90 percent. Though I had no way of verifying these claims, I suspected they were overblown.

The assumption of risk and pervasive criminality corresponded to practices of surveillance and regulation that affected *all* visitors to The Edge. Despite the club's problems, the police lauded its owner—a middle-aged South Asian man who had run the establishment for over a decade—for his security systems. In addition to an ample staff of bouncers and security guards, the owner had several tools to gather information about patrons. Upon entering the club, visitors had their identification scanned and a "red carpet" photo taken. Both Crawford and the owner explained to me separately that between these two methods, the owner could relay to the police a person's name, the time and date of their visit, their visit history, and photos of their associates. The owner had also installed an audio-video camera above the club's back door, and he provided the police with the IP address enabling them to view the footage at any time.[10] From the accounts of the police, it did not appear that law enforcement used these tools to surveil or punish activities in the club. They left internal incidents to the owner and his sizable security staff. But the police cited the documentation at The Edge as a resource for investigating external incidents. Moreover, they viewed the owner as cooperative. Sergeant Burkes said the owner had helped to take a suspect into custody by informing the FBI when the man had arrived at the club. With these systems in place, patrons of The Edge unknowingly contributed their information to a trove of documentation that could be easily accessed by the police.

Beyond this surveillance inside the club, the police were preeminently concerned with containing and controlling crowds when they left The Edge and entered public space. The owner closed The Edge fifteen minutes earlier than the bars at the intersection of Main Street, and this staggered timing enabled greater police presence during closing at both ends of the corridor. Officers spoke anxiously in anticipation of closing time at The Edge, and they aspired to clear the area as quickly as possible. During my ride-along with Sergeant Burkes, we watched as people began to stream out of the club. The Edge's security staff followed the crowd and urged them toward the nearby parking lots. An officer in a squad drove alongside the flow of people and announced through the megaphone that the bar was closed and anyone who did not continue moving would be arrested for loitering. Other officers approached individuals or groups who lingered, issuing loud directives and threats of arrest. As the sidewalk in front of the club cleared, Burkes drove to the parking lots and shined the squad's spotlight onto people who were not immediately getting into their vehicles. Through surveillance and threats, the police cultivated an uninterrupted flow of people from the club to the parking lot and, ultimately, out of the downtown.

The regulation of The Edge was not the only example of police collaborating with private businesses to contain or exclude Black people within the entertainment district. During a ride-along, Sergeant Crawford pointed out a parking lot near the Main Street intersection and described how people from "the ghetto" would essentially tailgate in the lot, with no interest in patronizing the taverns. As the parking lot belonged to a bank, the police had met with the bank's representatives to discuss the issue. Crawford said the meeting was cordial and friendly, though the police were ready to discuss liability issues if an incident occurred. The bank responded by raising the cost of parking in the lot from five to ten dollars and hiring a security guard on the weekends. Crawford said the situation had since improved. In this case, the police put their collaborative relationships and problem-solving ethos to use in managing race out of place. It also revealed that officers' helpful and protective orientation was reserved for those who "belonged" in the district. Spatial regulation in the downtown drew on ideas of threat and economic contribution imbued with racial undertones.

Policing Racialized People

The regulation of Main Street's intersection—a corridor where a majority of patrons were white—highlighted another racialized surveillance and control modality. While The Edge received attention as a potentially dangerous *place*, officers focused on potentially dangerous *people* at the Main Street intersection. This required identifying threats among the hundreds, if not thousands, of individuals in the area. The epicenter of the intersection included several blocks of nearly side-by-side bars and restaurants. Visitors often circulated among multiple establishments, producing a steady flow of pedestrians through the intersection. In many cases, police attention and activity unfolded as described in chapter 3. Officers worked with bar managers and bouncers to address problems on a case-by-case basis and watched for nuisance or safety concerns on the street. Much of this work was reactive: the police were summoned to bars, helped citizens who asked for assistance, and checked on people who appeared to be excessively intoxicated.

When the police took a more proactive approach, efforts to identify "threats" targeted people out of place. Officers said they made this distinction based on expectations of appropriate behaviors in the entertainment corridors: patronizing taverns, enjoying entertainment options, and generally engaging in consumption and exchange. Like Sergeant Crawford, East District officer Kevin Hickey explained that the police did not use race to identify people out of place; their attention was more nuanced and tied to indicators that people were in the downtown to contribute to the nightlife economy. Hickey said that all of the criminals he knew growing up in his small hometown were white rednecks—the kinds of people with mullets and Confederate-flag shirts. He suggested that such people would be more out of place and suspicious in the downtown than a group of well-dressed Black men clearly in the area to visit the bars. Hickey offered distinctions that drew on his extant knowledge of criminal patterns and class indicators, ostensibly transcending a focus on race.

Yet my observations indicated that Black individuals and groups received more scrutiny at the Main Street intersection. Moreover, it often appeared that officers were construing relatively common behaviors as suspicious rather than identifying objectively suspicious behaviors. For example, groups of people frequently lingered on the sidewalk in between visits to bars, but an officer pointed out four young Black men standing on the corner and said, "That's what we're worried about, the guys who are just lurking outside." We did not remain in the area long enough to discern whether the group was actually loitering or merely in transit between establishments, but regardless, the group did not appear to be doing anything unusual. During the ECD on Halloween, a small group of Black men costumed as various superheroes passed by an officer as they crossed the Main Street intersection. One of the men made a remark to a white woman, and the officer interjected, "She's not interested. You should move on." I was surprised by this intervention into the kind of event—a man speaking to a woman—that had to happen hundreds of times a night in the downtown. The officer's attention suggested the policing of gender relations on the basis of a notion of racialized threat. At bar closing time, the same officer took note of this group again as they marched theatrically down the block. He walked toward them hurriedly and suggested it was time to head home. Afterward, he explained to another officer that the group had been out earlier and "possibly causing problems." Again, the actual behaviors of the group appeared to be typical of friends going out on the weekend.

As described earlier, the depth of the associations between race and suspicion was most on display when the police used place-based language to draw attention to potential "problems." Here, constructions of threat transcended specific individuals and groups to mark Black people more generally. Though the police did not explicitly label race, they used geographic signifiers with clear racial connotations. Sometimes, they referenced The Edge with comments like, "The Edge is coming up Main Street." In other cases, officers used labels that corresponded to River City's distinctly segregated landscape, referencing the predominantly Black part of the city or the police districts that covered it. I did not observe officers arrest or cite people without further cause, however. This was consistent with previous research finding that race plays a role in the formation of suspicion but that behavioral criteria determine the decision to take action.[11] Yet police scrutiny could eventually result in the detection of a behavior that rose to the level of reasonable suspicion or probable cause. Disproportionate attention had the potential to lead to disproportionate enforcement. Though arrest data reported by the RCPD did not capture ECD activities specifically, it did show that the police made over five times as many arrests of Black people for curfew violations and loitering compared to arrests of white people and over three times as many arrests of Black people for disorderly conduct citywide.[12] Additional surveillance, verbal admonishments, and law enforcement activities directed toward Black individuals marked the Main Street intersection as an unwelcoming place.

The assumptions of criminality that inflected officer-initiated encounters with Black people at the intersection of Main Street stood in contrast to police engagement with white people, which remained generally reactive. One night, a young white man stood slumped against the façade of a bar and suddenly vomited inches away from an officer's boots. With a grimace, the officer muttered something about people making themselves potential victims and began to demand loudly that the man call his friends, who arrived soon after to guide him home. In another instance, officers detained a white man in his early twenties after a bar's bouncer told them that the man had been caught selling drugs in the bathroom. An officer learned that the young man had come in from a suburb and admonished him, "You can't come into my city and cause problems." While his comment evinced the common concern of keeping the entertainment corridor safe in service of River City's prospects, these interactions showed how ideas of "problems" varied. Excessively drunk white people were potential victims rather than signs of disorder. In order to pose a threat, they had to overtly engage in criminal behavior.

Together, the regulation of The Edge and Black people on Main Street revealed that constructs of economic value and potential *were* about race rather than place alone. Black visitors and residents of the downtown also spent money and participated in the city's nightlife scene, but they were perceived as criminal threats to the economic vitality of the downtown, instead of an audience for the city's revitalization efforts. Policing efforts subsequently attempted to contain Black patrons to sites where they could be regulated, like The Edge, to exclude them from the corridor, or to proactively ensure they did not interfere with the "legitimate" use of the entertainment corridor by white visitors. Even as the police claimed that they differentiated between those who caused problems and those who patronized the downtown establishments, my observations revealed that race served as an axis of distinction.

Racialized Organizational Practices

Racialized policing was not limited to the Entertainment Corridor Deployment: it was also evident in racial disparities in traffic stops in the East District. Reports of racial disparities in stops tended to emphasize citywide patterns in which Black and Latinx drivers were stopped at much higher rates than white drivers overall. The differences in the volume of stops conducted between districts played a central role in generating these disparities. For example, when the city's major newspaper analyzed traffic stops, it found that twice as many stops had occurred in the West District compared to the East District during the same several-month time frame. As chapter 4 described, this difference in volume was driven by the existence of proactive units tasked with making stops in the West District, while no comparable unit existed in the East District. But breakdowns of stops *within* each district revealed that the East District was characterized by the greatest racial disparities of any district. Black drivers constituted nearly half of all stops, even though they constituted less than 10 percent of the district's driving-age residents. By contrast, the West District actually had the smallest disparities in stops, though the volume of stops was much greater.[13] Racialized organizational practices were not just a matter of district-level deployments. Intradistrict dynamics also contributed to racial disparities.

A ride-along with Officer Marvin Elliott, a white man in his forties, highlighted potential sources of racial disparities in East District traffic stops. Elliott was assigned to one of the district's "traffic cars." Each district had a unit that was primarily responsible for traffic safety enforcement. Elliott was part of this unit, and he had expertise in traffic and vehicle laws. His primary tasks included responding to car accidents and conducting traffic stops. Elliott's stops were distinct from investigatory stops in that they were focused generally on addressing traffic and equipment violations instead of investigating other criminal activities. Elliott was responsible for a large proportion of the traffic stops in the East District. He showed me a recent breakdown of performance measures that indicated that East District day-shift officers had conducted an average of eight stops over a seven-week reporting period. By contrast, Elliot said he would probably have about three hundred stops for the upcoming period. Given this high volume of stops, the traffic cars played a role in contributing to the racial disparities reported in the area.

I asked Elliott how officers decided which cars to pull over, given the many violations they might observe; he explained that officers exercised their discretion. Elliott noted that he focused on equipment violations because they were harder to dispute in court compared to traffic violations. Throughout the evening, Elliott pointed out myriad violations, from missing license plates to defective lights to excessive window tinting. Elliott was particularly attentive to excessive window tinting, which could be verified as illegal using a tint meter that measured how much light passed through the window. Though he spent much of the shift backing up other officers and responding to traffic accidents, Elliott made four traffic stops during my observation, and three of them were for dark window tint.

As Elliott made the first stop for dark tint, he said that people often worried that the police were racially profiling during traffic stops. He asked me if I could tell who was in the car—if it was a man or a woman or a Black or white person. Elliott said that he had no idea; he could not see inside the vehicle. Then he elaborated, saying that when he made stops during the ECD on the weekend, drivers often accused him of pulling them over based on race, but this just was not the case. The night I observed, the first driver whom Elliott pulled over was a man who appeared to be of Middle Eastern descent. The second was a white man in his late twenties, and the third was a young Black woman. While this variation seemed to confirm Elliott's perception that stops were not based on race, research has shown that particular kinds of vehicles are coded in raced and classed ways.[14] Furthermore, critics have argued that window-tint enforcement is a mechanism that enables the disproportionate policing of people of color.[15] Taking at face value Elliott's assertion that the police were not engaged in racially profiling drivers themselves, his work nevertheless highlighted the possibility that the police targeted vehicles that signaled race and class in a subtler manner.

Elliott's traffic car was also outfitted with an automatic license-plate reader system (ALPRs). When my ride-along began, Elliott pointed out cameras on either side of the squad that automatically read the plate numbers of passing vehicles, returning a notification if the plate was associated with a violation like an expired registration or suspended license, a stolen vehicle, or an outstanding warrant. Later in the shift, Elliott said he would show me some of the city's public housing (ride-alongs sometimes entailed a touring component). He drove the squad car to a West District subsidized housing complex just across the boundary of the East District. Even though this neighborhood was adjacent to the downtown, its residents were over 80 percent Black.[16] As we drove past blocks of parked cars, the ALPRs pinged almost constantly. When we returned at the end of the shift, Elliott showed me that ALPRs had detected eighty-three vehicles with suspended plates and scanned over twelve hundred license plates that night. While Elliott had paid little attention to ALPRs during his shift, the squad car's outfitting with this system represented another source of compounding uneven law enforcement along lines of race, place, and class.

As the sociologist Sarah Brayne describes, technological tools like ALPRs create feedback loops that can amplify racial and economic inequalities.[17] For instance, poor people are less likely to be able to pay off tickets for minor equipment violations and thus risk having their license suspended.[18] Indeed, a technical report by a scholar at one of the universities in River City found that 60 percent of license suspensions in the state were for failure to pay forfeitures rather than for traffic violations.[19] Due to the overlaps between poverty and race, license suspensions were concentrated in predominantly Black, lower-income areas, as Elliott's tour of the public-housing complex in the West District revealed. If and when these vehicles crossed segregation boundaries into the jurisdiction of the East District's traffic enforcement, they could be detected by ALPRs and their drivers subject to further enforcement. Thus, the policing of race out of place in the East District was also driven by organizational practices that focused on indicators of race and class attached to vehicles rather than drivers themselves.

In sum, the policing of race out of place in the East District served to reinforce deeply entrenched associations linking Blackness to criminal threat and whiteness to economic value. Police attention to Black bodies was integral to the project of urban revitalization as officers sought to protect the commercial viability of the downtown from people and places constructed as threatening and disorderly. Yet the policing of race out of place also transcended the protection of the downtown to include organizational practices that compounded past patterns of disproportionate policing of poor people and people of color. In all cases, police attention concentrated on those who crossed segregation boundaries. The police did not necessarily act on their piqued suspicions, and I rarely observed them take formal law enforcement actions like arrests. Yet the projects of shepherding Black patrons of The Edge out of the downtown at bar closing time, admonishing Black men for innocuous activities at the intersection of Main Street, and stopping drivers for violations that could reflect an inability to pay fines all conveyed messages about where raced and classed people could and could not go in the city if they wanted to avoid police scrutiny.

Conclusion

The policing of race out of place in the East District is consistent with other research showing that "watching and warding off people who seem out of place in White areas are core aspects of police work."[20] The policing of race out of place has the effect of discouraging the crossing of segregation boundaries in daily life.[21] Moreover, policing can shape segregation in the long term by informing residential preferences. The sociologist and legal scholar Monica Bell describes policing as a "located institution," or a meaning-making lens that shapes perceptions of neighborhoods and communities: "by becoming embedded into neighborhood reputations, located institutions can function as a first-order heuristic through which certain neighborhoods become highly appealing or off-limits to particular groups."[22] Her research identifies a pattern in which Black individuals experience policing as a public nuisance that discourages them from visiting or living in certain neighborhoods. Work in this vein identifies the mechanisms linking the policing of race out of place to the endurance of racial segregation through residential preference and the routine avoidance of particular parts of the city.

The policing of segregation boundaries sent messages about the relative standing of racialized citizens in River City. It became clear—as police activities defined Black people in the downtown as sources of crime and danger rather than economic contribution—that urban-revitalization efforts did not equally include all residents. Growth discourse held that downtown development would eventually serve the entire city by renewing municipal finances and spilling economic benefits into adjacent areas. Yet this vision of growth relied on maintaining sanitized arenas for commerce, entertainment, and comfortable living that implicitly assumed white participants and beneficiaries. Exclusionary policing resulted, and disproportionate police encounters shaped hierarchies of urban citizenship. White residents, business owners, and visitors were free to enjoy the fruits of the city's growth and development, while Black individuals were subject to scrutiny and intrusions that limited their ability to participate fully in what the urban growth coalition understood to be the heart of River City's social and economic life.

It is also important to understand how the maintenance of segregation boundaries occurred through policing practices that conformed to departmental policies and legal standards. Even as the police attended to race out of place, they insisted they were not racially discriminatory. Technically, this could be the case. I did not observe officers acting on the basis of race alone, and many could identify behavioral criteria that met thresholds of reasonable suspicion or probable cause when explaining their formal activities. In the policing of segregated neighborhoods and segregation boundaries, bureaucratic rules, roles, and routines bolstered nonracial interpretations of work. Officers understood discrimination as a matter of treating *otherwise equal* units differently on the basis of race. However, in River City, officers understood real differences in crime rates and other social problems as meriting differential enforcement. Previous chapters have shown how such a logic motivated the divergent policing strategies between the East District and the West District. This chapter has demonstrated that the assumption of potential criminality transcended neighborhoods and became attached to Black people.

While officers did not perceive their work as discriminatory, a structural and institutional analysis of racism arrives at a different conclusion. Issa Kohler-Hausmann offers an alternative definition of discrimination based on categories like race, "as an action or practice that acts on or reproduces an aspect of the category in a way that is morally objectionable."[23] Discrimination, in this reformulation, "implicates social meanings in a way that constitutes some social kinds as degraded or disfavored, over many domains and times."[24] In River City, as in many other places, the policing of race out of place was part of the ongoing construction of physical and social spaces that reproduced racial differences, hierarchies, and inequalities. The racial realities of segregation, poverty, wealth, family disruption, economic opportunity, and criminalization were rendered actively through institutional practices, including those of the police. "Race" was not merely a matter of otherwise-equal units; racial categories were laden with a host of inextricable meanings produced through historical, political, and social processes.

Hence, policing in River City *was* racial. In a context where class, space, and race were so intertwined, political-economic projects to reconfigure space inevitably redistributed resources along racial lines and drew on racial logics. The constructs that distinguished between neighborhoods on the basis of their economic value or criminal propensities were not just about geographies; these ideas were also attached to physical bodies. Chapter 6 further illustrates the links between place and race by accounting for the policing of white people in the West District. It shows that segregation served as a powerful heuristic in policing— one that precluded racial integration and interracial social networks and instead assumed strict Black-white binaries and separation. Yet it also accounts for the shifting of segregation boundaries. As gentrification transformed the racial and economic character of certain neighborhoods, understandings of place shifted, and policing modalities followed suit.

6

Policing and the Social Structure of Segregation

Officers Will Rawlings and Stuart Weingarten, both white men in their thirties, worked in the West District antiviolence unit (AVU). Their duties primarily involved making proactive traffic stops and pedestrian stops, though they also engaged in longer-term investigatory work like building cases on potential drug houses. Weingarten was newer to the role, and he had a lot of admiration for Rawlings. At one point, Weingarten and I sat in the squad car while Rawlings searched a vehicle that the officers had pulled over. Weingarten watched him and explained to me that Rawlings was very thorough; he was also very smart. Weingarten speculated that Rawlings probably had a photographic memory. He later told me that Rawlings had been doing proactive work for the past decade. His comments conveyed the sense that Rawlings was exceptionally competent, based on both his natural capacities and his depth of experience.

As a cold rain began to fall, Rawlings suggested to Weingarten that they go "sit on a house" so they would not have to be outside. Sitting on a house involved surveilling an address and gathering evidence after there had been reports of drug dealing. If people were frequently coming and going from the house and staying for a short time, the officers might conduct an investigatory stop. If they found paraphernalia or drugs in the car, they could arrest the driver and then ask them to inform on what was happening at the address. If the information gave the police probable cause, they could secure a search warrant for the property. Rawlings explained this logic and process to me after setting up half a block away from a house. He had received the address from Officer Vester, the community-based officer, who compiled complaints from residents about potential drug dealing. Rawlings opened up a program on the in-car laptop and showed me a database of tips on potential drug houses. He also showed me how he worked on building casing, pulling up a file on the computer that included a list of people affiliated with an address.

Rawlings said that they would eventually try to make a traffic stop with the goal of getting the driver to give them information on the residents of the house. In selecting whom to stop, Rawlings explained that it was best to get a "whitey" because they always turned. He speculated that white people would act as informants because they had something to lose. I was surprised by the overt acknowledgment that the police targeted people on the basis of race, but Rawlings's standing among his colleagues suggested that this was a kind of common sense. And, indeed, I eventually found that Rawlings's perspective was shared by many officers. As in the East District, the policing of race out of place played a role in the West District, though it operated in different ways and had different consequences.

This chapter uses contrasting cases of policing white people in the West District to argue that officers' attention to race out of place transcended overt political-economic projects to more broadly reveal the power of segregation as a material structure and interpretive lens. Policing and segregation were mutually reinforcing: segregation created a series of associations that shaped police action, which, in turn, reified the realities of segregation. Police attention to white people in the West District revealed two new analytical points that together highlight the rigidity and dynamism of racial segregation as a social structure.

First, segregation acted as an enduring and potent heuristic in policing. Racial and spatial separation was so entrenched and naturalized that the police problematized any boundary crossing. While this was clearly the case for Black people in the downtown, the police also marked white people in predominantly Black neighborhoods as out of place. AVU officers tasked with investigating drug trafficking assumed that white people in such neighborhoods were drug users (not drug dealers) and, therefore, targeted them as potential informants. This assumption precluded the possibility of residential integration and interracial social networks not tied to crime. Moreover, I observed officers racially classify a person as "white" on multiple occasions when I thought they might actually be Latinx or multiracial. To the police, segregation was Black-and-white only, and the crossing of segregation boundaries was an indicator of potential criminal problems. As the police used evidence proffered by non-Black suspects to build cases about other crimes, they further criminalized Black residents. Hence, the policing of race out of place in both districts ultimately served to strengthen the associations between Blackness and criminal threat.

Second, even as segregation in River City endured, its geographic boundaries could shift, along with accompanying material resources and public services. On the eastern end of the West District, representatives of Riverside—a gentrified, predominantly white neighborhood—contested their inclusion in the West District. They argued that their community was more like River City's downtown than like other West District neighborhoods: crime was relatively low, and as a historic district, the neighborhood had great economic-development potential. The Riverside Neighborhood Association (RNA) initially considered pressuring the police department to redistrict again and to include the community in the East District. But the group eventually abandoned redistricting and instead sought to leverage policing resources within the West District toward the neighborhood. Residents eventually felt they received responsive and collaborative service from West District leaders and officers; the police approached the neighborhood with the community-service ethos of the East District, even though it remained within the West District. The case of Riverside shows that when segregation boundaries shift, meanings and resources follow in ways that maintain the material inequalities between Black and white neighborhoods. While white people in west-side neighborhoods raised flags for police when they *crossed* segregation boundaries, white people in Riverside advanced symbolic meanings and advocated for material resources until they *shifted* segregation boundaries. The following sections take up these two themes in turn.

Segregation as Rigid

Police attention to white people in marginalized, predominantly Black neighborhoods revealed how segregation was the norm in River City, and violations of this norm triggered suspicion. Specifically, the police assumed that white people were visiting Black neighborhoods to buy drugs. Like Rawlings, AVU officers who did proactive work could be surprisingly explicit about this assumption, explaining that white people only visited "the hood" to buy heroin and, thus, were legitimate targets for police stops and investigations. The expectation that white people were only in the area to engage in criminal activity was so strong that I observed the police mistake other officers for white drug users. One evening, two patrol officers drove past an undercover squad car with two white plainclothes officers inside. During a phone call between the pairs, one patrol officer said that he thought the undercover officers were white guys in the area to buy heroin.

"Whitey" in the West District

A ride-along with Officers Chris Conti and Luther Halliday, both white men in their thirties, further captured the dynamics of policing white people in predominantly Black neighborhoods. Conti and Halliday worked on an AVU squad engaged in medium-range investigations. Conti explained that their unit had more freedom than other AVUs because they worked with the district captain, the community policing unit, or the district's crime analyst to focus on particular problems. Conti cited robberies and heroin-based investigations as recent examples. Like Rawling and Weingarten, Conti and Halliday received tips from the district's community-based officer and followed up by surveilling and investigating potential problem addresses.

When I arrived at the district to observe the officers' work, Conti was finishing paperwork in the office. He showed me a description of a vehicle registered to an owner in a small town outside the city. Given the development of racial segregation in the state, the suburbs and towns around River City were majority white. Conti said that when white people were in the district, it often indicated drug-dealing activity because they came to buy heroin. Halliday popped his head into the office and asked if we wanted to start by getting some breakfast. As the meal concluded, Halliday announced, "Let's go find some white people!" Conti said he had explained the significance of this to me earlier, and Halliday corroborated that there was value in focusing on white people in the "hood." Once in the car and on patrol, the officers spotted a young white man in a gray hooded sweatshirt walking down the sidewalk. Halliday yelled, "White guy! White guy!" Conti, noting that the man was on his cellphone, speculated that he was talking to his drug dealer. The officers did not take any action, but their assumptions linking the man's mere presence in the area to criminal activities were on full display.

Soon after, the officers noticed a pickup truck parked in front of a house. They observed a white man enter the house, while a woman, who also looked white, sat in the passenger seat. Conti and Halliday conferred about whether they had seen the truck in the area before. Conti radioed dispatch to check the truck's license plate, and it came back as registered to a different kind of car. This provided sufficient basis for a stop. When the man returned to the truck and pulled out a few minutes later, Halliday drove after it. He turned the squad car's lights on a few blocks later. The driver did not pull over immediately, and when the truck finally did stop, Halliday and Conti jumped from their car. I heard Halliday exclaim, "He swallowed it!" He later explained that he had seen the man drink from a two-liter bottle of Coke before stopping the vehicle. Halliday and Conti yelled for the driver and passenger to exit the truck. Halliday frisked the man, and Conti squeezed the pockets of the woman's jacket. Halliday then searched the truck and returned with a packet of K2, a synthetic cannabinoid. While the woman insisted that they did not take drugs, her companion prodded her to tell the truth. Finally, she admitted, "It's my addiction."

The cops asked why the couple had been at the house. The man said they used to live in the area. He had lent money to his former neighbors, and they now patronized his roofing business to pay him back. The man eventually admitted he had a pill addiction that had started due to the physical intensity of his work. Halliday asked the man to take a walk with him. They moved about twenty feet away from the curb and conferred with their heads close together. After a few minutes, they concluded with a handshake. The officers let the couple return to the truck, with Halliday asking if the man needed to go to the hospital because of the pills he had swallowed. The man said he would be fine, and they drove off. Back in the car, Halliday explained that the guy had agreed to be an informant. He told Halliday that he had bought Percocet from a man in the house. Halliday said they made an agreement in which the man would "get him a pistol" (inform him about a suspect with an illegal gun) at some point in the future.

One interesting aspect of officers' attention to race out of place in Black neighborhoods was the rigidity of their Black-and-white perceptions. I observed several instances of officers assuming that an individual was white while I perceived other potential classifications and identities. This was the case with Halliday and Conti's traffic stop, where the man's dark hair and brown eyes suggested he could be a light-skinned Latino. But the officers had referred to the driver as white when they first spotted the truck. On another occasion, several officers were on a scene of a domestic-violence battery. As their work wrapped up, Officer Calvin Rhem, a white man in his midtwenties, stood at the window of the squad I was riding in, chatting with Officer Jason Mercer. A man with olive skin and wavy hair gelled into a pony-tail had been on the scene. He clearly knew the victim, a young Black woman, as he had given her a hug at one point. Now, the man walked past the squad. At first, Rhem mused to Mercer that it was a white guy who must be in the area for heroin. But as the man approached, Rhem seemed surprised and exclaimed, "Oh, maybe he's a Black guy!" In moments of racial ambiguity, officers reverted to a Black-white bi-nary. I suspect this reflected the intersections of racial ascription and the context of the city's majority Black-white demographics. Whatever the cause, officers' classifications naturalized the city's segregation and imbued the categories of "Black" and "white" with a nexus of assumptions about criminality.

The Consequences of Policing Race Out of Place

The policing of race out of place in both the East District and the West District underscored the power of segregation as a cognitive schema. In both districts, the presence of a person whose race was incongruent with officers' expectations was a sign of possible criminal activity. Yet the policing of white people in Black spaces versus Black people in white spaces was also characterized by contrasts. For one, the police overtly named race in the West District, while place-based signifiers often stood in for race in the East District. I suspect that this difference reflected the contours of colorblind racial discourse, with officers hesitant to name Blackness for fear of being labeled racist, even as they drew on racially coded language.[1] The overt naming of whiteness may not have seemed like such a taboo, particularly as most officers were also white. More-over, AVU drug investigations could bolster the associations between white people and known criminal patterns, perhaps increasing officers' certainty that attention to race was consistent with the department's fair and impartial policing policy. In any case, the signaling of racial bodies out of place occurred in both districts, albeit in different ways.

Officers also approached those who crossed segregation boundaries with different goals. In both the East and West Districts, officers saw boundary-crossers as potential sources of crime and disorder. But Black people in the East District were treated as criminal, while white people in the West District were coerced into collaborating with the police. White people could be exempt from criminal punishment if they could turn officers' attention to other subjects—typically residents of predominantly Black neighborhoods. Indeed, arrest data revealed stark disparities in drug enforcement, with the RCPD reporting over three times as many arrests of Black people as arrests of white people for drug violations citywide.[2] Hence, the policing of race out of place in both districts served to strengthen the associations between Blackness and criminal threat. In the East District, race out of place was tied to protecting the city's economic assets. While the policing of white people in the West District was more subtly implicated in urban revitalization, it nevertheless reinforced foundational underpinnings of uneven economic development by amplifying the assumption that Black neighborhoods were a source of criminal and civic problems.

The policing of "whitey" in the West District naturalized River City's segregation as a taken-for-granted reality. When the police identified white-appearing people in predominantly Black neighborhoods with criminal reputations, they assumed they were drug users visiting the area briefly and for a single purpose. Officers did not view them as potential residents or as visitors with prosocial familial or friendship networks in the neighborhood. They struggled to imagine the possibilities of residential integration and interracial social relations. For example, the man whom Conti and Halliday pulled over had previously lived in the neighborhood they policed. He had described relationships of mutual exchange with his past neighbors. Neither of these potential accounts for his presence in the area had arisen in officers' initial interpretations. Segregation was the norm, and policing activities reflected this assumption.

Yet not all white people in the West District were assumed to be drug users who could be turned into informants. In contrast to white people who were "out of place" in predominantly Black neighborhoods, white people who lived in certain areas of the West District asserted that they belonged and that they deserved the services and resources devoted to predominantly white parts of the city. The following section describes policing in Riverside, a majority-white community on the eastern edge of the West District. Gentrification and white residents' subsequent efforts to redefine the neighborhood and garner policing resources eventually shifted segregation boundaries.

Segregation as Dynamic

When the River City Police Department redrew the boundaries of its districts to follow neighborhood lines and crime patterns, many people saw the change as a logical reflection of the social distinctions between segregated neighborhoods. However, one group of empowered stakeholders did not agree. Riverside, a gentrified neighborhood that had previously been in the East District, was now on the eastern edge of the West District due to the redistricting. This change in police administrative boundaries sparked grassroots efforts to reclassify the community, as representatives of the Riverside Neighborhood Association argued that the neighborhood belonged in the East District. RNA representatives distanced themselves from the criminal and racial stigmas of the West District and emphasized the neighborhood's economic contributions and development potential. When they failed in their reclassification efforts, the RNA advocated for West District policing resources to protect the area's value and potential. Eventually, they successfully negotiated for the same community-service-style policing that East District residents received, even while they were still technically in the West District.

A Brief History of Riverside

Riverside had a long history as an evolving and contested space. During the early growth of the city, the neighborhood was a robust industrial area home to European-immigrant laborers and wealthy factory owners.[3] Some of the factory owners' mansions still stood. However, like neighborhoods throughout the city, Riverside had experienced a period of decline and transition accompanying deindustrialization. Businesses left or closed, and many homes were demolished. The population also shifted to eastern European immigrants and then to African Americans. In the 1970s, Riverside saw renewed interest through historic preservation and restoration efforts. Residents founded the Riverside Neighborhood Association and successfully lobbied for designation as a historic district. The neighborhood's large homes attracted newcomers who could afford to pay higher property taxes and invest in rehabilitation projects. The racial demographics changed yet again: though 80 percent of Riverside residents in 1970 were African American, by 2010, the population was around 60 percent white and 30 percent Black.[4]

Longtime Black residents expressed concerns about gentrification. Some felt that the demographic changes threatened the neighborhood's culture and history. In a local news article, a Black resident who grew up in Riverside described competing views emerging over who belonged in the neighborhood. He questioned why new residents looked at his family like they were "the visitors" and described how his mother, who had lived in the neighborhood since childhood, had been excluded from an RNA meeting because she did not use a computer and could not receive the association's email updates.[5] In another article on gentrification in the city, a resident of a nearby predominantly Black neighborhood cited fears of displacement like those Riverside had seen in the 1970s.[6] He described the history of Riverside as leaving a bad taste for residents in his neighborhood. For many, Riverside stood as a reminder of the risks that gentrification posed to communities of color.

Nevertheless, newcomers saw the influx of capital as sparking a renaissance for the area. Residents rehabbed historic homes, developers converted former industrial properties into condominiums, and new businesses cropped up in and around the neighborhood. Many growth aspirations and initiatives converged through the Riverside Neighborhood Association. The RNA focused on community development, beautification projects, and social engagement. Interviews with two leaders in the RNA, Debra Cook and Maurice Burke, captured the interests of the group. Debra, a white woman in her thirties, had initially moved to the city for graduate school. She and her husband had looked to Riverside when they were ready to buy a house. As the secretary of the RNA, Debra had become increasingly involved with the Safety Committee. Maurice, a middle-aged white man, had lived in Riverside for over fifteen years and played an integral role in several development projects in the neighborhood. As the president of a real estate company, he had purchased, rehabbed, and rented out multiple properties. Maurice also served on the board of a business improvement district on the edge of the neighborhood. He had been involved in the RNA throughout his time in Riverside and had also focused on public safety.

RNA leaders described Riverside as a desirable part of the city for many reasons, particularly its elegant housing stock and multiple forms of diversity. Debra explained, "I think there's always interest in living in our neighborhood. We have the old houses and the historic charm, and those types of houses don't come up for sale that often." Moreover, the neighborhood offered affordable access to the city's downtown amenities:

> We're within walking distance of so many great things our city has to offer. We're a single-family neighborhood that's affordable to live in com- pared to other places in the country where, if you see the skyline, you probably can't afford to live in that house. So it's a really neat dynamic.

This affordability contributed to the neighborhood's diversity, which both Debra and Maurice construed widely to include age, income, and occupation, in addition to race. As Maurice described, "Most of the residents are median income. I don't think any of us are rich because we wouldn't live here if we were rich." He described the neighborhood's residents as "a mix of just about everybody, from artists to architects, to doctors, lawyers, just about anything. Very diverse in that respect. Also race, as well. It's Black and white—it's kind of mixed together." Both saw this as part of Riverside's appeal. As Debra explained, "You can walk down the block, and it's a great feeling just to have diversity, whether it's income or race or housing style. I think everyone really appreciates that."

Despite the neighborhood's trajectory and assets, RNA representa- tives felt that Riverside remained outside the scope of the city's deeper redevelopment efforts. Debra described, "People say, 'Oh, it's an up- and-coming neighborhood' sometimes. But I think we had our big development heyday back in the '90s. And now you don't see much development focus going on in our neighborhood." She named three neighborhoods south of the downtown and elaborated that "they have a huge emphasis right now and enough traction for new development." With Riverside, she explained, "I think we're lacking on that. And we have some pretty big parcels of land that are still available for development, but I don't know if we're tracking that same level of interest in terms of the broader development community." Debra said the recession had hurt the neighborhood's commercial vibrancy, though she saw investments in the downtown, like the construction of a new arena, as having the potential to spread to adjacent neighborhoods, including Riverside: "Hopefully our neighborhood, too, can really bring some of those development interests." Though Riverside remained outside official development projects, the RNA sought to advocate to maintain and enhance the neighborhood's value.

Crime and Public Safety in Riverside

As public-safety issues were a central focus of neighborhood improvement efforts, crime patterns and relations with the police department were a preeminent concern. Maurice recounted how criminal problems had changed over time: when he had first moved to the neighborhood fifteen years ago, it had been "pretty rough—a lot of crime going on, a lot of prostitution." Maurice mentioned drug dealing and frequent home and garage break-ins. But now, he explained, "we don't have a lot of crime. It's way, way down from that." He noted the occasional more serious incident: "Last year we had an armed robbery, which really scares the neighbors. It was kind of a fluke, but it happened; and it made people really on edge for quite a while." In addition to the occasional high-profile armed robbery, Debra described the neighborhood's most pressing concern as drug dealing out of vehicles. Debra believed this to be largely a problem of people from outside the neighborhood: "They're doing that deal in our neighborhood because it's a safe middle point close to the freeway, so there's quick access." She continued, "I would think that's a consistent complaint for our neighborhood. And if one of those deals goes bad, it can get scary pretty quickly." Though crime generally appeared to be on the decline in Riverside, the neighborhood experienced periodic incidents that piqued residents' concern.

Yet efforts to address criminal issues in Riverside were complicated by the neighborhood's changing classification within the police department's administrative boundaries. As it was currently in the West District, many people saw Riverside as one of the "better" neighborhoods in the district. Thus, residents felt they were particularly prone to being overlooked by the police. Maurice explained,

> The West District, they've got a huge area to take care of a lot of bad stuff to deal with, which I understand. There's a lot of stuff going on, and they've got more than they can handle. But that shouldn't leave us uncovered because we've always been voicing that issue. We understand that we've got worse things [in the district], but we still want you to be here to make sure that things aren't happening here. If we call, that you actually come, which is a huge problem.

Debra made a similar point while emphasizing the consequences for neighborhoods: "I fully understand that there are some really serious issues going on with the West District, and neighborhoods are really struggling from the crime that's happening. I think everyone is cognizant of that. It's just frustrating when it's a competition for resources." Regarding Riverside's position, she explained, "We don't ever want to have our concerns seem like they're greater than any other neighborhood. But it's just recognizing what our concerns are—they're still valid." Debra suggested that most neighborhood residents understood that police must address more serious issues in other parts of the district, but this did not preclude frustration with faltering responses to Riverside's problems.

Riverside had experienced quite a different relationship with the police when it was a part of the East District. Maurice acknowledged that within the East District Riverside had been "the worst of their neighborhoods during the day" because burglaries, car break-ins, and garage break-ins would occur when residents were away from home. But the police had been equipped to address these problems through oft-desired visible patrols and rapid response. Maurice explained, "We would see cops all day long because they really didn't have a lot going on downtown because downtown has their own security during the day. So we had a lot more presence back when the East District was involved." He continued, "The response time was incredible in the East District. They were always just spot on. Whenever you called, they were there because they weren't that busy during the day." Thus, Riverside residents saw police service as contingent on the way their neighborhood compared to others within their police district. The changes in policing they experienced were directly related to the redistricting decision, which had classified Riverside as more akin to the "high-crime" neighborhoods of the West District than to the "low-crime" parts of the East District.

Contesting Classifications and Advocating for Resources

In the redistricting's aftermath, RNA stakeholders opposed the police department's district boundaries and offered alternative definitions of where Riverside fit in the city's overall landscape. Maurice argued that Riverside belonged in the East District: "I think it makes sense the other way around. We're more of a downtown neighborhood than a west-side neighborhood. Like I said, we don't have that much crime, so we're always the forgotten ones." In fact, the Riverside Neighborhood Association had considered formally requesting that the police department redraw the district boundaries *again*, with Riverside included in the East District. Captain Williams of the West District noted that such efforts to reclassify Riverside continued:

> Even up until last year, people would bring it up in community meetings, you know: "Can't we go back into the East District? They gave us better police service. We know you guys are busy and that you're trying; but you guys keep getting pushed out into the other parts of the district, and we don't get any service."

Arguments over administrative boundaries relied on commonplace distinctions differentiating high-crime neighborhoods from low-crime areas with economic assets. Residents classified Riverside as the latter. Lobbying to change the police-district boundaries was one path toward institutionalizing these distinctions to garner additional policing resources.

However, formal boundary changes were not the only means of ensuring investments in Riverside. The RNA eventually abandoned the effort to change the boundaries and turned instead toward lobbying for West District resources. Debra narrated this transition, describing how she spoke to a former captain of the East District about the redistricting process: "It was definitely not easy and could get very political." She recounted how the police also cautioned that the new East District now encompassed the university, so "even if you are in the East District, you still might be facing the same competition for resources because a lot of that is drawn to the university area." She speculated that police presence would have nevertheless been more consistent if the neighborhood was in the East District, but the association had eventually taken a different approach after learning of the challenges of redistricting: "Before we ever would want to pursue that, let's try and work with the West District and see what we can do to help some of the issues that were going on. So we went with that route."

A prime example of efforts to mobilize police response in Riverside occurred after an incident in which a resident confronted a suspected drug dealer in a vehicle, and the driver of the vehicle fired a gun in the resident's direction. The RNA called a special meeting that the West District captain attended, along with the day-shift lieutenant, Officer Vester from the community policing unit, and an AVU officer. According to the meeting minutes,[7] Captain Williams offered a detailed account of the police response to the incident, describing similarities between drug activity in the neighborhood and a particular crew's pattern of dealing. He discouraged residents from approaching vehicles and said the district had assigned a narcotics officer to the neighborhood as part of a long-term drug investigation. The officers encouraged residents to call in *all* suspicious vehicles and to let the police determine whether they were potentially tied to drug dealing. Captain Williams concluded by assuring the group that Riverside had the West District's attention—the police understood how much residents cared about their neighborhood and the investments they had made in their houses and the city—though he also acknowledged that the police had to work with limited resources.

While Captain Williams had described this meeting to me during my fieldwork, my interview with Debra occurred over a year after, so she could reflect on its impacts over time. She began by noting that the RNA had tried to "reengage not only [Officer Vester] but the captain and to get them in tune with what the neighborhood concerns were." She felt the police had been responsive:

In the last couple years, they've done a good job at listening to us and being able to dedicate resources. We had an undercover drug officer specifically for our neighborhood the last year, year and a half, and I can't even tell you what a big dent that made in the drug deals. I had a ton happening in front of my house, and so we worked with him, text messaging, being able to say, 'Hey, something's happening here.' He could work with what details we had. If he's undercover in the area, then it was a quick response time.

With the attention of district leadership and a direct line of communication available, response in Riverside had improved.

Debra nevertheless understood the battle for resources as an ongoing one: "Summer is coming up, you know. We always want to have that constant police presence, whether it's in the form of bike cops or regular patrols." She noted that the neighborhood had not experienced serious issues recently but reflected on what would happen if they arose and sparked residents' concerns: "Then we're kind of right back where we were before, with demanding resources be rededicated back to our neighborhood." She reflected, "It just seems like that is a constant concern—just how are these resources reallocated." While maintaining resources required ongoing attention, Debra nevertheless described Riverside's relationship with the West District police as positive. She elaborated in relation to reporting suspicious vehicles, "My neighbor and I, we always call, and we always seem to get really good responses from the officers, whether they follow up with us with a phone call or stop by. It seems like that hasn't gotten worse at all." Thus, residents benefited from targeted attention from the police, even if the resources devoted to Riverside seemed precarious.

Indeed, West District leadership was comparatively responsive to Riverside. This appeared to be, in part, a reflection of the neighborhood association's lobbying efforts. Captain Williams often mentioned working with the RNA when we met, and RNA leaders described actively cultivating this relationship. But the attention to Riverside was not merely responsive to lobbying pressure. It also tapped into the same ideas of economic potential and worthiness that inflected the police department's citywide priority-setting. During a driving tour of the district, Captain Williams pointed to some large homes, explaining, "Here, you got people out mowing their lawns. You got a lot of houses that are re-habbed." He continued,

> Most of the people that bought these bought them for very good prices, and it took them years of living in them. And most of them did it them-selves. They rehabbed them themselves and made them what they are. These people took tremendous risks, and they are very involved in this neighborhood.

He said that this investment contributed to the push to reclassify the neighborhood as part of the East District after the redistricting occurred.

Even as the RNA stopped pursuing a formal boundary change, the police recognized an internal boundary within the West District. During the driving tour, Captain Williams noted a thoroughfare on the bound-ary of Riverside, describing it as "the divider between the good part of the district and the higher-crime area." In another conversation, he said that Riverside was the only part of the district that was not "garbage." This classification distinguished Riverside and its residents as deserving, and the West District police devoted additional policing resources to the neighborhood. In short, Riverside residents advocated for the same community-service ethos in the policing of their neighborhood that East District neighborhoods experienced.

Lessons from Riverside

Riverside is a microcosm that emphasizes and extends key themes of this book. It shows the relational and contingent nature of spatial clas-sifications and resource distributions in River City. Because of the neighborhood's evolving and contested symbolic position, its clas-sification varied between stakeholders and across time. The police department's redistricting reform had grouped Riverside together with West District neighborhoods defined by their criminality. RNA rep-resentatives subsequently sought to redefine their neighborhood by distancing themselves from other west-side communities and posi-tioning the area as more similar to the downtown and East District neighborhoods. In the process, the RNA elevated widely circulating dis-tinctions that focused primarily on the economic viability and potential of particular places. It argued that the neighborhood was proximate, both geographically and socially, to River City's urban-revitalization efforts and could benefit from and contribute to economic growth. RNA representatives drew on the same logic that police officials had used when explicating the redistricting: "high-crime" areas drew policing resources away from "low-crime" neighborhoods, leaving them unprotected. Riverside residents fought for dedicated policing resources to address their concerns, thereby impacting the intradistrict distribution of police service.

Police responsiveness in Riverside also reveals the embeddedness of the police within the broader political-economic environment of the city, where stakeholders had different degrees of voice and power. Police leaders in the West District responded to Riverside residents' needs and demands, just as police executives responded to powerful citywide stakeholders' interests. As in East District neighborhoods, affluent white residents, business leaders, and developers in Riverside demanded police service. While they recognized the pressing needs of other communities, they nevertheless advocated for police response and protection. These stakeholders were vocal and empowered, and they saw the police as a public service to which they were entitled. They could exert a different kind of pressure than could residents of marginalized neighborhoods that had been historically brutalized and underserved by the police. The police, in turn, prioritized service in Riverside. As they did so, police officials and officers defined the neighborhood's residents as economic assets to the city, reinscribing ideas of value and deservingness that more broadly applied to well-resourced, predominantly white communities.

Finally, Riverside shows that divergent policing modalities ultimately overlapped with segregation boundaries instead of the administrative boundaries of police districts. The River City Police Department's redistricting reform had institutionalized divisions between places of value and those of violence, laying the foundations for disparate policing strategies. The boundaries of police districts had followed the lines of River City's segregation, but not precisely. Riverside was a discrepancy—a place where the natural boundary of the river, the socioeconomic boundaries of segregation, and the administrative boundaries of the police district failed to entirely align. While the police department had used the river as an administrative boundary, this did not preclude the recognition of socioeconomic boundaries. Rather than treating the area as similar to other West District neighborhoods, the police provided the responsive and thorough service that stakeholders in white communities desired. The geographic boundaries of segregation could shift, but distinctions characterizing some places as valuable and deserving, and others as criminal, endured. Policing strategies followed suit, reinforcing the gaps in the meanings and experiences attached to white versus Black neighborhoods.

Conclusion

The contrasts between the policing of white people in different parts of the West District revealed the contingency of race out of place in segregated spaces. While white people in predominantly Black neighborhoods were incongruent with officers' expectations and treated as potential criminals, race and class dynamics in Riverside had shifted until white people were no longer out of place. Riverside residents lobbied to have their neighborhood understood and classified as similar to other predominantly white places like the adjacent downtown and east-side communities. Their efforts succeeded insofar as police officials treated their neighborhood like an East District community: they devoted special resources, took a collaborative problem-solving approach, and prioritized service, even in the midst of the West District's resource constraints. White people in predominantly Black west-side neighborhoods were assumed to be temporarily crossing segregation boundaries, while white residents of Riverside shifted segregation boundaries by transforming the material and symbolic character of the neighborhood.

The policing of white people in the West District and many other empirical cases throughout this book demonstrate the simultaneous rigidity and dynamism of racial segregation. Segregation was rigid in the sticky associations the police deployed in their interpretations of racialized places and people. The symbolic ties between Blackness, criminal threat, economic noncontribution, and social dysfunction versus whiteness, value, and worthiness are tropes that have sustained segregation across time and place.[8] These ideas reflect systems of racial domination and subordination that continue to circumscribe the life chances of individuals and groups.[9] Policing was one of many institutional arenas in River City creating an uneven distribution of resources across segregated space. This happened at the organizational level, as police executives determined deployments and personnel allocations across the city, but it also occurred at the interactional level, as officers naturalized segregation and used it as a heuristic to determine what kinds of people and behaviors were congruent with their assumptions about racialized space. Policing converged with other institutional arenas—from housing to the labor market—to reinforce the symbolic and material foundations of River City's historical Black-white segregation patterns.

Segregation was also dynamic, however, as its boundaries were actively constructed, solidified, contested, and shifted. The police participated in these projects as they maintained segregation boundaries by criminalizing people who crossed them and as they altered their resource distributions to align with evolving segregation patterns. But the police were certainly not the sole or even the primary participants in these projects. City officials, private developers, empowered residents, and many other stakeholders sought to cultivate particular kinds of places in the city. As in Riverside, place-making efforts coalesced around visions of economic growth and revitalization. Though some of River City's place-making projects attempted to shift segregation boundaries, they did not fundamentally challenge the underlying associations that saw white neighborhoods as areas of growth potential and Black neighborhoods as criminal threats to it. Even as segregation boundaries changed, the character of segregation in River City endured.

Conclusion

When I began this research in 2013, I did not expect to write a book about urban growth politics. I was initially interested in investigating the institutional processes that drove mass incarceration and the overpolicing of race- and class-subjugated communities. The River City Police Department's redistricting reform offered a window into how the police defined and impacted such communities in the West District. I anticipated that decision-makers would draw on discourses of criminal threat, poverty governance, containment, and social control when explaining the rationale for the redistricting. I also expected that crime control in the West District would be a central motivator for the redistricting. To an extent, I found evidence consistent with these initial hypotheses: police executives and officers understood the West District as a violent place, and on-the-ground policing did have the effect of reinscribing historical patterns of overpolicing and underprotection in predominantly Black neighborhoods.

Yet, as I met with police executives, elected officials, business leaders, and representatives of community groups, the *East District* emerged as the heart of this story. In my early conversations with police officials, I was surprised that policing in the West District was almost an afterthought. Instead, police leaders elevated enhancing policing in the downtown and in white, middle-class residential neighborhoods. Their rationales aligned with a narrative I heard from many sources: River City was at an economic and social crossroads. It could revitalize, redevelop, and recover, or it could continue its descent into a postindustrial wasteland. In order to survive, the city had to retain middle-class taxpayers and attract new flows of capital by transforming the downtown into a global hub of commerce, culture, and entertainment. In this vision of urban growth, the police were a public service and urban amenity leveraged to enhance the economic value of the city's most vital geographies. Thus, a preeminent redistricting goal was to ensure adequate policing resources for the new "low-crime" districts that covered the downtown and white middle-class residential neighborhoods.

My empirical findings around the significance of policing in places that were home to the city's economically and racially *dominant* people and entities shaped my analysis and central argument in several ways. First, the findings unveiled the links between policing and neoliberal urban governance. In an era of urban austerity and growth politics, the police played a central role in providing essential public services and in cultivating new private investments. The River City Police Department embraced the project of urban revitalization: its strategic priorities, resource allocations, and daily practices interpolated the growth interests of the mayor, business associations, developers, and empowered residents with the effect of improving policing in well-off, predominantly white communities. The police were a key resource in a nexus of public and private investments that collectively amplified the symbolic and material significance of the East District. The connections between policing and uneven urban development show the utility of analyzing policing as embedded within the surrounding institutional field. Police departments are arms of municipal governments, which actively navigate broader national and global political-economic contexts.

Second, River City policing was *relational*: the policing of dominant places and people intertwined with the policing of marginalized communities. Symbolically, ideas of economic worth evoked corollary notions of criminal and civic threats that could compromise that value. Such narratives overlaid the city's racial geography and motivated practices that intensified the perceived value of the East District and the perceived criminality of the West District. Organizationally, the police department operated in a resource-constrained environment. Redrawing police-district boundaries to keep patrol officers in the quiet neighborhoods of the East District raised the question of whether there were enough officers to respond to the calls for service in the West District. Indeed, after the reform, patrol resources were not proportionately distributed in relation to the call volume of the East and West Districts. The police department's efforts to prioritize service and order maintenance in the downtown and middle-class neighborhoods had a ripple effect of limiting policing resources in other parts of the city. As this case shows, a full account of urban policing must include the role that white middle-class and affluent communities play in determining what the police do within their neighborhoods and citywide.

Finally, the connections between growth politics, police administration, and racialized policing practices tell an *institutional* story. While some individual officers used racial tropes, many could generate racial disparities without racial intent: they did so just by following their official duties within the circumscribed work environment of the police district. Racial outcomes in policing were facilitated by organizational structures like district boundaries, resource allocations, deployment decisions, formal policies, and legal standards. District boundaries crafted distinct work environments characterized by different pressures, from call volumes to residents' demands. Inequities in social control and service widened as proactive policing units concentrated in predominantly Black and Latinx districts and as patrol resources were devoted to predominantly white ones. Institutional structures and mandates, from district boundaries to specialized deployments, translated policing priorities into on-the-ground practices. These findings bolster work that sees organizational processes as key mechanisms in producing racial inequalities in policing outcomes.

Policing and the Construction of Place and Race

By aligning with urban-revitalization goals, the police attempted to shape the character of neighborhoods. Their spatial regulation in the East District and the West District had constitutive effects. In the East District, a community-service ethos elevated the area's economic and social importance. Officers managed a light call volume, sometimes responding to a single call over an eight-hour shift. Nevertheless, they felt that their workload was ample, describing demanding and politically connected citizens who expected thorough investigation and follow-up, even for minor incidents. When officers were not responding to calls, they engaged in preventive work, conducting traffic safety stops, checking on businesses, and walking foot patrols through downtown corridors. Beyond providing responsive service and a visible, stable presence, the police developed special initiatives for residents and businesses. A weekend deployment through the district's entertainment corridors focused on order maintenance in collaboration with bar owners. Furthermore, the district allowed university-area residents to bypass dispatch when calling with nuisance complaints. Stakeholders and residents described improved response times, professional service, and community-based policing. Police executives and others drew connections between policing in the area and continued investments in the downtown.

Across the river in the West District, the police were primarily concerned with suppressing violence. While violence constituted a real problem for some residents, many felt that the totalizing focus on crime overlooked attention to repairing police-community relations and enhancing the development potential of Black neighborhoods. Moreover, the RCPD's strategy of aggressive investigatory stops ultimately failed to address the root causes of crime and eventually heightened racial tensions. These proactive tactics contributed to overpolicing. Meanwhile, the West District was also underprotected. Patrol officers experienced relentless call-volume pressure: there were often several assignments waiting for a squad to be dispatched, and officers would sometimes be pulled from an assignment to be sent to a higher-priority call. Response times suffered, and citizens felt that their safety could be endangered and their problems overlooked. Faltering police service underscored that predominantly Black neighborhoods were comparatively underserved and undervalued by the city. Together, policing priorities in the East District and the West District amplified long-standing meanings and experiences attached to segregated neighborhoods, reinscribing race- and class-based inequalities in the process.

Protecting and serving areas of economic value while containing and controlling those of criminal threat was more than a spatial project. Policing also regulated race. Deep-seated associations between place, race, class, and crime motivated the policing of racialized bodies that were "out of place" and ultimately served to maintain segregation boundaries. In the downtown, officers suggested that "outsiders" to the district threatened nightlife corridors' economic vitality. Thus, they focused on clubs serving predominantly Black clientele and Black individuals in predominantly white spaces. Organizational practices targeted vehicles marked with indicators of race and class, fueling racial disparities in East District traffic safety stops. Black-white segregation was so naturalized that officers viewed any crossing of segregation boundaries as a sign of criminal activity. They assumed that white people in predominantly Black neighborhoods were drug users who could be turned into informants, and they classified people on the basis of a Black-white binary. Even when segregation boundaries shifted through gentrification, as they did in the Riverside neighborhood, symbolic classifications and material resources followed in ways that reified the meanings and experiences associated with the categories of "Black" and "white."

While the police did not invent segregation in River City, they were nevertheless players in the ongoing construction of race and place. Their institutional projects distributed resources along racial lines and maintained spatial boundaries. Patterned policing activities augmented the disproportionate surveillance and social control experienced by historically marginalized Black neighborhoods, on the one hand, and the robust public-service infrastructure available in affluent, predominantly white communities, on the other. As the police reinscribed and regulated segregation and its boundaries, they conveyed messages about the relative standing of racialized communities and citizens. Even if not solely responsible for the city's inequities, policing was a critical arena that further articulated racial and spatial differences, hierarchies, and inequalities. In the remaining pages of this conclusion, I situate River City within an analysis of dozens of police redistricting reforms, and I reflect on what this case tells us about the role of the police in the city.

Redistricting in River City and Beyond

I am often asked if the policing inequities in River City stemmed from the creation of race- and class-segregated police districts. While the relationships between district configurations and racial segregation should be investigated further in general, I found that racialized policing in the East and West Districts was not just a matter of police-district boundaries. Indeed, organizers have made arguments for aligning police-district boundaries with race-conscious community lines as a means of facilitating community control over police. In 1971, a Black Panther Party–inspired ballot initiative in Berkeley, California, proposed to divide the city into three police districts: "the predominately black community of West Berkeley, the student-dominated University of California district and the predominantly white community of North

Berkeley."[1] Each district would be overseen by an elected council of fifteen citizens, and officers would be required to live in the districts they policed. While the ballot measure was defeated, it highlighted the idea that community-specific districts and decentralized policing could serve the interests of specific groups.[2]

More recently, a 2016 proposal for Black community control over police similarly recognized the possibility of neighborhood-based police districts. In a law review article, organizers M. Adams and Max Rameau argue that "in order to maximize community control, municipalities can be divided into smaller policing districts, with residents of each district afforded the opportunity to select their own police force." Furthermore, Adams and Rameau note, "The precise locations of district lines is a political question and will vary from one municipality to the next but should reflect a general sense of community, which, in modern U.S. society, is most often a combination of income, race, and ethnicity." Hence, homogeneous districts might result from community-conscious projects, though Adams and Rameau also recognize that such districts have served inequitable ends: "Ironically, some of these police control districts will overlap significantly, if not entirely, with existing police districts, which are often designed with the intent of protecting wealthier communities from encroachment by poorer ones."[3]

The pitfalls of the River City redistricting stemmed more from subsequent policing priorities and resource distributions than from district boundaries themselves. Many stakeholders saw the promise of more democratic and equitable outcomes in police executives' emphasis on the links between the redistricting and community-based policing. Yet strategic priorities ultimately institutionalized goals of containment and control by aligning with the city's pursuit of growth. Police officials did not ultimately address the needs of marginalized communities on their own terms. Instead, they defined neighborhoods in relational and opposing ways that stemmed from the broader project of urban revitalization. By acting on the ideas of economic value and criminal threat, the police participated in the ongoing construction of racially segregated landscapes.

Though River City is one case, it represents several nationwide trends: localism in policing, the persistence of segregation and neighborhood inequality, and urban revitalization as an economic-development strategy. To illustrate, nine out of ten police departments serving jurisdictions with a population of over twenty-five thousand incorporate a community policing component in their mission statements.[4] While actual community policing practices vary widely, they all recognize spatial and social differentiation. Marking differences and identifying coherent "communities" occurs in the context of the ongoing realities of racial and economic segregation. Though declining since a peak in the 1960s and 1970s, Black-white segregation remains high nationally, particularly in Rust Belt cities across the Midwest and Northeast.[5] Segregation continues to correspond to enduring inequalities in neighborhood conditions. Moreover, many cities have responded to the exigencies of neoliberal globalism by attempting to cultivate their most desirable neighborhoods. The competition for entrepreneurial capital extends beyond New York, Los Angeles, Seattle, and other prototypical "global cities," reaching Indianapolis, St. Louis, and Cleveland.[6]

River City's redistricting offered an analytical window into how these trends intersect. Redistricting required police executives to mark boundaries within the city and, in the process, grapple with shifting roles and functions of the police, imperatives flowing from the surrounding political-economic environment, and legacies of segregation and racial inequity. But River City is not the only site where redistricting has taken place. To better situate River City's reform, I worked with a student research assistant to analyze forty-two implemented and proposed police redistricting reforms in thirty-four major US cities. We found that a majority of redistricting reforms continue to reflect the goals of the incident-based response model by focusing on balancing calls for service and reducing gaps in response times. Sometimes, city or state governments made balancing calls for service a redistricting requirement. For example, the San Francisco Board of Supervisors enacted legislation in 2006 mandating that the police department review its district boundaries every ten years, with the first stated objective being to "consider workload parity across the districts (e.g., the number of calls for service)."[7]

Though rare, redistricting around specific communities' needs did occur. A 2018 reform in Seattle, Washington, reunited the historic Chinatown-International District, which had been split between two precincts.[8] A 2013 redistricting in Oakland, California, institutionalized citywide, place-based, community-oriented policing. The Oakland Police Department divided the city into five "areas," where it had previously been divided into two large regions. District leaders were empowered with control over district-level policing resources. A memorandum from the city administrator's office elaborated on the goal of this change: "District commanders will deploy crime reduction and prevention strategies tailored for the areas they command in order to provide as much focused, problem-oriented and community-driven police service delivery as possible."[9] The formal logic of the Oakland reform was similar to the official account of the River City Police Department's redistricting. Whether the Oakland reform facilitated democratic community-based policing or fell prey to the pitfalls of the River City reform is a question for another study.

While the redistricting in River City was exceptional in its departure from the incident-based response model, our analysis revealed that police redistricting reforms across the country were embedded in broader contexts of urban governance. Several police redistricting reforms consolidated districts as part of urban austerity measures: closing facilities and eliminating layers of bureaucracy allowed city governments to save money. For instance, a 2009 redistricting in Portland, Oregon, reduced the number of police precincts from five to three. A local news article explained, "The proposal would slice $2.8 million from the bureau's budget. Chief Rosie Sizer says consolidating the bureau's five precincts into three is necessary to avoid deep cuts to the agency's 90 programs."[10] Such reforms revealed the clear links between police administration and the economic health of the city. Though police services are more resistant to cuts than other public services are, they are not immune in times of fiscal crisis.

We also found several reforms clearly inflected by growth politics and responsive to dominant economic interests. For example, a 2019 redistricting in Atlanta, Georgia, shrank the size of a zone that encompassed Buckhead—one of the wealthiest and most exclusive areas of the city—after residents reported rising crime. To improve service, the redistricting removed two "problematic" beats while retaining the same number of officers.[11] In Austin, Texas, the police department cut the size of the downtown-area command to "focus their efforts on the heart of the district."[12] In Omaha, Nebraska, the police department created a new precinct covering the predominantly white neighborhoods of the city's west side after complaints of lack of police presence, long response times, and increasing property crimes.[13] Each of these reforms prioritized improving policing in already-wealthier neighborhoods and commercial areas. They included justifications about the need to serve neighborhoods most impacted by growth.

Finally, we found that police redistricting reforms were *not* arenas in which police executives and city officials openly worked through central questions of racial equity and redress. As with River City, racial considerations lay in the background or entered implicitly through the language of place. Attention to place could facilitate more racial parity. For instance, while race was never explicitly mentioned, a 2011 redistricting in New Orleans aimed to "level the playing field in terms of the service received by citizens in disparate neighborhoods," by focusing on evening response times.[14] But reforms could also reinscribe the inequalities of urban growth politics. When the Omaha Police Department created the new West Precinct, it did so based on projections of growth. A local news article described, "The new precinct's area receives fewer calls for service than the other four, though that's expected to change as the city continues to grow through annexation and development."[15] The precinct would serve the Elkhorn area, which was almost 99 percent white, per the 2000 census.[16] This meant that a subset of Omaha's white residents was served by a district with proportionally more resources given its workload. Racial redress could happen through redistricting, but the absence of race conscious checks could also open the door for continued disparate resource distributions.

Our analysis of police redistricting reforms in River City and beyond does not conclusively address how police districts *ought* to be structured. Arguably, district boundaries could follow the neighborhood lines of segregated landscapes, as advocates for community control over police suggest, though segregated police districts risk amplifying racialized policing and urban inequalities, as this study has shown. Alternatively, the sociologist and legal scholar Monica Bell describes how police-district boundaries that cross segregation lines could enhance democratic control over the police by engaging white and more affluent stakeholders across more districts. However, as Bell notes, these same stakeholders who tend to be empowered and vocal could co-opt policing to serve their own needs *within* their district.[17] Our analysis of police redistricting clarifies that these reforms have received insufficient attention as processes that shape spatial and racial regulation. This invites new questions into how district configurations and place-based policing strategies mitigate or amplify the structural, institutional, and interactional inequalities of segregated landscapes.

The ties between police redistricting reforms and the politics of urban austerity and growth also highlight the embeddedness of policing in the broader context of neoliberal urban governance. As local governments grapple with shrinking municipal budgets and strive to attract new forms of capital, they deploy the police to serve many functions: suppressing crime, providing emergency services, and cultivating the economic value of space through order maintenance. Shifts in the national field of policing have enabled the proliferation of policing tactics by elevating local approaches to discrete problems and places. These intentional strategic divergences also intersect with organizational processes like resource constraints, narrow performance measures, and siloed professional roles to intensify the uneven distribution of policing resources, be they for service or surveillance. The following section recounts the various roles that the police played in River City—as problem-solvers, crime fighters, and service providers—and identifies some organizational dynamics that contributed to an overemphasis on particular functions within different neighborhoods.

Findings from this case bear on evolving debates over police reform and abolition. While they identify organizational leverage points for change within policing, they also point to deeper questions of how the police came to play so many varied roles in the city and whether they must continue on this path. Such questions encourage a broader analysis of how cities invest in and distribute many kinds of services and resources across disparate neighborhoods.

The Roles of the Police in the City

The River City Police Department embraced national strategic innovations in the policing field corresponding to new police roles and tactics. Though police have always performed a variety of functions—including order maintenance and service provision—they claimed a

narrow mandate of crime control through most of the twentieth century. In the twenty-first century, they have explicitly widened their
mandate to include reducing fear, resolving conflicts, and enhancing
community capacity. As the police expand their array of activities and
emphasize collaborative relationships with new stakeholders, they open
themselves to the surrounding institutional environment, which can
push them in multiple directions. Such was the case in River City, as
various, sometimes conflicting goals were incorporated into official
measures, organizational roles, and formal and informal rewards. External political-economic pressures and problems of institutionalization
concentrated particular policing roles and functions in different parts
of the city.

The Police as Community Problem-Solvers

RCPD leaders appeared exceptional in their commitments to community policing. Indeed, Chief Lancaster was hired because of his national
reputation as an innovator who would bring cutting-edge best practices
to the city. He immediately incorporated community-based problem-
solving into the department's mission statement, and the redistricting
aligned the department's structure with a focus on tailored local efforts.
In the aftermath of the redistricting, community policing initiatives
unfolded in both the East and West Districts. Stakeholders described
collaborations with district captains, community-based officers, and
community policing units. Representatives from neighborhood agencies
lauded these initiatives, citing benefits ranging from specific problem-
solving capacities to improved police-community relations.

Despite these apparent successes, the River City case shows the
limits of popular police reforms like community-based policing and
problem-oriented policing. These strategic innovations were robustly
implemented in some parts of the city but limited or undercut in others.
Strategic innovations were ultimately undergirded by a localist approach
that invited divergent tactics, contributing to racialized policing. The
problems of partial implementation were particularly overt in the case of
community policing. Initiatives in both districts were rooted in the logic
of neighborhood-level problem-solving, but they varied in the extent to
which they were actually community-based. Policing in the East Dis-

trict aligned with an ethos of responsiveness to residents and collaboration with local stakeholders, while proactive patrol in the West District
developed without community control and ultimately alienated many
residents, even as it technically aimed to solve a problem of violence.

Several dynamics limited the implementation of community policing
citywide. First, as with many departments, community policing initiatives were relegated to a small subset of officers in the West District.
Second, community-based initiatives confronted the challenges of local
histories and differentially empowered stakeholders. Residents in the
East District were vocal and confident that the police could assist them,
while those in the West District grappled with decades of mistrust and
estrangement. Third, community policing had varying degrees of efficacy. In the East District, information-sharing and special initiatives
could meaningfully impact the quality-of-life issues at the heart of many
residents' concerns. However, the community policing unit in the West
District lacked the resources to address the full scope of citizens' concerns, ranging from problems of nuisance to risks of violence. In short,
ideal-typical community problem-solving concentrated in the East District, where it became an ethos that transcended the specific officers assigned to community-based work.

Though community policing remains rife with limitations, even in
more robust implementations,[18] police reformers continue to see value
in efforts to make policing more responsive to the needs of marginalized
communities. Their work identifies avenues for change in River City and
beyond. Some proposals, like those of President Obama's Task Force on
21st Century Policing, emphasize traditional tenets of community policing: building trust and legitimacy, enhancing procedural justice, diversifying police forces, creating opportunities for positive community
engagement, and collaboratively developing public-safety strategies.[19]
The inroads of the West District's community policing unit reflected
the incorporation of these principles in the unit's work. Robustly imple-
menting community policing in the West District and in other race- and
class-subjugated neighborhoods in River City would require making
community engagement a priority and practice for every officer, not just
those in a siloed unit. The police would also need to address barriers
to trust by ending racialized practices like stop-and-frisk.[20] Activists in
River City advocated for more positive engagement between the police

and residents of marginalized communities and saw community policing as a logical goal of reform.[21]

Other proposals, like those outlined by Adams and Rameau earlier,
focus on community control over police. Community control goes further than information-sharing and procedural justice, advocating for civilian oversight of policing policy. For instance, the Movement for Black
Lives includes in its platform a call for "direct democratic community
control of local, state, and federal law enforcement agencies, ensuring
that communities most harmed by destructive policing have the power
to hire and fire officers, determine disciplinary action, control budgets
and policies, and subpoena relevant agency information."[22] Community
control involves fundamental shifts in power that would require redesigning institutional arrangements.[23] While the forms that new institutional arrangements take are subject to experimentation and debate,
the legal scholar Jocelyn Simonson argues that we should center visions
emerging from grassroots movements and critical contestation. This is
where "we can hear the most profound reimaginings of how the system
might be truly responsive to local demands for justice and equality."[24]

The Police as Crime Fighters

Additional limitations to robust implementations of community policing in River City stemmed from other institutional pressures on the
police. One primary demand is that the police control crime. The police
themselves have historically staked claim over crime control, and hence,
many parties now expect police work to home in on this goal. In cities
across the country, elected officials look to police chiefs when violent
crime increases. Local media often focus on crime stories and inevitably
link these narratives to police responsibilities through law enforcement
imagery. Though the police actually have little ability to eradicate crime,
they must manage public expectations by emphasizing their crime-
fighting activities.[25] Formal law enforcement tactics like stops, searches,
and arrests become proxies for crime reduction. Indeed, in River City,
police executives routinely presented data that correlated stops to a variety of crime control gains. The embrace of proactive patrol in the West
District aligned with perennial expectations that the police take immediate and demonstrable action around crime.

One way to catalog crime fighting was through performance measures, and the emphasis on crime control pervaded key formal and informal success indicators. Like many departments around the country, River City used Compstat, a performance management system that identified district-level crime problems and held captains accountable for efforts to address them.[26] In addition to tracking crime patterns, the system compared officers in each district across four performance measures: arrests, incident reports, traffic stops, and subject stops. Thus, Compstat concentrated on technologies of formal law enforcement, creating pressures for proactive activity down the chain of command. Beyond this formal system, crime fighting was also rewarded in subtler ways. Officers considered assignments to proactive units and investigative teams to be a privilege. Those who were assigned this work, like Hayes and Bachman, were seen as particularly smart, intuitive, and competent. Crime fighting was a motivator and aspiration for many officers. Yet the crime-fighter orientation contributes to a warrior mentality characterized by symbolic divides between police and citizens.[27] Hence, even as police executives claimed a commitment to community policing, many organizational rewards and incentives enshrined crime control tactics versus community engagement.

While crime fighting targeted parts of the city on the basis of uneven criminal patterns, it also further *produced* criminality by oversaturating the West District with law enforcement. Certainly, a comparison of the East District's one homicide to the forty in the West District demonstrates differences in residents' exposure to violence.[28] Yet the distinction between "high-crime" and "low-crime" areas institutionalized assumptions that further constructed crime—or lack thereof—in racialized ways. The West District included violent hotspots, but it also included quiet residential neighborhoods. The lines between the two blurred in theory and practice as investigatory stops occurred throughout the district. The devotion of resources to proactive patrol also meant greater detection of criminal violations, like possession of firearms or drugs, that may not have been reported otherwise. By contrast, the East District's community-service ethos meant that officers could overlook violations of municipal ordinances and criminal laws. Indeed, the ECD's approach to nightlife establishments explicitly deprioritized sanctioning taverns and their predominantly white patrons. Moreover, while university campuses are frequently sites of underage drinking, illegal drug use, and sexual violence, students were rarely subjected to criminal sanctions for such activities. As crime fighting was distributed unevenly across space, so too was criminalization.

Ironically, while the proactive strategy produced criminality, it was less effective at crime control. As described in previous chapters, crime fluctuated independently of stops, rising even when proactive tactics were pervasive. While the structural antecedents of violence were beyond police control, proactive patrol failed in more immediate ways. Research on violence has revealed its highly networked and place-specific character. For example, gang-related shootings occur at the intersections of several social and spatial processes: turf proximity, conflict histories, and reciprocated acts of violence.[29] Some variations of proactive policing can account for these processes. For instance, problem-oriented strategies that seek to change the underlying criminogenic conditions of specific hotspots have been shown to reduce crime.[30] But investigatory stops in River City were not that sophisticated. Even as the chief recognized the importance of targeting specific people and places, stops blanketed the West District in a scattershot approach.

Given these realities, how should cities address violent crime? New approaches should incorporate more nuanced theories of the underlying causes of violence. While policing in River City could develop strategies based on criminological research, some of the most promising models of violence intervention exist outside of law enforcement entirely. Cure Violence, a program that operates in cities in the United States and internationally, takes a public-health approach that understands violence as a contagious problem spread through exposure. The program's interventions recognize the networked and reciprocal nature of gun violence, in particular. Trained "violence interrupters"—often from the same communities in which violence occurs—work with victims, their friends and families, and other stakeholders to prevent retaliations and mediate conflicts. Several evaluations show marked reductions in shootings in areas where the program operates.[31] This model's success showcases the power of understanding the underlying causes of gun violence. It offers insights that could be translated into policing and, perhaps more importantly, reveals solutions outside of policing.

Indeed, scholarship on violence identifies institutional and structural dynamics that serve as other points of intervention. The sociologist Robert Vargas shows that violence is shaped by relations among neighborhood residents, nonprofits, and public officials. Communities with strong ties to their ward politician can channel public resources for violence prevention into their neighborhoods, while those that are split across gerrymandered districts struggle to develop the organizational and political infrastructure to bolster residents' work to end violence. This points to the need to strengthen the political power of marginalized communities within the city and implicates political ward redistricting as another consequential process.[32] Vargas's work highlights a set of mediating factors in a relationship that has long been documented by social scientists: the ties between violence and neighborhood structural conditions like poverty, unemployment, and family disruption.[33] Interventions that address concentrated structural disadvantage by investing myriad resources—for housing, education, jobs, and child care, among others—into historically marginalized communities could meaningfully transform the underlying conditions that correspond to violence.

The Police as Service Providers

The dearth of such resources contributed to another set of pressures on the police: citizens' demands for service. Even as strategic innovations purport to shift policing away from incident-based response, patrol endures because the police must respond to 911 calls. Nationally, requests for assistance constitute half of all police-citizen contacts.[34] People continue to rely on the police when they experience crime, suspicious activities, neighborhood disturbances, and noncriminal emergencies. The situations to which officers are summoned range from life-threatening to truly mundane. During fieldwork, I watched officers prepare accident reports, investigate noise complaints, address mental health crises, counsel victims of domestic violence, resolve disputes between neighbors, and once, drive around chasing a dog. Many pressures in both districts stemmed from the calls for service. Indeed, the patrol function continued to dominate daily work, despite the chief's efforts to move the department away from incident-based response.

One of the most striking inequalities in River City policing was the variation in workload pressures based on call volumes. West District officers ran between calls like "chickens with their heads cut off," as an officer had described. East District officers did not have the same workload, but they nevertheless felt pressure due to citizens' political and economic status. Organizational decisions played an important role in shaping these workload patterns: the East District centered the importance of its geography and population, while the West District clearly lacked the personnel to provide comparably rapid and thorough service. Though the police department could not control the uneven spatial distribution of calls themselves, it did have the power to allocate resources proportionally.

However, inequalities in service provision are difficult for police leaders to appreciate because the work of patrol officers continues to be institutionally and normatively undervalued. While Compstat systems often capture outcomes like arrests or incident reports, many calls for service end with no formal law enforcement action. Therefore, important dynamics of patrol work are not accounted for in performance measures. In River City, officers' conduct on scene was periodically supervised by sergeants and could be reported by citizens, but there were few official indicators of the timeliness, nature, or quality of assistance rendered. Even the simple and available measure of response time, if compared across priority levels, could have identified district-level disparities in service provision; I did not find evidence that this comparison occurred routinely.[35] Ensuring equitable resources for response to citizens' calls across the city could have intervened in the sense of undervaluation that West District stakeholders expressed.

Moreover, changes to the relative standing of patrol work could improve the service-provision skills and capacities of officers. Patrol remains at the bottom of the police organizational hierarchy. Though every officer begins their career in patrol, many pursue promotions into investigatory work or supervisory roles. Few recognize or laud the routine work of responding to calls, even though patrol is immensely complex. As first responders and service providers, patrol officers' work often resembles a nurse's or social worker's responsibilities.[36] During my fieldwork, I witnessed the power of sociability, compassion, and adaptability required of this work—characteristics that some officers had in more abundance than others but that received little lip service or institutional recognition. Replacing the crime-fighter image with an emphasis on public service and community caretaking could change whom the profession attracts and how it socializes its members. This could move the police toward the "guardian" role and mind-set, which many reformers see as a key shift in enhancing police legitimacy and relations with marginalized communities.[37]

The incredible range and variation in the work of patrol officers also raises the question of whether this should be the responsibility of the police. People call the police to address problems of mental health, homelessness, family conflicts, and many other challenges with structural origins. While the police may have little capacity to shift the landscape of affordable housing or mental health services, they could improve their training and ties to extralegal resources. But perhaps an actual nurse, social worker, or peer crisis responder would be better equipped in many cases. Some cities have begun exploring alternative emergency response. For instance, in Eugene, Oregon, the CAHOOTS program dispatches a medic and a mental health professional to 911 calls involving psychological crises.[38] Community groups across the country have also developed systems of crisis response, harm repair, and accountability that operate at the grassroots level. Organizations like Critical Resistance, Philly Stands Up, and Generation Five engage community members in practices of restorative and transformative justice to address problems including mental health crises, gender violence, and child sexual abuse.[39] These organizations point to alternative models of emergency response and community safety. Yet, in cities across the country, much of this work continues to fall to the police. This reality invites the question of how cities manage their deeper structural inequalities.

What Comes Next?

Cities rely on the police because of exigencies flowing from the surrounding political-economic environment. Earlier chapters have described the global and national transformations that have rendered many cities vulnerable to fiscal crises. Deindustrialization, globalization, and the turn to neoliberal governance undercut the economic foundations of industrial centers like River City. Segregation and mass incarceration concentrated the social and economic consequences of these changes within central-city neighborhoods. The rollback of federal aid to cities left municipal governments to address social problems on their own, and many turned to private development and growth to salvage their economic prospects. In River City, the police became the "social agency of first resort for the poor," according to one police executive. However, the police capacity to provide services depended on the overall economic health of the city, and police officials, therefore, turned their attention to enhancing the city's commercial corridors and middle-class neighborhoods. The situation of the River City Police Department is not unique. Redistricting reforms in many cities have highlighted pervasive ties between police administration, urban austerity, and growth politics. These links suggest looking beyond policing in considering racial and economic inequity and redress in the city.

Such questions have evolved alongside the resurgence of the Movement for Black Lives and the COVID-19 pandemic, which have altered the constraints and potentials for municipal governments. Recent events in River City speak to debates and questions yet to be resolved, even as they point to new possibilities. One set of considerations focuses on responding to and preventing the myriad problems the police are often left to address. The murder of George Floyd in the summer of 2020 catalyzed attention to the ongoing racial violence of policing and punitive state interventions. In response, social movements have elevated calls to divest in policing and invest in communities.[40] This idea gained traction in River City, where a majority of the City Council signed a proposal to cut the police department's budget and redirect funds toward public health and housing programs.[41] Many stakeholders recognized that the challenges officers encountered in the West District and other race- and class-subjugated communities reflected concentrated poverty and a dearth of institutional resources like jobs, education, housing, and transportation. In River City and across the country, momentum built for the idea of shrinking punitive state interventions through robust investments in social services and community-based institutions.

River City's mayor and City Council ultimately approved a 2021 budget that reduced the number of police officers in the RCPD. It also funded a new program to support home ownership, a violence-interrupters initiative, and a pilot project to increase outreach and access to mental health services.[42] However, the city's budget did not reflect a straightforward story of divesting from policing and investing in social services. It was shaped by the city's fiscal constraints: River City would lose police officers through attrition; changes to the police department's budget remained nominal due to increased costs associated with salaries, benefits, and other personnel expenses.[43] Meanwhile, the city government faced the loss of tens of millions of dollars due to the pandemic, while state restrictions limited sources of revenue.[44] The tone of the mayor's budget address was not one of optimism. He cited "serious challenges," "few options," and cutbacks on services that would impact quality of life in the city. The city government simply did not have the economic resources to provide robust social services, and cuts to policing were framed as a financial necessity rather than a reorientation of approaches to public safety.[45] River City showcased the ongoing challenges of fiscal austerity that local governments face in their efforts to reconfigure public services.

However, shifts in the national political landscape suggest changes in governance that will impact cities and their residents. The coronavirus pandemic brought US social inequalities into sharp relief and motivated a dramatic expansion of federal aid. Many Americans experienced the benefits of this directly, as they received support for rent, food, and health care, and public opinion warmed to the idea of increased government intervention.[46] Beyond coronavirus relief, the Biden administration introduced economic proposals that would allocate trillions of dollars to infrastructure, child care, education, family leave, health care, and poverty relief. These programs would be funded through tax increases on the wealthiest Americans.[47] In contrast to decades of austerity politics, the federal government's proposals turned toward expanding the social safety net and providing pathways for economic mobility. Many analysts noted that federal programs would be a boon for cities.[48] Beyond the benefits from job creation, infrastructure overhaul, and other social services, Biden's economic stimulus proposals included hundreds of billions of dollars of aid to municipal governments.[49] The pandemic ushered in discussions of a renewed role for the federal government in urban life. Whether a fundamental shift occurs remains to be seen, but federal proposals have hinted at the possibility of a stronger redistributive state.

Expanding the arm of the welfare state may be a means of shrinking its punitive arm by opening access to opportunity structures and mitigating the inequalities within cities. But many scholars have described how the welfare state is also a mechanism of surveillance and social control, often working in tandem with carceral systems to regulate and redistribute the poor across institutional spaces.[50] Social services can reinscribe and amplify racial inequalities. And government redistribution does not necessarily lead to racial redress, as history has shown. Indeed, while the Keynesian welfare state helped build the American middle-class, it also played a fundamental role in constructing racial segregation.

Hence, if there is a final lesson to be taken from the case of River City, it is that conversations about reform and redistribution must go hand in hand with conversations about dismantling segregation and structural racism. Proposals without an explicit racial-redress focus run the risk of augmenting racial inequalities. The story of the River City Police Department's strategic innovations offers a cautionary tale about seemingly progressive reforms that fail to meaningfully engage with legacies of anti-Blackness. This caution transcends policing and applies to considerations around urban inequalities more generally. The racial disparities of today reflect a history of discrimination and racial domination. Racist policies and practices constructed segregation, and efforts to redress its harmful impacts on wealth accumulation, residential mobility, job access, health care, criminalization, and myriad other outcomes require corollary attention to racial and economic redress. Whether this takes the form of policies that undo past barriers to racial integration or those that enhance Black collective ownership over the resources and institutions in Black neighborhoods,[51] what comes next must trouble the spatial and racial logics of segregation. Ultimately, reimagining a just city may transcend policing altogether.

METHODS APPENDIX

Conducting a Critical Police Ethnography

"Studying up" is difficult. Conducting fieldwork inside a police department for over a year was exceptional as a research experience and also fraught with ethical, methodological, and practical dilemmas. In this appendix, I offer candid reflections on the behind-the-scenes processes of the ethnographic component of this project. I do this primarily for epistemological reasons. In naming the assumptions and dynamics underlying data collection, I offer a foundation to assess the claims made in this book. These claims have been shaped by the theoretical frames informing research design and by the micropolitical processes involving my own social position and those of the people with whom I interacted.[1] I also have practical motivations for this appendix. Several graduate-level courses in qualitative methodology did not fully prepare me for fieldwork. I faced countless decisions, large and small, for which there was no technical direction. The experience was messy—far more conditional and unpredictable than I had imagined. I hope that recounting my choices offers some guidance for those who are considering similar projects.

CHOOSING THE OBJECT OF ANALYSIS
A rich research tradition explores the intersections of race and the criminal justice system through ethnographic methods.[2] Much of this work asks how race- and class-subjugated individuals and communities experience, respond to, and resist the deep reach of the punitive state in daily life. Scholarship in this vein has named and described processes of criminalization and marginalization, and it has revealed counter-practices of survival and resistance. It problematizes disadvantage by highlighting its structural causes and consequences, and it can help dismantle stigma by representing the heterogeneous and multidimensional people and places often depicted through diminishing stereotypes. Such research also has important implications for knowledge production. It

takes seriously the struggles and subjectivities of groups that are often discredited by mainstream institutions. It prioritizes the experiences and voices within marginalized communities and challenges traditional hierarchies of credibility in the process.[3]

However, ethnographies of race- and class-subjugated populations also carry significant risks. They can verge into exploitation, as researchers with relative educational advantages—often among other race- and class-based privileges—extract data from vulnerable communities to use in advancing their status and career. Representations in research can perpetuate reductionist stereotypes, portraying subjects as dangerous or pitiable.[4] Study findings can also be leveraged to actually enhance state power and regulatory control over disenfranchised groups.[5] While these outcomes may represent the worst-case scenario, they implicate broader questions of power and the politics of representation that pervade ethnographies more generally.

Attentive to the hazards of urban ethnography, I turned my gaze upward toward an arm of the state. While recent studies have investigated the racialized logics and practices within police departments, courts, and prisons,[6] such analyses of powerful institutions and actors remain relatively rare. "Studying up," or seeking to understand "the processes whereby power and responsibility are exercised,"[7] is an important complement to research that investigates the lived consequences of mass incarceration and overpolicing. It reveals how these phenomena emerge and how they are justified and maintained through organizational decisions and everyday practices. It can render processes of governance and the exercise of power more transparent and, thus, accountable to the public. As the anthropologist Laura Nader argued in her canonical piece *Up the Anthropologist*, "The quality of life and our lives themselves may depend upon the extent to which citizens understand those who shape attitudes and actually control institutional structures."[8] With such goals in mind, I selected policing processes as my object of analysis.

Studying the police avoids the complicated power dynamics of researching those who are most impacted by racialized policing: historically marginalized Black and brown communities of which I am not a part, as a multiracial Asian American who grew up in a predominantly white, upper-middle-class town in the Bay Area, where the police were primarily preoccupied with traffic enforcement and breaking up high school parties. Yet "studying up" was also laden with epistemological and ethical challenges. Chief among them, it risked giving a platform to people at the top of the "hierarchy of credibility"—people like police executives, elected officials, and business elites who have more access and power to shape mainstream narratives and whose accounts are often taken at face value.

To mitigate the likelihood that I would simply reproduce dominant narratives of policing, I employed a critical approach. An emerging community of sociolegal scholars describes their work as "critical police studies." This research explicitly examines dynamics of race and class in law enforcement administration. It interrogates the history and role of the police in society and asks how policing processes contribute to ongoing processes of racialization. In addition to drawing on analytical frames consistent with this body of research, I also sought to empirically triangulate and compare police officials' accounts against those offered by researchers, evaluators, the media, elected officials, and, importantly, city residents. While I focus on the police, my interviews with representatives of neighborhood associations, community organizers, and other stakeholders offered accounts of policing that could be compared to the official logics presented by police executives.

While my theoretical commitments motivated me to examine policing and take a critical approach, practical realities shaped how the research unfolded. In what follows, I offer a chronological overview of my fieldwork, while emphasizing an analytical point: even though I was "studying up," power dynamics in my research relationships were varied, and they shaped what I could see and hear in the field. I encountered barriers common to researching powerful institutions and actors, who can use their resources to limit access, relationships in the field, and representations of findings. But I also found heterogeneity and diversity among "the powerful." Officers were embedded in a stratified and hierarchical organization with ranks characterized by different degrees of agency, and many had working-class backgrounds. Police officials themselves navigated a broader field of urban elites and faced many pressures and constraints of their own. Also in the equation were citizens, some of whom were the traditional subjects of police power and violence, while others treated the police like a public service that they purchased with their tax dollars.[9]

I was a part of this mix, navigating the field as a civilian, as a researcher, and as a young Asian American woman. I brought theoretical orientations shaped by enormous educational privilege and dispositions cultivated through my upbringing. All these factors impacted my relations in the field, some in ways that I could perceive and others in ways about which I can only speculate. The following discussion aims to situate the data and claims found in this book by attending to the contingencies of power relations in the field.

The Origins of This Project

My interest in the relationships between segregation, urban governance, and policing emerged after I relocated from the Bay Area to the Rust Belt. As I settled in, I was struck by how powerfully Black-white segregation served as a heuristic for the people around me. I rented a room in a predominantly white neighborhood but frequently traveled to predominantly Black and Latinx neighborhoods as part of my work with a nonprofit that focused on community organizing. Many of my white acquaintances—generally recent college graduates and young professionals from the metro area—never ventured into these areas. They described the wide swath of the city's predominantly Black neighborhoods as "ghetto" and dangerous, insinuating that nothing of value could be found there. I wanted to better understand how such powerful and homogenizing racial typifications of place developed and how they contributed to segregation at the institutional level and in everyday life.

After I began graduate school, I embarked on a project examining the links between perceptions of urban space and daily mobility patterns. Through interviews with residents of segregated neighborhoods, I found that white respondents stereotyped and flattened Black neighborhoods into unidimensional containers of criminality, while Black residents described a nuanced geography of crime and elevated the resources, social networks, and sense of community they found within their communities. Moreover, this project honed my interest in the role that policing played in regulating segregated space. Black respondents described police encounters as a deterrent to crossing segregation boundaries. For instance, one respondent, a middle-aged Black man named Jacob, explained how he intentionally avoided affluent white neighborhoods because of his personal and vicarious experiences of policing. Jacob described a traffic stop in a white neighborhood that had ended with the officer telling him, "The next time, you find a different route home." Max, a young Black man, also suggested that he avoided potentially being racial profiled because, as he put it, "I stay where I'm supposed to stay." These accounts centrally implicated policing in the active maintenance of segregation and furthered my interest in the way policing varied along racial and spatial lines.

River City Police Department's redistricting reform presented a perfect opportunity to explore questions around segregation and policing practices. The clear alignment between police-district boundaries and racial-segregation boundaries was surprising. It seemed obvious that creating racially homogeneous police districts would risk amplifying disparate practices. Initially, I was curious about the predominantly Black West District, where the dynamics of mass incarceration and over-policing were potentially playing out on the ground. Yet, as I began data collection, the redistricting emerged as part of a larger story about the ties between policing and urban growth. Ultimately, the reform offered an analytical window into several broader processes: the symbolic and institutional partitioning of a segregated landscape, the articulation of strategic policing priorities, the construction of consequential work environments, and, ultimately, the ties between policing and the political economy of the city. While some of these insights developed through the research-design stage and others surfaced during the research, the redistricting offered an entry point for my inquiry.

Initial Access

From the moment I pitched this project to the police, I began navigating the complicated world of the police bureaucracy and the many relations—both hierarchical and shifting—within it. Some experiences confirmed expectations that the police agency, as a powerful institution, would assert control over the research process in various ways. Yet other experiences departed from my assumptions, particularly in the case of gaining access. Police departments are notoriously guarded when it comes to external actors, but social networks and favorable circumstances resulted in a relatively straightforward entrée. My access began through personal connections. One of my professors, a national expert in the policing field with ties to police executives around the country, offered to set up a meeting with the River City Police Department chief of staff. During this meeting, I proposed a project that would include a year of ethnographic fieldwork to investigate the redistricting, focusing on how the reform altered the experience of police work and police-community relations in the East District and West District. The chief of staff was enthusiastic and seemed particularly compelled by the idea of having an embedded researcher within the police department. He described the RCPD as a "teaching department" open to external evaluation and committed to evidence-based best practices. After this introduction, he remained my key point of contact. He set up a meeting with Chief Lancaster and authored an institutional letter of support as part of my application to the Institutional Review Board. When the project was approved by the university IRB in fall of 2014, he introduced me to the East District and the West District captains.

The chief of staff instructed these two district captains to permit me "full access" to the districts. After this directive, the captains became my primary points of contact. Both were exceptionally accommodating, and as I began to make initial visits to the district stations, they introduced me to lieutenants, sergeants, and officers. Similar to the chief of staff, the captains told supervisors that I would be doing ride-alongs for a year and that my requests should be honored. I began to meet many officers through observations at the district stations. As I did, I explained that I was a student studying the redistricting and comparing police work in the East District and the West District. Many people were quite willing to share their thoughts on their work, their perceptions of the districts, and their recollections of the redistricting. If I sensed openness, I asked if they would be comfortable if I observed a shift with them. I also relied on sergeants to assist in scheduling, which meant that some ride-alongs were assigned. Soon, I was scheduling multiple ride-alongs per week, with a great deal of cooperation and support from personnel in each district.

In short, gaining access to the police department was almost shockingly simple, and access was expansive once granted. This stands in stark contrast to the barriers that many researchers face when studying powerful institutions. I suspect that my experience reflected several dynamics. My initial entrée was facilitated by personal connections among colleagues with enduring relationships, rather than cold calls that could be easily ignored. The police department was also in a period of reform and optimism. Crime in the city had been on the decline, and the chief and other stakeholders saw the department as a bastion of innovative policing. They may have been open to external research and evaluation assuming that it could only bolster the department's reputation as transparent and data driven. Moreover, I negotiated access *before* the country was rocked by the 2014 police killings of Michael Brown, Eric Garner, and Tamir Rice and subsequent Black Lives Matter protests. Perhaps the police would have been less open to the scrutiny of a researcher had the request come amid the scrutiny they have since faced through our nation's collective reckoning over racism and police violence.

Shifting Relations with the Police Department
Changing circumstances eventually led to new restrictions and research challenges, however. The initial conditions of my entrée changed considerably over the time it took to complete the research and write up my findings. The chief of staff who had negotiated my access left for a job in the private sector. Generally, transfers, promotions, and retirements meant that I had fewer connections to relevant offices in the police administration. Eventually, Chief Lancaster retired as well. The department also faced growing public critique, some in light of the Movement for Black Lives and some specific to River City. Compared to the early enthusiasm for the chief, the final years of his tenure were characterized by resistance and criticism from civic groups, elected officials, and even officers. Media accounts and evaluations of racial disparities began circulating, and several of the chief's policy choices came under fire during public meetings. Personnel turnover, external conditions, and other unseen dynamics within the police bureaucracy resulted in greater uncertainty around how the department would respond to me and the project over time. This proved to be particularly difficult when it came to navigating the department's expectations around products from the research.

When I initially negotiated access, police officials expressed no expectations around how I would convey the findings of the work beyond supporting my IRB application, which specified that I planned to write academic publications based on the research. Months after the fieldwork was completed, I made a request for some administrative data to contextualize the ethnography. At this point, the police department's research office drafted a memorandum of understanding (MOU) to govern the research. This appeared to be a run-of-the-mill agreement specifying that the department would provide data for the project, but it included a provision that I share forthcoming publications so that the department could offer feedback and propose revisions. I agreed to the conditions of the MOU, feeling that the department did have a right to see the research based on the access I had been granted. Moreover, the MOU did not require changing written reports on the basis of the department's comments.

However, after sending an early draft of a paper about the redistricting reform to the department, I received a memo directly from Chief Lancaster requesting that I deidentify the project. The memo took issue with my description of the department's proactive approach, emphasizing again that deployments were made in relation to patterns of crime and criminal victimization. It also asserted that I had misrepresented my aims in pitching the research. I did not believe this to be the case, as the MOU itself indicated that the project would examine the redistricting—including the motives for the reform, its impact on the organization of police work and community relations, and the effectiveness of the changes with regard to workload, distribution of crime, and demographic characteristics—and these themes *were* at the heart of my inquiry. I suspect that my focus on racial inequity was surprising, though it seemed that racial dynamics would inevitably arise in any analysis of geographic policing because of the city's stark segregation.

Yet I also acknowledge that I did not explicitly foreground my intentions to analyze the redistricting in relation to segregation when I proposed the project to the police department. This remains an ethical gray area for me. It raises thorny questions around information sharing and transparency within the research relationship, and I have no neat answers. However, I argue that governing institutions should be subject to study and critique and that such an enterprise may require researchers to navigate barriers to access in ways that differ from how they would approach sites and people with less capacity to exclude them.

Ultimately, the chief's request highlighted a risk of studying up, as participants have the institutional resources and power to attempt to control research outcomes. In a project so deeply rooted in a specific place, compromising precision and verifiability by deidentifying the site was an immense analytical sacrifice. In consultation with my mentors and colleagues, I agreed to abide by the request rather than jeopardize the project. This has not stopped me from being specific about the dynamics of River City or from including as much detail as possible about my source material, even if I cannot cite sources explicitly. Indeed, the police department's concerns over identifiability appeared to largely focus on using the city's name; in a review of an early draft of this manuscript using the "River City" pseudonym, a department representative did not take issue with the information I have otherwise included in the book. I received only a brief note that the department had reviewed the draft and had no proposed revisions.

While the response of the police department to the research has varied dramatically over the years, the MOU generally had the effect of making the police department one of the audiences for the work. This could clearly have serious epistemological consequences if I felt compelled to censor my findings on the department's behalf. This was not the case, however; I certainly have not suppressed unflattering findings. If anything, the potential scrutiny of police officials encouraged me to be *more* rigorous in my analysis—to ensure that my claims were well substantiated through data, so my arguments could perhaps convince a critical reader, as well as a sympathetic one. I ultimately framed the MOU as a means of being accountable to the participants in the study. Feedback from the police could serve as a kind of member check, even if the exchanges were agonistic or rooted in opposing perspectives.[10] For instance, though Chief Lancaster's memo objected to my argument, it also served to confirm my findings around the spatial patterning and organizational logics of proactive patrol. Hence, I saw potential benefits in having the police department provide additional data or explanations in response to my findings. I also must admit, however, that I felt relief when I sent the draft manuscript and did not encounter additional resistance from the police administration.

NAVIGATING RIDE-ALONGS

Beyond overarching considerations of access and my position vis-à-vis the police bureaucracy, the research process entailed daily decisions about my role during ride-alongs. These decisions were laden with questions of power, which were shaped by my interactions with participants, their position within the police hierarchy, and my proximity to their work. Navigating relations with participants and my role in the field also had epistemological consequences insofar as they structured my observations. I grappled with practical and ethical challenges by relying on my best judgment, the advice of my mentors and colleagues, and conversations with participants in the research.

Dynamics of hierarchy were particularly acute in securing officers' voluntary participation in the study. The officers I hoped to observe were embedded within a paramilitary organization that circumscribed their agency, and I recognized that the top-down approval of the research could pressure those who were lower in the organization to participate. As part of negotiating study participation, I raised this concern in conversation with officers themselves. Many explained that the chain of command was integral to police administration, so approval from the top was actually of paramount importance. Nevertheless, I tried to clarify that I was not affiliated with the police department and that their participation was voluntary. Conveying this message was particularly crucial at the stage of arranging ride-alongs. When sergeants assigned my ride-along with an officer, it precluded a more direct arrangement that made the research aims clear. I worried about the imposition, but officers explained that this practice was not unusual; they were periodically assigned civilian ride-alongs like journalists, prosecutors, dispatchers, and student interns. Whether a ride-along was officer initiated or assigned by a sergeant, I explained that my observations would only be included in the research with the officers' consent.

In an effort to negotiate consent in an ongoing way, I tried to make my role as a researcher as clear as possible. At the beginning of each ride-along, I offered a verbal overview of the project. I shared a consent form and asked for permission to take notes, explaining that I would type up a longer narrative of the ride-along when I went home. This would include a description of everything we did on the shift and a summary of the conversations we had, though I would honor requests to keep comments "off the record." I kept a notebook out and scribbled jottings while in the squad. Officers were aware of my note taking, and they did occasionally ask me to omit certain comments from my notes. These requests were rare, but when they occurred, it was often in discussions of internal departmental politics like critiques of superiors or police-agency policies. Generally, officers understood that I intended to publish academic products from the research, and as I spent more time in the districts, they would ask how my paper was coming or reference my future book. By making my role unambiguous, I sought to ensure that officers could make informed choices about study participation. Though they might have to encounter me at the district station or host me as a ride-along, they could decide whether these interactions would constitute data to be included in the project.

In general, I found police to be surprisingly open to observation. Part of this surely reflected selection effects. Officers who volunteered to host a civilian observer may have been more personable or less likely to do or say things that would garner scrutiny. Sergeants who assigned me to particular squads were probably attentive to which officers would reflect well on the department. I also found that I developed a better rapport with some officers, and particularly in the early days of fieldwork, I would arrange ride-alongs with those whom I suspected would be amenable. Because of this, I assume I potentially missed officers prone to more extreme or troubling behaviors and attitudes, though it is possible that the proportion of such officers was low. What I was and was not able to observe as a researcher became a central issue in this work, a conundrum that is not unique to this project. All research is shaped by the social location and standpoint of the researcher, and recognizing "limited location and situated knowledge," as the feminist scholar Donna Haraway describes, "allows us to become answerable for what we learn how to see."[11] This section explores considerations of social location and social relations that emerged in studying the police.

Being a Nonparticipant Observer

One particularly important set of relations involved my positioning between police and civilians. While I was a civilian, I was still proximate to the police and, in some ways, affiliated with their work. This position shaped the nexus of interactions between me, officers, and the people they encountered. In contrast to police ethnographies conducted by researchers who are also police officers, I did not receive or pursue training in law enforcement, and I had no intentions of acting in that capacity. Within the police department, my role as an academic researcher was clear from the beginning, and I sought to be a nonparticipant observer in the field. While I followed officers when they exited their squad car, I often stood a few feet away from the main locus of an encounter and remained quiet unless addressed directly. When citizens asked who I was, I said I was a student conducting a ride-along. Officers often preemptively introduced me as such. I aimed to cultivate an appearance consistent with this identification, generally wearing jeans, sneakers, and a plain jacket while in the field.

Even with the goal of nonparticipation in mind, I recognized that I could be and occasionally was implicated in policing. My general commitment not to act was tempered by concerns that I might witness or even exacerbate safety risks for citizens and officers. For instance, when I was embarking on fieldwork, I asked a seasoned police ethnographer what would disqualify me from the work; he said that I could not stand by while a cop was hurt. I also felt that my lack of training in situations that involved trauma, tension, and other strong emotions could enhance the risks to all parties. The potential need for me to act in emergency situations was bolstered by the police. During several ride-alongs, officers showed me how to use the radio and told me what to say should they be incapacitated. One sergeant went so far as to teach me how to unlock the shotgun in the squad car in case I needed to use it, though I had no intention of doing so and I probably lacked the ability, given that I have little knowledge of or experience with guns.

I am thankful that these preparations proved unnecessary. Nevertheless, I tried to mitigate safety risks. As I developed relationships with police personnel, I candidly discussed with them concerns around how my presence increased risk, inviting their input about how to handle potentially tenuous situations. Many reassured me that they were used to managing ride-alongs with nonpolice personnel. They said their training prepared them to navigate complex situations and encouraged me just to follow their instructions. In short, officers generally appeared nonchalant about my presence, so I aimed to follow suit. I trusted the situational knowledge of the police and abided by their instructions. For example, if I was told to stay in the car, I did. I also relied on my own judgment and tried to avoid putting myself in dangerous situations, which often meant that I stood physically removed from the center of contentious interactions. For instance, the officers I was shadowing one night took a call for a wanted person whose girlfriend had reported his whereabouts at a house. While the officers approached the front door and went to check the back of the house, I remained on the sidewalk where I could see and hear exchanges at the front of the house but where I would be out of the way, rather than in the midst of an arrest. This practice may have sacrificed detail in my fieldnotes, but it reduced the probability of becoming entangled in a difficult situation.

While I tried to avoid scenarios that would increase the need to take action, I did participate in policing in more mundane ways, such as re- viewing and relaying information from the computer-aided dispatch system and looking out for cross-traffic while on patrol. On a few occa- sions, officers filling out traffic-accident reports on the in-squad com- puter would ask me to input information. I generally complied with these minor requests for the sake of a smooth ride-along experience, though I drew the line when officers asked for my input into discretion- ary decisions. For instance, some officers would ask me to identify cars for potential traffic stops, and I always declined. Occasionally, police asked me if there was anything I would like to do or see during the rides; I always responded that I wanted to do whatever they would usually do. Officers often suggested that aspects of their work are boring—report writing, meetings, surveillance of drug houses—and I assured them that I wanted to observe this too, as these tasks were part of their routine ac- tivities. While trying to maintain access to mundane work, I also sought to preclude any sense that officers should avoid particular kinds of situ- ations on my behalf. I reassured officers that I had permission to observe extensively and that I was comfortable accepting the risks, including a frequent refrain of "I signed all the waivers."

Impacting Police Work
Though I cannot say how a shift would have been different if not for my observation, I have evidence that I impacted officers' work, both orga- nizationally and normatively. Procedurally, officers' shifts were altered when I was riding along in a few ways. According to policy, squads with ride-alongs were not sent as the primary unit to priority-one calls when the suspect was still on scene. However, I still observed how such situ- ations unfolded on occasion; officers I rode with responded as backup squads to fights, armed robberies, and other incidents with the suspect

on scene. Sometimes, this policy seemed loosely enforced, as when an officer I was riding with was sent as the primary squad to an assignment about a man threatening his mother with a knife. Nevertheless, the policy limited my observation of incidents with a higher risk of use of force and, hence, police violence. Other procedural dynamics altered "typical" work. Officers were also occasionally unable to transport citizens if I was riding in the backseat. In some cases, officers had to change the conditions of their usual shift, as when two officers assigned to bike patrol took a squad car out so that I could ride with them. There are probably additional ways that officers were organizationally constrained while I was conducting research.

Beyond these organizational limitations, I encountered indicators that my presence altered normative practices. Officers occasionally mentioned that they would typically do something were it not for my presence. For instance, during one ride-along, a sergeant pointed out a group of men he "knew were dirty" and said that he would have made a stop if I were not with him. I am unsure if this was because it would present a risk or an inconvenience. One officer suggested that having a ride-along was a good excuse to avoid certain kinds of work. In a few instances, officers radioed dispatch to remind them that they had a ride-along present, suggesting that they were trying to invoke the discretion of the dispatcher in selecting their next assignments.

In addition to influencing the kind of work officers did, my presence probably had an effect on their interactions with citizens, though the extent of the impact is difficult to measure. I suspect my civilian-outsider status potentially dampened inappropriate or problematic behaviors due to social desirability concerns and the risk that I would report these actions. But I was occasionally surprised by the severity of the way officers spoke to and interacted with citizens, despite my presence. I attribute this to what the sociologist Mitchell Duneier calls the "Becker Principle," which holds that interactions are largely structured by their own imperatives and routines and that these eventually supersede the presence of the ethnographer.[12] This was particularly noticeable when I rode with partners, who were prone to fall into shared patterns of conversation and decision-making that did not include me. For example, during Conti and Halliday's investigatory stop described in chapter 6, the officers spoke aggressively to the driver and his female companion.

At one point, Conti told the woman brusquely to "shut the fuck up," as she insisted that they did not have drugs on them. Later in the afternoon, Conti told me he had become conscious of how I might perceive what they had said to the couple. I told him about my process of writing up fieldnotes, and he said he was comfortable with me writing anything, as long as his name was not attached to it. This interaction reflected both the way I was visible to officers and the way my presence could be overlooked.

In short, the data I gathered do not capture pure, unadulterated police work as it would without the organizational and normative constraints of an observer. Nevertheless, what I could observe still speaks to the heart of this project: the existence of workload disparities and the ways officers managed responding to calls for service, the different routine activities undertaken by special units and deployments, and the interpretations and meanings officers deployed to understand their work environments. In fact, some dynamics and inequalities I described might be *more* extreme if I had not been present; perhaps officers would use more derogatory or overtly racist language, initiate additional aggressive stops, or "lay in the weeds" and avoid work for longer periods if left to their own devices. While this is speculative, it is notable that many of these dynamics still occurred to some degree during my observation, often to the effect of widening inequalities in racialized policing.

Candid Conversations?
Aside from observational effects, there is a question of whether officers represented their "true" perspectives in conversation. I was frankly surprised by how forthcoming many officers were, though perhaps the desire to share work-related frustrations is a universal phenomenon. During the vast majority of ride-alongs, officers had few reservations about discussing their experiences on the job and in their district. Some went further, telling me how most civilians could not understand how difficult policing was and noting how nice it was to talk to someone who was interested and not a colleague. As I generally observed for an entire eight-hour shift, the amount of time we spent together permitted wide-ranging talk. In some cases, I did ride-alongs with the same officer on several occasions. Hence, we had ample time to discuss a range of topics, from personal career histories to district-level gossip to our hometowns

and families. While I tended to ask work-related questions, I engaged in more free-wheeling discussions and responded to inquiries about myself when asked. Given our conversational scope, I am confident in asserting that I captured several important interpretive frames that officers deployed in making sense of their work.

Still, I assume that officers engaged in a degree of impression management. Discussions of racial dynamics in policing offer a case in point. During my fieldwork, protests unfolded in Ferguson, Missouri, and in cities across the country, and the growth of the Black Lives Matter movement made race salient to the way officers understood and experienced their jobs. Thus, racial dynamics arose as a topic of conversation. While individuals are generally unlikely to express overtly racist attitudes due to social desirability bias, I still encountered many interpretations of racial inequality that drew on colorblind frames explicitly. Officers naturalized segregation and accounted for the social problems they witnessed in predominantly Black neighborhoods by citing failing families and cultural deficiencies. One officer's comments captured this dynamic succinctly: "It's frustrating watching people live off of the state without making any effort to try and get work." As I describe in more detail shortly, I suspect that officers may have been more open in sharing these attitudes with me because I am not Black or brown. Rather than presume hidden motivations or options, however, I focus on the value in analyzing the frames and discourses that *did* emerge in police talk. Even assuming that these accounts are "public facing," they provide insight into how certain work conditions and particular interpretive frameworks serve to bolster one another.

Other Thoughts on Positionality

My interactions were also shaped by my social location, which often differed from officers along lines of class, gender, and race. Though the following discussion examines these identity categories discretely, they are not wholly distinct from one another or rigid in their operation. Systems of social differentiation are "interlocking, non-additive and often contradictory," and hence, the power dynamics in the research process were contingent and fluid.[13] Power emerged as salient through interactions and practices, rather than simply reflecting particular fixed attributes.

In some cases, officers explicitly invoked our differences in social location. For instance, several officers brought up my educational background with apparent self-consciousness. Some said they had struggled
in school and made self-deprecating remarks about their intelligence.
One officer admitted that he was embarrassed when sending me text
messages to arrange ride-alongs because his grammar was "horrible." In
this case, I assured him I would never judge his texting and shared that
I was also a terrible speller (true). In general, I tried to narrow any perceived educational gulf: I joked that my skills were actually quite limited
and that most of my time was spent sitting in a chair and reading. After
I had observed the complexities of police work, it was easy to highlight
how partial my routine activities were compared to those of officers and
to emphasize that their work required skills and intelligences that I did
not possess.

I also understood our discussions of education as tied to class backgrounds. While I grew up in an upper-middle-class community with
abundant access to educational resources, many officers described their
working-class or middle-class backgrounds. Some had become police
officers because they liked the profession or had family members in law
enforcement. But others pursued the job because, as one officer put it,
it was one of the best options for what was essentially blue-collar work.
This officer described working as a bartender before joining the department and joked that he would probably be pouring concrete were he not
a cop. Another officer, recently out of the academy, said he had previously been a janitor and in pest control. The differences between my opportunities and the experiences and narratives of many officers helped
me attune to the salience of class in officers' occupational trajectories.

Gender was another major axis of distinction between me and the
police. As a woman studying a traditionally hypermasculine space, I
dealt with occasional comments that could be construed as flirtatious or
sexualizing, usually by brushing them off. I also experienced fieldwork
as thoroughly gendered because the dynamics of ethnographic research
lent themselves to behaviors that have historically been constructed as
feminized. For instance, I sometimes acted as a compassionate listener
and offered emotional support during difficult discussions that arose
during ride-alongs. I also felt pressure to be relentlessly accommodating for the sake of maintaining access. Some days, I sat for several hours

in the public area of the district after my plans got lost in translation, waiting for a sergeant to reschedule a ride-along. On one occasion, a sergeant assigned me to shadow an officer who conducted a walking beat on a day when the weather was forecast to be about seven degrees Fahrenheit, with a windchill advisory. I felt compelled to take any opportunity I was offered with a smile, lest I appear ungrateful or burdensome. In general, I constricted my physical and social presence. This was exhausting, even though it is likely that these gendered expectations and interactions facilitated data collection. My position as a student and a relatively young woman—and perhaps some corresponding assumptions of naivete—made it easy to elicit officers' perspectives as experts, and I embraced their tendencies to explain things to me.

Race also probably played a role in the way officers engaged with me. As I mentioned, they might have limited their descriptions of Black neighborhoods as pathological—even if in colorblind terms—if I were a member of a community with a more historically fraught relationship to the police. Instead, I encountered familiar dynamics as people struggled to place me, as an Asian American and as a multiracial person, within the racial ontology of the United States. These dynamics have included inquiries into "what I am" or "where I'm from," comments on my "exotic" appearance, and tacit assumptions of proximity to or affinity with whiteness. In general, I had the sense that my race was a point of vague curiosity rather than a major delimiting factor in the way the police interacted with me. For instance, a white officer asked about my racial background as we were sitting in the district station before a ride-along. He explained that his wife was from a Southeast Asian country and said that I could be his daughter's sister. In discussions of race, I saw benefits of potentially more open talk if white officers assumed that my racial social location aligned more closely with theirs than with the Black residents they policed.

This was one area I struggled with representing myself to study participants. In reality, my own experiences and observations of racialization and years of studying race and ethnicity in the United States had cultivated a perspective that often diverged from those I heard from officers; I was more attuned to structural racism and enduring discrimination in contrast to colorblind explanations of inequality. Politics was another area of profound chasms in perspectives; for instance, I did not relate to an officer describing himself as an "ultraconservative gun nut." When themes of race or politics arose in conversation, I prioritized the goal of data collection and sought to facilitate further discussion without endorsing or negating an officer's perspective. I often asked follow-up questions, and I responded to officers' probes into my own viewpoint in ways that I felt were genuine, even if they were not entirely forthcoming. For instance, an officer with whom I had rapport told me explicitly that he sometimes wondered if I had ulterior motives and if I planned to write some "liberal" book about awful police culture, one in which he would recognize himself and the things he said in the text. I responded sincerely that I felt like it was my duty as a social scientist to represent people accurately and with dignity.

While conversations on touchy themes could be fraught ethically, they were relatively rare. I did not generally raise sensitive or potentially controversial topics, and I certainly did not try to provoke "gotcha" moments. When such topics arose, I saw them as important to understanding officers' backgrounds and social contexts and as germane to the way they made sense of their occupational identities. Perhaps I could have brought more of my full self into fieldwork. But I recognized that my presence as a researcher could easily be seen as an imposition and a burden, so I prioritized smoothing interactions. This goal was captured in a candid conversation with an approachable officer a few months into fieldwork. I asked how he and his colleagues felt about having me around, trusting that he would offer some honest feedback if I could do something differently. He said he would not invite me to ride with him if he did not enjoy it, suggesting I had an "easy presence" that people appreciated because I brought a smile into the room. This perception was surely informed by attributes like gender, race, and age. But it was also one that I actively tried to cultivate to facilitate the relationships required of the research.

My Role with Civilians

While my ethnographic goal was to describe the activities and attitudes of police officers, my observations invariably involved the public. Per my IRB approval, I could not disclose data that could potentially identify victims and offenders, and hence, I recorded only general, nonidentifying demographic descriptors when describing civilians in my fieldnotes.

But my concerns about the way I was perceived by and engaged with civilians extended beyond the formal requirements of the various institutional agreements I had signed; this was particularly difficult terrain to navigate given the immense situational power differentials between civilians and the police.

At a surface level, I focused on the optics and impact of my presence on the street. I was probably perceived as a police affiliate while in the field. Though I did not wear a uniform or carry a weapon, I wore a department ID badge and a bulletproof vest. I came and went freely from the district stations, rode in squad cars, and stood near the police on the street. I recognized that adding one more police-affiliated body to a situation could enhance the sense of state power that citizens experienced. I observed several instances in which many officers converged on a scene, their numbers communicating messages—often racialized—about how threatening or dangerous the police perceived a person to be and about how much force they might use in response.

At the same time, though I could bolster the visual representation of state power, I did not actually have any law enforcement capacity, and so I could not offer services or assistance to civilians. These dynamics were complicated further by my social location and the raced and gendered nature of policing and service provision, which must have also factored into the way people perceived me, potentially shaping their expectations of my ability to hurt or help them. For instance, citizens might have perceived my presence as a non-Black person as enhancing the risks that anti-Blackness could come into play in encounters with the police. Or some might have looked to me for assistance given gendered assumptions about providing care in times of crisis.

When the police responded to calls and engaged with citizens, I still attempted to be a nonparticipant, though in this realm, I also recognized that I would need to act if someone's safety was in jeopardy. I did not witness instances of police brutality or excessive force, though I imagined how I might respond by recording, reporting, or even trying to intervene in a situation if I had. Again, thankfully, no such situation unfolded during fieldwork. Instead, as I did with the police, I engaged in small practices in response to the situational needs I perceived. In most interactions, people directed their attention to officers. But when they included me in their audience, I listened actively and responded when addressed. In many situations, the police encountered people who had recently experienced a traumatic event or, at a minimum, a major inconvenience. People often desired an opportunity to express their pain, fear, or frustration, and I tried to serve as a sympathetic, albeit quiet, ear— making eye contact, nodding, and trying to nonverbally communicate that I heard their message and understood their emotional response to the incident.

In some cases, I felt compelled to engage directly with a citizen, often when I was briefly left alone with someone and wanted to provide some reassurance or explain my presence. As an example, an officer responded to a mental-observation call for a thirteen-year-old girl whose mother thought she needed to be taken to the county mental health facility. In preparing to transport her, the officer brought the girl to the backseat of the squad car. He briefly left to consult his partner in another car while I sat in the squad car with the girl. I asked her if she was all right. She nodded. I tried to reassure her that the officers wanted to help, figuring that being in the back of a police car could be an unsettling and scary experience. While this arguably further affiliated me with the police and endorsed their actions, I believed they were handling the situation to the best of their abilities given the circumstances, and I wanted to ease the girl's potential anxieties.

In another case, an officer agreed to drive a young Black woman to her grandmother's house after responding to a call for a battery in which she was the victim. She described being physically abused by her boyfriend, who had hit her in the chest and pushed her out of his car. The officer stopped at a gas station and left the car to buy the woman a coffee. In his absence, I told her I was sorry to hear that this had happened to her and that she did not deserve to be treated that way. The woman began to describe the incident again, crying as she did so, while I listened and tried to validate her pain and anger. When we arrived at her grandmother's house, she thanked the officer for the ride and thanked me for listening. In these instances, I saw the risks of compounding harm by acting indifferently toward a person who had experienced trauma as greater than those of abandoning the nonparticipant role. Indeed, these situations and the others described earlier reveal the limits of nonparticipation. Even though I was not a police officer, I was nevertheless a presence and therefore could not avoid some degree of participation in a scene.

I also grappled with observing police-initiated interactions. The stops, searches, and arrests that I witnessed—while legal as far as I could tell and within police mandate—could nevertheless seem intimate, invasive, and humiliating. To provide citizens with a modicum of additional privacy during these moments and to potentially reduce the chance that I bolstered the sense of police power, I stood farther away and averted my eyes, trying to focus my attention primarily on the police while still noting the contours of the interaction. This was particularly the case when officers took people into the booking room, where they would be searched more thoroughly, fingerprinted, and photographed. In these moments, I took a position where I could see the officer conducting the booking and the arresting officer but could not see the person being booked removing their top layer of clothing and being searched. While I did not observe how citizens navigated the booking process, such an omission is consistent with my overarching focus on police behaviors and attitudes.

REPRESENTATION AND WRITING

All ethnographic work requires researchers to interrogate their assumptions and allegiances. When a researcher's affinities or sympathies lie with the people being studied, there may be a temptation to ensure that research subjects appear in a positive light. However, this project started from a different premise: that powerful institutions and actors merit additional scrutiny. On this basis, my orientation was more critical from the outset, which surely shaped what drew my attention during observations, in analyzing the data, and in presenting these data. For instance, as I was interested in the practices and representations that could reinforce racial differences and hierarchies in River City, I was attentive to the possibility of demeaning treatment of nonwhite citizens and patterned differences in the outcomes of police-citizen encounters. Nevertheless, I aimed to check my presuppositions through an openness to negative cases and disconfirming evidence throughout the research process. I tried to pursue an inquisitorial stance rather than an adversarial one.[14]

I found it easy to be open to the surprise of the field, given the sheer novelty of the experience. As someone whose prior knowledge of policing was shaped by scholarly accounts, media representations, and the occasional traffic stop, fieldwork offered insight into the realities of on-the-ground policing in a much deeper way. I left the experience under-standing police work, particularly the patrol function, to be incredibly complex. It required officers to be adaptable and ready to respond to a range of situations—from serious crises to truly mundane incidents—with limited tools. Many officers navigated this work with respect to-ward citizens; a few did so with what I saw as exceptional compassion. In general, I felt that many of the police personnel I observed and inter-viewed were dedicated public servants doing a very difficult job. Never-theless, in analyzing and weighing all of the evidence I gathered, I still had to conclude that policing in River City was maintaining segregation and amplifying race- and class-based inequalities.

In summary, my goal was to understand people in this ethnography as complex, full humans instead of archetypes or tropes. I focused on people in their various contexts: as shaped by their personal histories and social locations, as enabled and constrained by institutional pres-sures and repertoires for action, and as embedded within a specific time and place. This applies to officers who navigated the powerful organiza-tional and normative context of a deeply hierarchical state institution. It also applies to police executives, who had to steward a department through an urban landscape characterized by entrenched social inequal-ities and myriad political and economic pressures. Finally, it applies to the city's political and economic elites, who responded to the realities of neoliberal urbanism by fighting to keep their city competitive and viable through growth and redevelopment. This contextualist perspective does not aim to absolve agentic decision-makers of their role in contributing to practices and policies that reinscribe race- and class-based inequali-ties. But I argue that these decisions cannot be divorced from the social structures in which these actors are embedded. Indeed, these structures are key leverage points for change.

ACKNOWLEDGMENTS

In many ways, this book feels like the culmination of a collective effort. I could not have carried out this project without the intellectual, emotional, and practical support of an incredible network of colleagues, mentors, friends, and family members. I am afraid I cannot do them justice in a brief acknowledgment. With this in mind, I consider the following a snapshot of a few of the ways that many people contributed to this project, rather than a complete account, and I apologize for any oversights.

Perhaps most apparently, I am indebted to the administration and members of the River City Police Department. The opportunity to do fieldwork with the police is rare; I am grateful that the police executives who granted me access believed in the value of research. Many members of the police department worked on my behalf in myriad ways—assisting with scheduling, ensuring access to data and sites, making connections and introductions to others. I could not have accomplished such breadth and depth of observation without their aid. I am also grateful to the individual officers who allowed me to accompany them as they worked. They shared with me insights both occupational and personal, and they introduced me to the realities of policing through their lived experiences. This project would not have been possible without them.

Before even entering the field, I benefited from the academic mentorship of faculty members at the University of Wisconsin. Foremost, my advisor, Pamela Oliver, has been a constant source of support since my first semester as a graduate student. Beyond shaping the intellectual trajectory of this project, she guided me through IRB applications and grant proposals, answered hundreds of emails, talked me through difficult fieldwork moments, and read countless drafts, including a full version of this manuscript. I am grateful for her enduring confidence in me as a scholar and a person. Sida Liu has also been a mentor of unparalleled generosity. His sharp theoretical insight always pushed my work forward. Myra Marx Ferree's training and advising in methods shaped my approach in this project and my perspective on the discipline more broadly. Access to the police department would not have been possible without assistance from Michael Scott, whose expertise in policing provided much foundational knowledge. Keith Findley and Michael Massoglia offered advising and feedback as members of my dissertation committee, and Jane Collins served as a discussant on a paper draft to come out of the fieldwork. I drew inspiration for this project from courses with Michael Bell, Katherine Curtis, Mustafa Emirbayer, Bob Freeland, Alice Goffman, and Gray Green. I also learned a great deal about conducting rigorous research through my work with Tonya Brito and David Pate.

During my time in graduate school, I was lucky to meet a group of fellow students who have been my primary interlocutors ever since. An account of what we shared through the years would take pages, so I will limit myself to noting that these friends have integrally shaped who I am as a scholar. Many have labored with me over this book. Casey Stockstill and katrina quisumbing king each read so many chapter drafts and provided near-daily commiseration and celebration during coworking sessions in the final months of writing. Casey also expertly facilitated a book workshop on my behalf. Esther HsuBorger, Johanna Quinn, and Amanda McMillian Lequieu offered feedback on chapters and excerpts. My work evolved through discussions with Ian Carrillo, Katie Fallon, Jordan Garner, Garret Grainger, Annabel Ipsen, Emma Shakeshaft, and the students of the Race and Ethnicity Brownbag, FemSem, Solidarity, and the ILS Law and Society Graduate Fellowship Program. Finding and making community with other students was one of the most valuable things to come out of my time at the University of Wisconsin.

This project also developed through the insights of many incredible scholars whose work on policing, law, race, and the city I deeply admire. Monica Bell and Amada Armenta provided essential feedback on an early draft of this manuscript during a many-hour book workshop over Zoom. Their generous and thoughtful comments shaped the core argument of the book and improved every single chapter. Robert Vargas's careful read pushed me to develop key themes. Chuck Epp and Steve Herbert both responded to the email equivalent of a cold call, and their mentorship at the earliest stages of writing clarified my vision for this work. Chris Smith and Mona Lynch offered helpful comments on early paper drafts at workshops. Sarah Brayne provided some much-needed guidance and reassurance as I managed my ongoing relationship with the RCPD. I benefited from the comments of Veronica Horowitz, Austin Kocher, Corinne Schwartz, and Kevin Woodson at the 2019 Law & Society Association Junior Scholars Workshop. I am continuously learning from and inspired by the Critical Police Studies Working Group. My small group through the NCFDD Faculty Success Program was a great source of encouragement. In general, it has been a privilege to connect with a network of remarkable scholars and to benefit from their expertise and wisdom in the course of carrying out this work.

I am fortunate to call Tufts University my current academic home. I am so grateful for the many forms of support offered by my colleagues in the Department of Sociology: Kathy Blake, Freeden Blume Oeur, Felipe Dias, Victoria Dorward, Paul Joseph, John LiBassi, Helen Marrow, Caleb Scoville, Rosemary Taylor, Natasha Warikoo, and Jill Weinberg. A special thanks goes to Sarah Sobieraj, who has been an amazing mentor, offering substantive feedback on a draft of this manuscript and many other forms of guidance, and to Anjuli Fahlberg, for her comments on the appendix and our many generative conversations. I have also received support from many groups on campus: I am privileged to be a member of the Department of Studies in Race, Colonialism, and Diaspora; I have benefited from the programming of the Center for the Enhancing of Learning and Teaching; I am heartened by the work of the Tufts Action Group; and I have been connected to new opportunities by Bárbara Brizuela and Jim Glaser. Thank you to my colleagues from across the university who have offered encouragement, advice, and friendship through this process, including Madina Agénor, Kim Bain, Hilary Binda, Sarah Fong, Kareem Khubchandani, Sarah Luna, Keith Maddox, Kris Manjapra, Diana Martinez, Lily Mengesha, Ryan Rideau, and Sam Sommers.

Many students shaped my thinking about this work, but special shout-outs go to Gabe Reyes and Anthony Davis-Pait for their exceptional research assistance. Gabe read drafts of nearly every chapter of this manuscript, synthesized relevant literatures, and took meticulous notes during the book workshop. Gabe's thoughtful comments contributed to my revisions and pushed me toward greater reflexivity. Anthony was my collaborator in the comparative study of police redistricting reforms in major US cities. He played a foundational role in data collection and analysis. This book would not be what it is without their contributions.

It has been a joy to work with my editor, Ilene Kalish, and her team at New York University Press. From our first phone conversation and in many exchanges since, Ilene has seen the promise of this work. It is through her advice and advocacy that it has finally reached this stage. Thank you also to the anonymous New York University Press readers, whose reports helped strengthen the manuscript at several points. I am also very grateful for the development and stylistic editing of Rose Ernst. Exchanging chapters with Rose was an integral part of the final months of drafting; her efficient and effective work did much to improve the writing and encourage me across the finish line.

Funding to support this project came from many sources, including the Neubauer Faculty Fellowship, the Bernstein Faculty Fellowship, the Tufts Faculty Research Award Committee, and the CELT mutual mentoring program. At the University of Wisconsin, this work was supported by the Center for Engaged Scholarship, the National Science Foundation under Grant No. 1602697, the Delamater Award, and the Mellon-Wisconsin Summer Fellowship.

Finally, many dear friends and my incredible family have anchored me through the years as eternal sources of perspective, joy, and love. This work truly would not have been possible without their enduring support. My family has created the opportunities that allowed me to walk this path. And they have been there to appreciate every challenge and celebrate every accomplishment that I have experienced along the way. While words cannot express the depths of my gratitude, I see the words in this book as a reflection of their efforts, as much as they are a reflection of mine.

NOTES

INTRODUCTION

1. All names are pseudonyms. This includes the names of individuals, organizational entities, initiatives, places, etc.
2. I capitalize "Black" because many understand this as a shared racial, ethnic, or cultural identity that should be treated like other names of ethnic or national groups like "Asian" or "Native American." Throughout the text, I occasionally use "Black" and "African American" interchangeably, though it is worth noting that these categories are not fully overlapping, nor do they capture the complex history of diverse Black communities and people in the United States. For instance, African immigrants or Black people from Latin American or the Caribbean may not see themselves as "African American." These tensions reflect the reality that racial categories evolve, they are contested and imprecise, and they refer to heterogeneous groups of people. Yet their use in this project is essential given its interest in racial disparities and inequities.
3. I suspect that parts of Snow's description were hyperbolic. Snow was not specific in the details of the event, so it was difficult to verify. During the fieldwork period, I checked several local news sources daily and did not recall seeing reports about a fight involving hundreds of people. This ride-along also occurred many months into my observations, and I had not heard about this event from other officers, who often discussed major incidents. At the same time, Snow's recollection probably included truthful elements. Officers often described homicide scenes as challenging because citizens would gather and emotions would run high. I had also observed a situation in which dozens of people on a block confronted the police. I interpreted Snow's comment as conveying the sense of overwhelm and conflict that officers in the West District could encounter.
4. Logan and Molotch 2007.
5. Peck, Theodore, and Brenner 2009.
6. Fainstein and Fainstein 1989; Caraley 1992.
7. W. Wilson 1996.
8. Alexander 2010.
9. Peck 2012; Donald et al. 2014.
10. Harvey 1989.
11. Sassen 2006; Glaeser and Gottlieb 2006.
12. Wilson and Wouters 2003.

13. Clark 2004.
14. D. Wilson 2007, 3.
15. Wilson and Wouters 2003.
16. Though segregation has affected all racialized groups in the United States, this book focuses specifically on Black-white residential segregation as it emerged and endures in Rust Belt cities.
17. Massey and Denton 1993; W. Wilson 1996.
18. Kobayashi and Peake 2000, 394. For further discussions of the coconstitution of space and race, see Delaney 2002; and Inwood and Yarbrough 2010.
19. D. Wilson 2007, 6; Schmidt 2011.
20. D. Wilson 2007, 6.
21. Buchanan, Bui, and Patel 2020.
22. Williams and Murphy 1990; Bass 2001; Hadden 2003; Owusu-Bempah 2017.
23. Weitzer and Tuch 2005; Brunson and Weitzer 2009; Kochel 2019.
24. Omi and Winant (1994) explain that racial rule in the US has evolved from dictatorship to hegemony. For much of US history, racial rule was accomplished through the coercive subjugation of nonwhite populations. Following the civil rights movement, racial projects—representations of racial dynamics and efforts to redistribute resources along racial lines—relied increasingly on consent instead of coercion. While strategically incorporating the interests of subordinate groups into the ruling apparatus, dominant groups nevertheless maintained control of institutional and cultural spheres. Mechanisms of racial exclusion have evolved to operate in more covert, albeit persistent ways.
25. K. Miller 2013.
26. Gilmore 2007; Simon 2007.
27. Garland 2001; Wacquant 2009.
28. Vargas and McHarris 2017.
29. Beck and Goldstein 2018.
30. Simon 2007; Stuart 2016.
31. Cordner 2010; Beck and Goldstein 2018.
32. Wilson and Wouters 2003.
33. For an overview of the theory of "Broken Windows," see Wilson and Kelling 1982; for work on the ties between order-maintenance policing and neoliberal urban governance, see Herbert and Brown 2006; Samara 2010; Sharp 2014; Laniyonu 2018.
34. Beckett and Herbert 2008, 2009.
35. Soss and Weaver 2017, 571.
36. Alexander 2010.
37. Rios 2011; Prowse, Weaver, and Meares 2020.
38. Soss and Weaver 2017, 573.
39. US Department of Justice 2015. On the rise of court-ordered monetary sanctions and their role in perpetuating racial and economic inequality, see Harris 2016.
40. Weisburd and Braga 2006; Weisburd 2008.

41. Kelling and Moore 1988.
42. Bureau of Justice Assistance 1994, vii.
43. Skogan 2006; Cordner 2014.
44. Rios 2011; Lynch et al. 2013; Stuart 2016.
45. Bell 2020a, 2020b.
46. Emirbayer 1997, 287.
47. Omi and Winant 1994, 55.
48. Soss and Weaver 2017, 579; Fields 1990; Hall 1992; Omi and Winant 1994; Mills 2014; Glenn 2015. These and other scholars of race and ethnicity describe the origins of the race concept in colonial conquests across the globe. In the United States, specifically, settler colonialism relied on the appropriation of Native lands and the establishment of a private-property regime that commodified both territory and the people forced to extract its resources. The idea of race emerged from the tensions between European settlers' ideologies of freedom and equality and the violent and exploitative treatment of indigenous peoples and enslaved Africans. Bodies came to be marked as civilized versus savage, superior versus inferior, agentic versus passive. These dichotomies justified white domination over racial "others," and they laid ideological foundations for myriad future projects of erasure, containment, and control.
49. For example, in an insightful ethnography of a penal institution, Michael Walker (2016) describes how deputies sort inmates into three racial constructs—Blacks, woods, and sureños—that combine disparate ethnic identities into discrete categories that then serve as the basis for segregated housing assignments and daily racial projects.
50. Epp, Maynard-Moody, and Haider-Markel 2014; Justice and Meares 2014.
51. Brunson 2007; Epp et al. 2014.
52. Wakefield and Uggen 2010; R. Miller 2020.
53. Russell-Brown 2009; Brayne 2017.
54. Lamont and Molnár 2002.
55. Weisburd and Braga 2006.
56. Klinger 1997.
57. Epp et al. 2014.
58. Armenta 2017a, 2017b. The 287(g) program is a US Immigration and Customs Enforcement program that authorizes state and local law enforcement agencies to directly enforce civil and criminal immigration laws (Armenta 2017a, 29).
59. Victor Ray's (2019) theory of racialized organizations has drawn important attention to the meso-level processes that contribute to racial stratification. Racialized organizations are those that activate "schemas delineating racial sub- and super-ordination" when distributing resources (32). In doing so, they "limit the personal agency and collective efficacy of subordinate racial groups while magnifying the agency of the dominant racial group" (36). Ray identifies several processes that interrelate organizations, racial stratification, and racial ideologies. Consistent with the broader literature on race and organizations, Ray generally focuses on

two avenues of stratification: how organizations themselves are hierarchized on the basis of racial schemas and how members within an organization get sorted on the basis of race. This project and others like it draw analytical attention to another modality of resource distribution: how organizations channel resources throughout the broader urban environment.

60. Tansey 2007; Collier 2011.

61. Collier 2011, 823.

62. Nader 1972.

63. The redistricting also affected the North District, an area that was redrawn to include a majority of the city's Latinx population. I did not conduct a comparative ethnography of policing in the North District, largely due to feasibility constraints. But I highlight some of the parallels between the logics that applied to the North District and the West District, and I draw in data that examines citywide racial disparities for Latinos as well as African Americans when possible.

64. State policies of Indian removal, Asian exclusion, Jim Crow, Japanese internment, and Mexican deportation offer a few examples of how spatial and racial boundaries have been regulated to the effect of excluding, containing, or controlling racialized "others" in the United States. Bass (2001) offers an overview of the role of the police in some of these projects. For examples of research on the experiences of various groups, see Song 1992; Perry 2009; Rios, Prieto, and Ibarra 2020.

65. These figured were taken from a news article published in the city's major newspaper in 2017. It included data on police-department demographics over several years. The numbers reported reflect the department's demographics during the year when the fieldwork was conducted.

CHAPTER 1. URBAN GOVERNANCE, POLICING, AND THE MAKING OF A SEGREGATED CITY

1. Harvey 1989; Fainstein and Fainstein 1989; D. Wilson 2007; Peck et al. 2009; Peck 2012.

2. Kelling and Moore 1988; Greene 2000; Weisburd and Braga 2006.

3. Massey and Denton 1993; W. Wilson 1996; Charles 2003; Alexander 2010; Rothstein 2017.

4. This project relies on many different kinds of publicly available materials that cannot be fully cited due to the condition that I deidentify the study site. In an effort to provide historical context, while avoiding identifying the site, I identify publicly available sources by offering a brief description of each and labeling it with a code (e.g., Video 01, Document 04, News Article 03, etc.). This allows me, at a minimum, to note when information came from the same source. In the case of this reference, I synthesized the history of indigenous peoples in the River City area from an entry on Native Americans in an online encyclopedia project that sought to comprehensively document River City's history (Document 01). The encyclopedia was funded by the National Endowment for the Humanities, a major

university in the city, and a philanthropic organization. Its entries were compiled and edited by several academics, many affiliated with the city's universities.

5. Warner 2016.

6. I characterize the city's early economy on the basis of an article about the economic history of River City in the encyclopedia project described in note 4 (Document 02).

7. Wilkerson 2011.

8. I offer this account of the participation of Black laborers in River City's industrial economy on the basis of a book by a historian that analyzes the experiences of Black residents in River City during the first half of the twentieth century, specifically in relation to their status as industrial workers (Academic Book 01).

9. This description of River City's Black belt was synthesized based on an article about the Black belt (Document 03) and an article on African Americans (Document 04) in the River City encyclopedia project.

10. These recollections were recounted on a webpage on the history of the Black belt hosted by the River City municipal government and published in 2019. The city maintains a website dedicated to the neighborhood, which includes tabs on visiting, news, development, and business, in addition to history (Document 05).

11. Drake and Cayton 1945.

12. Drake and Cayton 1945.

13. Massey and Denton 1993; Wacquant 2000.

14. Meyer 2000.

15. Rothstein 2017.

16. Rothstein 2017.

17. A long-form journalistic article in one of the city's alternative newspapers included a redlining map and an account of the origins of segregation in River City published in 2020. The article described national trends of redlining, racial covenants, and the development of the suburbs and included many specific details on how these dynamics played out in River City (News Article 01).

18. This account of redlining in River City was featured in an article on a website hosted by the state's public broadcasting and public radio services. It was prepared by two researchers from the state's flagship public university. It included an overview of redlining and specific examples of HOLC grades in the River City metro area (Document 06).

19. Quoted in Rothstein 2017, 65.

20. I synthesized this description of the development of River City's suburban ring on the basis of an article about suburbanization in the River City encyclopedia project (Document 07).

21. News Article 01.

22. Gotham 2000.

23. Document 06.

24. The use of zoning as an exclusionary mechanism was described in a 2005 report prepared by a private, nonprofit organization focused on promoting fair hous-

ing in the River City metropolitan area. The report covered demographic and economic patterns in the metro area, impediments to fair housing within the city and based on suburban policies, state and federal policies, and barriers originating from the private market (Document 08).

25. Avila and Rose 2009.
26. I drew this description of urban renewal in River City from an article on the subject in the River City encyclopedia project (Document 09).
27. Document 05.
28. This description is based an article on the history of public housing in River City in the River City encyclopedia project (Document 10).
29. High 2003.
30. W. Wilson 1996.
31. I complied the description of the economic landscape of River City on the basis of a technical report prepared by an academic affiliated with an economic-development research center at one of the city's universities. It provided an overview of key economic forces in the city and included discussions of the impacts of deindustrialization, regional changes in job opportunities, labor-market and income stratification by demographic variables, and other topics (Technical Report 01).
32. W. Wilson 1996; see also Massey and Denton 1993; Sampson and Wilson 1995.
33. The statistics were derived from Technical Report 01.
34. Lever 2001.
35. Peck et al. 2009, 50.
36. Fainstein and Fainstein 1989.
37. Wacquant 2009.
38. Tonry 1995; Beckett and Sasson 2004; Alexander 2010.
39. Alexander 2010.
40. Alexander 2010.
41. Sentencing Project 2020, 2.
42. The Sentencing Project (2020) reports an incarceration rate of 655 per 100,000 on the basis of a 2019 source. Wakefield and Uggen (2010) note a rate of 751 per 100,000 in 2006.
43. Sentencing Project 2020, 2.
44. Sentencing Project 2020, 5.
45. Pettit and Western 2004.
46. Tonry (1994) explains that, in poor minority neighborhoods, drug arrests are easier to make than in working-class or middle-class white neighborhoods, for several reasons. Drug dealing is more likely to occur in visible outdoor spaces, undercover officers can penetrate drug distribution networks, and arrested dealers are often quickly replaced, providing new targets for enforcement. In short, drug arrests in neighborhoods that experience social disorganization are more politically expedient.

47. Labor market: Pager 2003; Western 2006. Family life: Pattillo, Western, and Weiman 2004. Participation: Manza and Uggen 2008. Instability: Rose and Clear 1998.
48. Quillian and Pager 2001; Sampson and Raudenbush 2004.
49. Wacquant 2000, 384.
50. I took the statistics on levels of incarceration for African Americans from a technical report prepared by two academics affiliated with one of the city's universities, published in 2013. The report focused on the consequences of mass incarceration for Black men in the workforce, specifically. While characterizing patterns in the state, much of the report focused on River City. The authors provided many descriptive statistics to quantify the scale of incarceration and trends over time. It drew on data from the state department of corrections to quantify Black men in the county who had been incarcerated in the 1990s and 2000s (Technical Report 02).
51. I found the information on River City's Latino population in a technical report prepared by an academic affiliated with an economic-development research center at one of the city's universities, published in 2016. The report offered a statistical portrait of the metro area's Hispanic population, describing trends in population growth, segregation, poverty, employment, health care, education, incarceration, and others. It largely relied on data from the American Community Survey (Technical Report 03).
52. Fainstein and Fainstein 1989.
53. Peck 2012; Donald et al. 2014.
54. Harvey 1989.
55. Fainstein and Fainstein 1989, 41.
56. Peck et al. 2009, 57.
57. Glaeser and Gottlieb 2006.
58. Sassen 2006.
59. Glaeser and Gottlieb 2006.
60. Wilson and Wouters 2003.
61. Logan and Molotch 2007, 37.
62. Logan and Molotch 2007.
63. Florida 2005.
64. Clark 2004.
65. Wilson and Wouters 2003, 127.
66. Peck 2005; MacLeod 2011.
67. Schmidt 2011.
68. Levine (1987) reviews the logic of downtown redevelopment before critiquing its consequences through a case study of Baltimore. He notes that proponents identify four primary benefits of this growth strategy: symbolic enhancement of the local business climate, tax-base broadening and job creation, ripple effects through surrounding neighborhoods, and adjustments to global economic trends.

69. Tighe and Ganning 2015.
70. Castells 1996; Sassen 2006.
71. Reardon and Bischoff 2011.
72. D. Wilson 2007.
73. Melamed 2011; Hashimoto 2021.
74. I developed the account in this paragraph form an academic journal article that described River City's stabilization planning during the 1970s. The article drew on public documents, interviews with planners, and other materials and argued that the city's planning functioned to stabilize and enhance better-off white neighborhoods, while redlining predominantly Black neighborhoods (Academic Journal Article 01).
75. I synthesized this description from an academic journal article that described the trajectory of River City's development strategy in the early 2000s. The article highlighted the influence of Richard Florida's creative cities thesis and presented an account of how private and public entities within the city's growth coalition reinforced the emphasis on downtown development by adopting this vision (Academic Journal Article 02).
76. The ongoing emphasis on downtown redevelopment was captured in a news article published in a national outlet in 2017. The piece describes the myriad projects under way in the downtown and quoted the current mayor explaining the goal of rebuilding from the center (News Article 02).
77. I synthesized this description of more recent redevelopment projects from an academic journal article that described the racial character of River City's reliance on courting the creative class as a means of economic growth. The piece drew on participant observation, analysis of public documents, and interviews with government officials and representatives from businesses and nonprofits (Academic Journal Article 03).
78. I took this information from a document reporting demographic data as part of an official citywide policy plan. It was accessed through the city's website. The document drew from data from the 2008 American Community Survey and made demographic and employment projections through 2025 (Document 11).
79. These findings were reported in a technical report prepared by two academics affiliated with one of the city's universities. The report focused on disparities in economic outcomes within the county, comparing the city's poorest zip codes to the wealthiest suburban zip codes (Technical Report 04).
80. Fyfe 1991; Herbert 1997a, 1997b.
81. Herbert 1997a, 13.
82. Smith 1986; Terrill and Reisig 2003.
83. Fagan and Davies 2000; Beckett and Herbert 2009; Novak and Chamlin 2012.
84. Meehan and Ponder 2002, 402.
85. Ericson 1982, 3.
86. Hadden 2003.
87. Bass 2001.
88. Williams and Murphy 1990; Bass 2001; Williams 2015.

89. Black Lives Matter 2020.
90. Wadman and Allison 2004.
91. Kelling and Moore 1988.
92. Kahn and Martin 2016.
93. Weisburd and Braga 2006; Walker and Archibold 2020.
94. Agee 2020; Gascón and Roussell 2019.
95. I drew much of the summary of the history of the River City Police Department from an academic book authored by a prominent policing scholar that reviewed the trajectory of the department from its inception through the early 2000s. Unless otherwise noted, the descriptions specific to River City come from this account (Academic Book 02).
96. Kelling and Moore 1988.
97. Kelling and Moore 1988.
98. Kelling et al. 1974; Spelman and Brown 1984.
99. Greene and Pelfry 1997.
100. Greene 2000; Scott 2000.
101. Skogan 2006.
102. Skogan 2006, 27–28.
103. Skogan and Hartnett 1997; Sunshine and Tyler 2003; Cordner 2014.
104. These two examples were drawn from one of the River City Police Department's annual reports, published a year after the chief began his first term (Document 12).
105. Weisburd 2008.
106. Braga, Papachristos, and Hureau 2014.
107. Epp et al. 2014; Tyler, Fagan, and Geller 2014; Huq 2017.
108. Beckett and Herbert 2009.
109. Lefebvre 1991; Lipsitz 2007.
110. Meyer and Rowan 1977; McQuarrie and Marwell 2009.

CHAPTER 2. THE PROMISES AND PERILS OF THE RIVER CITY REDISTRICTING

1. Canon 1999; Bullock 2021.
2. Okonta 2017.
3. Frankenberg 2009; Owens 2018.
4. Saiger 2010, 537; Viteritti 2012.
5. Mastrofski and Willis 2010; see also Go (2020), who describes how US imperial projects abroad informed the militarization of police tactics and organization in the twentieth century.
6. Klinger 1997; Hassell 2006.
7. Klinger 1997, 272.
8. Bruce 2009, 1.
9. Bruce 2009, 2.
10. Several academic sources describe technical models for police-district design and patrol-resource allocation focused on the goal of workload balance. For instance,

see D'Amico et al. 2002; Curtin, Hayslett-McCall, and Qiu 2010; and, for a review, see Liberatore, Camacho-Collados, and Vitoriano 2020.

11. This review examined media accounts and publicly available records for any redistricting reform undertaken by a police department in any of the largest fifty cities of the United States. It concentrated on reform efforts within the past twenty years. While the review is not exhaustive, it provided a basic overview of the outward logics of many redistricting efforts.

12. Kelling and Moore 1988.

13. Weisburd and Braga 2006.

14. In saturation patrols, a large number of officers are deployed into a small geographic area to create a sense of ubiquitous police presence.

15. Skogan 2006, 37.

16. Bruce 2009.

17. Moore and Poethig 1999; J. Wilson 1968; Stucky 2005; Klinger 2004.

18. Irwin 2011; Wacquant 2009; Beck and Goldstein 2018.

19. Samara 2010; Sharp 2014; Laniyonu 2018.

20. This is based on an empirical review of twenty-first-century police redistricting reforms, where I found little evidence of reforms departing from a goal of workload balance.

21. As this was a public meeting, footage of the presentation of the redistricting before the Safety Committee of the City Council was published and available through the city's Legistar system. I use the video footage from this presentation as the basis for much of the following discussion (Video 01).

22. I found this description on a page on the River City government's website that described "public safety" as one of the key issues addressed by the mayor's office (Document 13).

23. This article was published in the city's primary newspaper a year after the chief began his appointment. It noted that the city's homicides had fallen to their lowest total in decades and included quotes from the police chief that suggested that police deployments were having an impact on crime, and from the mayor, also citing the police department's work (News Article 03).

24. I accessed these meeting minutes through the Civilian Review Board's website. They contain a narrative description of the chief's presentation of the redistricting proposal (Document 14).

25. Video 01.

26. This footage came from a hearing of the City Council's Licensing Committee. One segment of the hearing focused on problems associated with a downtown bar and included a presentation by the captain of the East District on the department's approach to nightlife policing. I accessed this video through the city's Legistar system (Video 02).

27. Reskin 2012.

28. Sutherland 1983; Rothe and Kauzlarich 2016.

29. Lauritsen, Rezey, and Heimer 2016; Desmond, Papachristos, and Kirk 2016.

30. Tonry 1994; Beckett et al. 2005.

CHAPTER 3. POLICING THE EAST DISTRICT

1. Cole 1999; Rhode 2004.
2. US Department of Justice 2009.
3. Skolnick 1966; Westley 1970; Manning 1978.
4. Sierra-Arévalo 2021. For instance, the River City Police Department evaluated officers using performance measures that captured key crime control tactics like police stops, arrests, and incident reports. Performance measures did not include indicators of community-policing activities or measures of police service during response to 911 calls. The implications of this are described further in the book's conclusion.
5. Martin 1999.
6. Martin 1999.
7. District-level demographic data were pulled from an online public mapping application available through the city government's website. In addition to aggregating demographic data by police district, the application allows the user to generate a summary report of major criminal incidents submitted through the state-specific version of the FBI's National Incident-Based Reporting System. I generated reports for the East District and the West District for a year-long period that corresponded to fieldwork, and I draw on these reports to characterize patterns in demographics and reported crimes (Document 15).
8. Document 15.
9. These numbers were reported in a River City Police Department's annual report, published a year after the boundary changes took place (Document 16).
10. The priority system distinguished among types of calls. "Priority one" calls involved life-threatening conditions; "priority two" calls included major-property-threatening conditions, accidents involving injuries, and nonspecific injuries or illnesses not resulting from criminal activity; "priority three" calls referred to situations that did not require an immediate response to prevent injury or property loss; and "priority four" calls designated other situations of a minor nature.
11. I calculated these differences from reports of dispatched calls included in two consecutive RCPD annual reports. The report published the year of the redistricting included counts of calls for service by district for the prior year. This captured the volume of calls in each district before the boundary changes, and these represent the baseline numbers (Document 12). The subsequent annual report captured calls within the new district boundaries the year following the redistricting (Document 16).
12. This article was published in the city's major newspaper. It described the Entertainment Corridor Deployment, which was a new initiative at the time, and included interviews with both the chief of police and the captain of East District (News Article 04).
13. Video 02 (see note 26 to chapter 2).
14. This article was published in a local business-news outlet. It included the history of the deployment, a description based on observations of a shift, and interviews with several police officials and downtown business owners or managers. The ar-

ticle quoted the chief describing ECD as a "good business investment." It generally noted the economic goals of police executives and the positive impacts perceived by downtown stakeholders (News Article 05).

15. News Article 04.
16. News Article 05.
17. These developments were quantified and reported in a "market profile" compiled by a national economic development and planning firm, in collaboration with the major business improvement district in the city's downtown. In addition to describing trends in growth over a decade, the report emphasized the significance of the downtown to the city's overall tax base and labeled it "the City's single most important economic resource" (Document 17).

CHAPTER 4. POLICING THE WEST DISTRICT
1. Bonilla-Silva 2006.
2. Proactive policing is defined in contrast to reactive policing. It includes "policing strategies that have as one of their goals the prevention or reduction of crime and disorder" (National Academies of Sciences, Engineering, and Medicine 2018). Tactics that fall under the umbrella of proactive policing can be varied. Most commonly, they include activities like investigatory traffic stops, business checks, and directed patrols (Koper et al. 2020).
3. I use the terms "proactive stops" and "investigatory stops" as interchangeable umbrella terms that refer to both investigatory traffic stops (distinguished from traffic safety stops) and pedestrian stops.
4. As in chapter 3, district-level demographic and crime data corresponding to the fieldwork period were pulled from an online public mapping application available through the city government's website. See note 7 in the chapter 3 (Document 15).
5. Document 15.
6. Braga et al. 2014.
7. Fagan and Davies 2000; Epp et al. 2014; Tyler et al. 2014; Fagan et al. 2016.
8. Fagan and Geller 2015.
9. Skolnick 1966; Jones-Brown 2007; Russell-Brown 2009; Muhammad 2010.
10. Brunson 2007; Bell 2017.
11. I drew on footage from the publicly available video posted to the RCPD's YouTube page to describe this meeting. It included a presentation by the chief of police, who was accompanied by several other high-level police executives. The chief outlined the official logic of the department's proactive strategy and traffic-stop practices in relation to crime control efforts (Video 03).
12. These numbers were included in a set of slides prepared by the police department as part of an annual presentation to the City Council Safety Committee on racial data and traffic stops. I accessed them through the Legistar record associated with the meeting where the data was presented (Document 18).
13. Video 03.

14. The article was published in the city's major newspaper. In an original investigation, the article drew on several months of police stop data and reported marked racial disparities in traffic stops citywide. It also included district-level analyses that unveiled racial disparities within districts. In addition to documenting racial gaps, the article included responses to the investigation's findings from multiple stakeholders, including the chief of police, elected officials, and leaders of civic organizations (News Article 06).

15. The NAACP offered this public statement in response to News Article 06. It was included in a series of response letters that were published alongside the article in the city's paper (Document 19).

16. Document 18. It also bears noting that, while the reduction in complaints could indicate citizens' increased satisfaction with the police—as the chief suggested—it could also reflect other dynamics, for instance, difficulties in utilizing the complaint system or the sense the complaints would not be meaningfully handled.

17. Video 03.

18. In addition to district-level proactive resources, two citywide crime control efforts contributed to the total volume of stops in the West District. First, the district housed an FBI task force where four West District police officers and several detectives collaborated with federal agents around crimes committed by street gangs. While the captain had requested this collaboration, the task force was overseen by the FBI and operated relatively independently from other district-level activities. As Lieutenant Gill explained, "We're really hands-off with that." However, he noted that the task force had an impact on the district's resources because the four patrol officers assigned to it were no longer available to respond to calls for service. Second, the chief of police had established a citywide unit—the Targeted Neighborhood Unit (TNU)—that consisted of motorcycle officers and squads that could be deployed to saturate high-crime areas. After identifying target areas, TNU officers would conduct proactive patrol in hotspots. The TNU could be sent to neighborhoods throughout the city, and the hotspots in West District made it a likely candidate for periodic deployments. While the work of the TNU fell outside the scope of this project, the unit nevertheless represented an additional source of traffic and pedestrian stops that concentrated in "high-crime" districts.

19. The AVU combines officers assigned to a squad car that took special assignments from the district's captain, those assigned to gang interventions, and those assigned to violent-crime squads, as they conducted similar proactive work. Descriptions and quantifications of personnel are based on a breakdown provided by Lieutenant Gill during the summer of 2015. Staffing in the district evolved over the course of the year, and so this represents a snapshot that captures a general sense of how the district allocated resources.

20. These numbers came from a technical report prepared by an academic as part of an investigation into racially disproportionate stops. The analysis relied on several years of data provided by the police department (Technical Report 05).

21. Articles published by two local television news stations described high rates of gun recovery in River City, compared to other cities (News Article 07; News Article 08).
22. I took these numbers from the 2015 RCPD annual report that drew on FBI Uniform Crime Report data to document changes in incidents and rates of crime over a nine-year period (Document 20).
23. Manning 1978, 8.
24. Bayley 1994. Consistent with other canonical works of policing scholarship, David Bayley explains, "That the police are not able to prevent crime should not come as a big surprise to thoughtful people. It is generally understood that social conditions outside the control of the police, as well as outside the control of the criminal justice system as a whole, determine crime levels in communities" (10).
25. Papachristos, Hureau, and Braga 2013; Papachristos, Wildeman, and Roberto 2015.
26. News Article 06.
27. Technical Report 05.
28. I found this data using the FBI's Crime Data Explorer, which compiles statistics from individual law-enforcement agencies. I searched for arrests reported by the RCPD in 2015 and examined select subcategories. The RCPD reported a total of 18,882 arrests of Black individuals and 5,947 arrests of white individuals in 2015.
29. A survey of eight hundred River City residents conducted by the ACLU reported a correlation between experiences of being stopped and negative views of the police. It found that approximately 45 percent of those who had experienced a stop had negative views and 15 percent had positive views of the police; for those who had not experienced a stop, 27 percent had negative views and 30 percent had positive views (Document 21). A survey conducted by a university research center in collaboration with the Civilian Review Board reported that 38 percent of Black respondents were not very satisfied or not at all satisfied with the police, compared to 17 percent of white respondents (Document 22).
30. The class-action lawsuit filed against the police department is Document 23.
31. This was described in an article published in one of the city's Black-owned newspapers. The article included comments from several Black public figures in the city, in response to the lawsuit alleging racial disparities and unconstitutional practices in the police department's use of stop-and-frisk (News Article 09).
32. This article was published in one of the city's alternative newspapers. It also described the lawsuit, and it identified several groups and initiatives pushing for police reform (News Article 10).
33. Video 03.
34. This article was published in a major national newspaper. It described the lawsuit against the police department and included a statement by the chief of police defending the use of investigatory traffic stops (News Article 11).
35. This article was published in the city's major newspaper. It described lagging response times in most major call categories and highlighted several dramatic

cases of slow police response. It correlated slowing response times to the devotion of additional units to proactive policing, though it noted that crime had declined since the chief's arrival (News Article 12).

CHAPTER 5. POLICING SEGREGATION BOUNDARIES

1. Attention to those who are "out of place" is a common phenomenon that has long been observed in studies of policing; see, for instance, Werthman and Piliavin 1967; Alpert, Macdonald, and Dunham 2005; Carroll and Gonzales 2014; Bell 2020a.
2. *Tennessee v. Garner*, 471 U.S. 1 (1985).
3. Alpert and Smith 1994, 1.
4. Goldstein 1963.
5. Gelman, Fagan, and Kiss 2007; Epp et al. 2014.
6. Kohler-Hausmann 2018, 1167 (emphasis added).
7. Kohler-Hausmann 2018, 1193.
8. Kohler-Hausmann 2018, 1187.
9. Video 02 (see note 26 to chapter 2).
10. Video 02.
11. Alpert et al. 2005.
12. I found this data using the FBI's Crime Data Explorer (see note 28 to chapter 4). The RCPD reported a total of 232 arrests of Black individuals for curfew violations and loitering, compared to 41 arrests of white people; 2,829 arrests of Black people and 932 arrests of white people were reported for disorderly conduct. These data are citywide, so they do not only refer to activities that occurred during the Entertainment Corridor Deployment; but they do demonstrate disparities in quality-of-life offences that officers could be particularly attentive to in the downtown.
13. News Article 06 (see note 14 to chapter 4).
14. Epp et al. (2014) argue that a driver's vehicle is the most visible symbol of the driver's class. They also note that certain car models and makes, for instance, domestic luxury cars like Cadillacs, are culturally associated with Black Americans. Swanton (2010) also describes vehicles as part of "how social differentiation is performed on the road" (447).
15. Santo 2015.
16. I took this statistic from a "neighborhood profile" report prepared by a River City data-analysis firm in collaboration with a citywide youth-serving nonprofit. Neighborhood demographics were compiled based on American Community Survey five-year estimates (Document 24).
17. Brayne 2020.
18. Regoeczi and Kent 2014. For a broader analysis of the relationships between legal monetary sanctions and economic inequalities, see also Harris, Evans, and Beckett 2010; and Harris 2016.
19. I found this statistic in a technical report prepared by two researchers at one of the city's universities. The authors analyzed data from several sources, includ-

ing the state department of transit, the county sheriff, and municipal courts. It focused specifically on trends and consequences of license suspensions for failure to pay forfeitures (Technical Report 06).

20. Bell 2020a, 696.
21. Gordon 2018.
22. Bell 2020b, 918.
23. Kohler-Hausmann 2018, 1172.
24. Kohler-Hausmann 2018, 1223.

CHAPTER 6. POLICING AND THE SOCIAL STRUCTURE OF SEGREGATION

1. Bonilla-Silva 2006.
2. I found this data using the FBI's Crime Data Explorer (see note 28 to chapter 4). The RCPD reported 1,819 arrests of Black people compared to 590 arrests of white people for drug violations.
3. I synthesized this historical description of Riverside from an entry in the online encyclopedia project described in note 4 to chapter 1 (Document 25).
4. Document 25. I took 2010 demographic estimates from StatisticalAtlas.com, a website that aggregates US Census data within a variety of geographic scales, including the neighborhood (Document 26).
5. This article was published in an online newspaper. It described concerns over gentrification and tied these to downtown growth projects. The article included the perspectives of a long-term Black resident of Riverside (News Article 13).
6. An article published in one of the city's alternative newspapers described current concerns about gentrification and referenced Riverside in the 1970s as a classic example of the displacement of longtime residents (News Article 14).
7. Meeting minutes summarized the presentation by the West District captain and several other police personnel. I accessed them through the website of the Riverside Neighborhood Association (Document 27).
8. Kobayashi and Peake 2000; D. Wilson 2007.
9. Massey and Denton 1993; Bonilla-Silva 1997.

CONCLUSION

1. *New York Times* 1970.
2. Williams 2015.
3. Adams and Rameau 2016, 533.
4. Reaves 2015.
5. Logan and Stults 2011.
6. Wilson and Wouters 2003.
7. Public Safety Strategy Group LLC 2015.
8. Clayton 2018.
9. Santana 2013.
10. Brink 2009.
11. Ruch 2019.

12. M. Wilson 2019.
13. Moring 2017.
14. McCarthy 2011.
15. Moring 2017.
16. CensusViewer 2020.
17. Bell 2020a.
18. Herbert 2006; Gascón and Roussell 2019.
19. President's Task Force on 21st Century Policing 2015.
20. Kleinfeld et al. 2017.
21. An article published in the city's major newspaper noted that leaders of a community-based coalition on police reform felt optimistic about the implementation of community-oriented policing policy in River City (News Article 15).
22. Movement for Black Lives 2021a.
23. Rahman and Simonson 2020.
24. Simonson 2016, 1609.
25. Manning 1978; Bayley 1994.
26. Weisburd et al. 2004.
27. Stoughton 2014.
28. These numbers came from city data and represented criminal incidents that occurred during a year-long period that corresponded to the fieldwork (Document 09). It is also important to note that measures of homicides tend to be more accurate than counts of other crime types, which vary in whether they are reported to the police and how they are classified in crime statistics (Lauritsen et al. 2016).
29. Papachristos et al. 2013.
30. Braga et al. 2014.
31. Butts et al. 2015.
32. Vargas 2016.
33. Sampson and Wilson 1995; Krivo and Peterson 1996.
34. Durose and Langton 2013.
35. Though police executives might point to the fact that rapid response to calls has little effect on rates of crime or the apprehension of offenders, it nevertheless plays an important role in citizens' levels of satisfaction during police encounters. Certainly, as previous chapters have illustrated, residents of West District felt strongly about slow police response.
36. Bittner 1990.
37. This was a recommendation from the President's Task Force on 21st Century Policing (2015), which encouraged law enforcement agencies and officers to "embrace a guardian—rather than a warrior—mindset to build trust and legitimacy both within agencies and with the public" (1).
38. White Bird Clinic 2021.
39. Critical Resistance 2021; Philly Stands Up 2021; Generation Five 2021.
40. Movement for Black Lives 2021b.

41. A news article published in the city's major newspaper described several City Council members signing on to explore budget cuts to the police department in response to the protests following the murder of George Floyd. It noted that many stakeholders in the city were calling for divestment from the police budget and investment in housing services, public-health campaigns, and other programs that would address the root causes of crime (News Article 16).
42. An independent newspaper published Mayor Taylor's budget address in full. The address described key aspects of the budget and situated its creation with the fiscal constraints created by the pandemic and by the state's budget formulas (News Article 17).
43. An article published on the website of the state's public radio station described the 2021 budget and explained that, though the police department would lose officers, overall spending on the police would remain nearly the same as the previous year (News Article 18).
44. A local TV channel published an article describing furloughs and other cutbacks necessitated by over $25 million of lost city revenue several months into the COVID-19 pandemic (News Article 19).
45. News Article 18.
46. Brenan 2020.
47. Tankersley 2021.
48. Fulton 2021; VerHelst 2021.
49. Albright 2021.
50. Soss, Fording, and Schram 2011; Headworth 2019; Kurwa 2020; Lara-Millán 2021.
51. Regarding the former, Richard Rothstein (2017) proposes several solutions focused on racial integration: federal subsidies to incentivize home ownership for Black Americans in suburbs that have been racially exclusive, bans on zoning ordinances that limit multifamily housing, requirements for inclusionary zoning, and others. Such policies target the many barriers to residential mobility that were actively constructed to exclude Black people from predominantly white neighborhoods. Other policy interventions aim to redress the institutional exploitation and neglect of Black communities. For instance, the Movement for Black Lives (2021a) demands economic justice through tax codes and job programs that radically redistribute wealth. The platform also calls for divestment from punitive institutions and investments in Black communities that promote education, health, and safety by ensuring that basic needs are met.

METHODS APPENDIX
1. Haraway 1988; Bhavnani 1993; Stoetzler and Yuval-Davis 2002.
2. For an overview of ethnographic work on race, crime, and justice, see see Rios, Carney, and Kelekay 2017.
3. Stuart (2020) offers a thoughtful reflection on these themes in the "Authors Note" of his book *Ballad of the Bullet*.
4. Small 2015.

5. Wacquant 2002.
6. Police departments: e.g., Armenta 2017a; Brayne 2020. Courts: e.g., Van Cleve 2016; Clair 2020. Prisons: e.g., M. Walker 2016.
7. Nader 1972, 284.
8. Nader 1972, 284.
9. Cousin, Khan, and Mears (2018) argue for greater attention to diversity within "elites" and analysis of how social structures act on them.
10. Vitus 2008.
11. Haraway 1988, 583.
12. Duneier 1999.
13. Conti and O'Neil 2007, 67.
14. Priyadharshini 2003.

REFERENCES

Adams, M. and Max Rameau. 2016. "Black Community Control over Police." *Wisconsin Law Review* 3:515–539.

Agee, Christopher Lowen. 2020. "Crisis and Redemption: The History of American Police Reform since World War II." *Journal of Urban History* 46(5): 951–960.

Albright, Amanda. 2021. "American Cities See Their Luck Turn with a Biden Administration." *Bloomberg News*, January 15.

Alexander, Michelle. 2010. *The New Jim Crow: Mass Incarceration in the Age of Colorblindness*. New York: New Press.

Alpert, Geoffrey, John Macdonald, and Roger Dunham. 2005. "Police Suspicion and Discretionary Decision Making during Citizen Stops." *Criminology* 43(2): 407–434.

Alpert, Geoffrey and William Smith. 1994. "Developing Police Policy: An Evaluation of the Control Principle." *American Journal of Police* 13(2): 1–20.

Armenta, Amada. 2017a. *Protect, Serve, and Deport: The Rise of Policing as Immigration Enforcement*. Berkeley: University of California Press.

Armenta, Amada. 2017b. "Racializing Crimmigration: Structural Racism, Colorblindness, and the Institutional Production of Immigrant Criminality." *Sociology of Race and Ethnicity* 3(1): 82–95.

Avila, Eric and Mark Rose. 2009. "Race, Culture, Politics, and Urban Renewal: An Introduction." *Journal of Urban History* 35(3): 335–347.

Bass, Sandra. 2001. "Policing Space, Policing Race: Social Control Imperatives and Police Discretionary Decisions." *Social Justice* 28(1): 156–176.

Bayley, David. 1994. *Police for the Future*. New York: Oxford University Press.

Beck, Brenden and Adam Goldstein. 2018. "Governing through Police? Housing Market Reliance, Welfare Retrenchment, and Police Budgeting in an Era of Declining Crime." *Social Forces* 96(3): 1183–1210.

Beckett, Katherine and Steve Herbert. 2008. "Dealing with Disorder: Social Control in the Post-Industrial City." *Theoretical Criminology* 12(1): 5–30.

Beckett, Katherine and Steve Herbert. 2009. *Banished: The New Social Control in Urban America*. Oxford: Oxford University Press.

Beckett, Katherine, Kris Nyrop, and Lori Pfingst, and Melissa Bowen. 2005. "Drug Use, Drug Possession Arrests, and the Question of Race: Lessons from Seattle." *Social Problems* 52(3): 419–441.

Beckett, Katherine and Theodore Sasson. 2004. *The Politics of Injustice: Crime and Punishment in America*. Thousand Oaks, CA: Sage.

Bell, Monica. 2017. "Police Reform and the Dismantling of Legal Estrangement." *Yale Law Journal* 126(7): 2054–2150.

Bell, Monica. 2020a. "Anti-Segregation Policing." *New York University Law Review* 95:650–765.

Bell, Monica. 2020b. "Located Institutions: Neighborhood Frames, Residential Preferences, and the Case of Policing." *American Journal of Sociology* 125(4): 917–973.

Bhavnani, Kum-Kum. 1993. "Tracing the Contours: Feminist Research and Feminist Objectivity." *Women's Studies International Forum* 16(2): 95–104.

Bittner, Egon. 1990. *Aspects of Police Work.* Boston: Northeastern University Press.

Black Lives Matter. 2020. "Herstory." Retrieved Aug. 3, 2020 (https://Blacklivesmatter.com).

Bonilla-Silva, Eduardo. 1997. "Rethinking Racism: Toward a Structural Interpretation." *American Sociological Review* 62(3): 465–480.

Bonilla-Silva, Eduardo. 2006. *Racism without Racists: Color-Blind Racism and the Persistence of Racial Inequality in the United States, Second Edition.* Lanham, MD: Rowman and Littlefield.

Braga, Anthony, Andrew Papachristos, and David Hureau. 2014. "The Effects of Hot Spots Policing on Crime: An Updated Systemic Review and Meta-Analysis." *Justice Quarterly* 31(4): 633–663.

Brayne, Sarah. 2017. "Big Data Surveillance: The Case of Policing." *American Sociological Review* 82(5): 977–1008.

Brayne, Sarah. 2020. *Predict and Surveil: Data, Discretion, and the Future of Policing.* New York: Oxford University Press.

Brenan, Megan. 2020. "New High 54% Want Government to Solve More Problems in the U.S." *Gallup News*, September 28 (https://news.gallup.com).

Brink, Benjamin. 2009. "Police Precinct Consolidation Worries Portland Residents." *Portland Oregonian*, April 21.

Bruce, Christopher. 2009. "Districting and Resource Allocation: A Question of Balance." *Geography & Public Safety* 1(4): 1–3.

Brunson, Rod. 2007. "'Police Don't Like Black People': African-American Young Men's Accumulated Police Experiences." *Criminology & Public Policy* 6(1): 71–101.

Brunson, Rod and Ronald Weitzer. 2009. "Police Relations with Black and White Youths in Different Urban Neighborhoods." *Urban Affairs Review* 44(6): 858–885.

Buchanan, Larry, Quoctrung Bui, and Jagula Patel. 2020. "Black Lives Matter May be the Largest Movement in U.S. History." *New York Times*, July 3.

Bullock, Charles. 2021. *Redistricting: The Most Political Activity in America.* 2nd ed. Lanham, MD: Rowman and Littlefield.

Bureau of Justice Assistance. 1994. *Understanding Community Policing: A Framework for Action.* Washington, DC: Bureau of Justice Assistance.

Butts, Jeffrey, Caterina Gouvis Roman, Lindsay Bostwick, and Jeremy Porter. 2015. "Cure Violence: A Public Health Model to Reduce Gun Violence." *Annual Review of Public Health* 36:39–53.

Canon, David. 1999. *Race, Redistricting, and Representation: The Unintended Consequences of Black Majority Districts*. Chicago: University of Chicago Press.

Caraley, Demetrios. 1992. "Washington Abandons the Cities." *Political Science Quarterly* 107(1): 1–30.

Carroll, Leo and M. Lilliana Gonzalez. 2014. "Out of Place: Racial Stereotypes and the Ecology of Frisks and Searches Following Traffic Stops." *Journal of Research in Crime and Delinquency* 51(5): 559–584.

Castells, Manuel. 1996. *The Information Age: Economy, Society, and Culture*. Vol. 1. Oxford, UK: Blackwell.

CensusViewer. "Elkhorn, Nebraska Population: Census 2010 and 2000 Interactive Map, Demographics, Statistics, Quick Facts." Retrieved August 17, 2020 (http://censusviewer.com).

Charles, Camille Zubrinsky. 2003. "The Dynamics of Racial Residential Segregation." *Annual Review of Sociology* 29:167–207.

Clair, Matthew. 2020. *Privilege and Punishment: How Race and Class Matter in Criminal Court*. Princeton, NJ: Princeton University Press.

Clark, Terry. 2004. *The City as Entertainment Machine*. Oxford, UK: Elsevier.

Clayton, Tracy. 2018. "Walking the Beat in the CID and Upcoming Boundary Changes." *SPD Blotter* (Seattle Police Department), January 18.

Cole, David. 1999. *No Equal Justice: Race and Class in the American Criminal Justice System*. New York: New Press.

Collier, David. 2011. "Understanding Process Tracing." *Political Science and Politics* 44(4): 823–830.

Conti, Joseph and Moira O'Neil. 2007. "Studying Power: Qualitative Methods and the Global Elite." *Qualitative Research* 7(1): 63–82.

Cordner, Gary. 2010. *Reducing Fear of Crime: Strategies for Police*. Washington, DC: US Department of Justice, Office of Community Oriented Policing Services.

Cordner, Gary. 2014. "Community Policing." Pp. 148–171 in *The Oxford Handbook of Police and Policing*, edited by M. Reisig and R. Kane. Oxford: Oxford University Press.

Cousin, Bruno, Shamus Khan, and Ashley Mears. 2018. "Theoretical and Methodological Pathways for Research on Elites." *Socio-Economic Review* 16(2): 225–249.

Critical Resistance. 2021. "Addressing Harm, Accountability, and Healing." Accessed May 25, 2021 (http://criticalresistance.org).

Curtin, Kevin, Karen Hayslett-McCall, and Fang Qiu. 2010. "Determining Optimal Police Patrol Areas with Maximal Covering and Backup Covering Location Models." *Networks and Spatial Economics* 10(1): 125–145.

D'Amico, Steven, Shoou-Jiun Wang, Rajan Batta, Christopher Rump. 2002. "A Simulated Annealing Approach to Police District Design." *Computer & Operations Research* 29:667–684.

Delaney, David. 2002. "The Space That Race Makes." *Professional Geographer* 54(1): 6–14.

Desmond, Matthew, Andrew Papachristos, and David Kirk. 2016. "Police Violence and Citizen Crime Reporting in the Black Community." *American Sociological Review* 81(5): 857–876.

Donald, Betsy, Amy Glasmeier, Mia Gray, and Linda Lobao. 2014. "Austerity in the City: Economic Crisis and Urban Service Decline?" *Cambridge Journal of Regions, Economy and Society* 7:3–15.

Drake, St. Clair and Horace Cayton. 1945. *Black Metropolis: A Study of Negro Life in a Northern City*. Chicago: University of Chicago Press.

Duneier, Mitchell. 1999. *Sidewalk*. New York: Macmillan.

Durose, Matthew and Lynn Langton. 2013. *Requests for Police Assistance, 2011*. Washington, DC: Bureau of Justice Statistics.

Emirbayer, Mustafa. 1997. "Manifesto for a Relational Sociology." *American Journal of Sociology* 103(2): 281–317.

Epp, Charles, Steven Maynard-Moody, and Donald Haider-Markel. 2014. *Pulled Over: How Police Stops Define Race and Citizenship*. Chicago: University of Chicago Press.

Ericson, Richard. 1982. *Reproducing Order: A Study of Police Patrol Work*. Toronto: University of Toronto Press.

Fagan, Jeffrey, Anthony Braga, Rod Brunson, and April Pattavina. 2016. "Stops and Stares: Street Stops, Surveillance, and Race in the New Policing." *Fordham Urban Law Journal* 43(3): 539–614.

Fagan, Jeffrey and Garth Davies. 2000. "Street Stops and Broken Windows: Terry, Race, and Disorder in New York City." *Fordham Urban Law Journal* 28:457–504.

Fagan, Jeffrey and Amanda Geller. 2015. "Following the Script: Narratives of Suspicion in *Terry* Stops in Street Policing." *University of Chicago Law Review* 82(1): 51–88.

Fainstein, Susan and Norman Fainstein. 1989. "The Ambivalent State: Economic Development Policy in the US Federal System under the Reagan Administration." *Urban Affairs Quarterly* 25(1): 41–62.

Fields, Barbara. 1990. "Slavery, Race and Ideology in the United States of America." *New Left Review* 181(1):95–118.

Florida, Richard. 2005. *Cities and the Creative Class*. New York: Routledge.

Frankenberg, Erica. 2009. "Splintering School Districts: Understanding the Link between Segregation and Fragmentation." *Law & Social Inquiry* 34(4): 869–909.

Fulton, William. 2021. "Here's How the Biden Administration Will Be a Boon for American Cities." *Urban Edge*, January 21 (https://kinder.rice.edu).

Fyfe, Nicholas. 1991. "The Police, Space and Society: The Geography of Policing." *Progress in Human Geography* 15(3): 249–267.

Garland, David. 2001. *The Culture of Control: Crime and Social Order in Contemporary Society*. Chicago: University of Chicago Press.

Gascón, Luis Daniel and Aaron Roussell. 2019. *The Limits of Community Policing: Civilian Power and Police Accountability in Black and Brown Los Angeles*. New York: New York University Press.

Gelman, Andrew, Jeffrey Fagan, and Alex Kiss. 2007. "An Analysis of the New York City Police Department's 'Stop-and-Frisk' Policy in the Context of Claims of Racial Bias." *Journal of the American Statistical Association* 102(479): 813–823.

Generation Five. 2021. "Who We Are." Accessed May 25, 2021 (http://generationfive.org).

Gilmore, Ruth Wilson. 2007. *Golden Gulag: Prisons, Surplus, Crisis, and Opposition in Globalizing California*. Berkeley: University of California Press.

Glaeser, Edward and Joshua Gottlieb. 2006. "Urban Resurgence and the Consumer city." *Urban Studies* 43(8): 1275–1299.

Glenn, Evelyn Nakano. 2015. "Settler Colonialism as Structure: A Framework for Comparative Studies of U.S. Race and Gender Formation." *Sociology of Race and Ethnicity* 1(1): 52–72.

Go, Julian. 2020. "The Imperial Origins of American Policing: Militarization and Imperial Feedback in the Early 20th Century." *American Journal of Sociology* 125(5): 1193–1254.

Goldstein, Herman. 1963. "Police Discretion: The Ideal versus the Real." *Public Administration Review* 23(3): 140–148.

Gordon, Daanika. 2018. "Daily Mobility in the Black-White Segregated City: Linking Material Realities and Repertoires of Meaning." *Sociological Perspectives* 61(4): 661–680.

Gotham, Kevin Fox. 2000. "Urban Space, Restrictive Covenants and the Origins of Racial Residential Segregation in a US City, 1900–50." *International Journal of Urban and Regional Research* 24(3): 616–633.

Greene, Jack. 2000. "Community Policing in America: Changing the Nature, Structure, and Function of the Police." Pp. 299–370 in *Criminal Justice 2000*, edited by J. Horney. Washington, DC: US Department of Justice, National Institute of Justice.

Greene, Jack and William Pelfrey. 1997. "Shifting the Balance of Power between Police and Community: Responsibility for Crime Control." Pp. 393–423 in *Critical Issues in Policing: Contemporary Readings*, edited by R. Dunham and G. Alpert. Prospect Heights, IL: Waveland.

Hadden, Sally. 2003. *Slave Patrols: Law and Violence in Virginia and the Carolinas*. Cambridge, MA: Harvard University Press.

Hall, Stuart. 1992. "The West and the Rest: Discourse and Power." Pp. 275–332 in *Formations of Modernity*, edited by B. Gieben and S. Hall. Cambridge, UK: Polity.

Haraway, Donna. 1988. "Situated Knowledges: The Science Question in Feminism and the Privilege of Partial Perspective." *Feminist Studies* 14(3): 575–599.

Harris, Alexes. 2016. *A Pound of Flesh: Monetary Sanctions as Punishment for the Poor*. New York: Russell Sage Foundation.

Harris, Alexes, Heather Evans, and Katherine Beckett. 2010. "Drawing Blood from Stones: Legal Debt and Social Inequality in the Contemporary United States." *American Journal of Sociology* 115(6): 1753–1799.

Harvey, David. 1989. "From Managerialism to Entrepreneurialism: The Transformation of Urban Governance in Late Capitalism." *Geografiskia Annaler: Series B, Human Geography* 71(1): 3–17.

Hashimoto, Yui. 2021. "Racing the Creative Class: Diversity, Racialized Discourses of Work, and Colorblind Redevelopment." *Urban Geography* 42(4):528–550.

Hassell, Kimberly. 2006. *Police Organizational Cultures and Patrol Practices*. New York: LFB.

Headworth, Spencer. 2019. "Getting to Know You: Welfare Fraud Investigation and the Appropriation of Social Ties." *American Sociological Review* 84(1): 171–196.

Herbert, Steve. 1997a. *Policing Space: Territoriality and the Los Angeles Police Department*. Minneapolis: University of Minnesota Press.

Herbert, Steve. 1997b. "Territoriality and the Police." *The Professional Geographer* 49(1): 86–94.

Herbert, Steve. 2006. *Citizens, Cops, and Power: Recognizing the Limits of Community*. Chicago: University of Chicago Press.

Herbert, Steve and Elizabeth Brown. 2006. "Conceptions of Space and Crime in the Punitive Neoliberal City." *Antipode* 38(4): 755–777.

High, Steven. 2003. *Industrial Sunset: The Making of North America's Rust Belt, 1969–1984*. Toronto: University of Toronto Press.

Huq, Aziz. 2017. "The Consequences of Disparate Policing: Evaluating Stop and Frisk as a Modality of Urban Policing." *Minnesota Law Review* 101:2397–2480.

Inwood, Joshua and Robert Yarbrough. 2010. "Racialized Places, Racialized Bodies: The Impact of Racialization on Individual and Place Identities." *GeoJournal* 75(3): 299–301.

Irwin, Darren. 2011. "The Showdown with Shrinking Budgets: Police Departments in Economic Downturns." Pp. 195–212 in *Economic Crisis and Crime* (Sociology of Crime, Law and Deviance 16), edited by M. Deflem. Bingley, UK: Emerald Group.

Jones-Brown, Delores. 2007. "Forever the Symbolic Assailant: The More Things Change, the More They Remain the Same." *Criminology and Public Policy* 6(1): 103–122.

Justice, Benjamin and Tracey Meares. 2014. "How the Criminal Justice System Educates Citizens." *Annals of the American Academy of Political and Social Science* 651(1): 159–177.

Kahn, Kimberley Barsamian and Karin Martin. 2016. "Policing and Race: Disparate Treatment, Perceptions, and Policy Responses." *Social Issues and Policy Review* 10(1): 82–121.

Kelling, George and Mark Moore. 1988. "The Evolving Strategy of Policing." *Perspectives on Policing* 4:1–16.

Kelling, George, Tony Pate, Duane Dieckman, and Charles Brown. 1974. *The Kansas City Preventive Patrol Experiment: A Summary Report*. Washington, DC: Police Foundation.

Kleinfeld, Joshua, Laura I. Appleman, Richard A. Bierschbach, Kenworthey Bilz, Josh Bowers, John Braithwaite, Robert P. Burns, R. A. Duff, Albert W. Dzur, Thomas F. Geraghty, Adriaan Lanni, Marah Stith McLeod, Janice Nadler, Anthony O'Rourke, Paul H. Robinson, Jonathan Simon, Jocelyn Simonson, Tom R. Tyler, and Ekow N. Yankah. 2017. "White Paper of Democratic Criminal Justice." *Northwestern University Law Review* 111:1693–1706.

Klinger, David. 1997. "Negotiating Order in Patrol Work: An Ecological Theory of Police Response to Deviance." *Criminology* 35(2): 277–306.

Klinger, David. 2004. "Environment and Organization: Reviving a Perspective on the Police." *Annals of the American Academy of Political and Social Science* 593:119–136.

Kobayashi, Audrey and Linda Peake. 2000. "Racism out of Place: Thoughts on Whiteness and Antiracist Geography in the New Millennium." *Annals of the Association of American Geographers* 90(2): 392–403.

Kochel, Tammy Rinehart. 2019. "Explaining Racial Differences in Ferguson's Impact on Local Residents' Trust and Perceived Legitimacy: Policy Implications for Police." *Criminal Justice Policy Review* 30(3): 374–405.

Kohler-Hausmann, Issa. 2018. "Eddie Murphy and the Dangers of Counterfactual Causal Thinking about Detecting Racial Discrimination." *Northwestern University Law Review* 113(5): 1163–1228.

Koper, Christopher, Cynthia Lum, Xiaoyun Wu, and Noah Fritz. 2020. "Proactive Policing in the United States: A National Survey." *Policing: An International Journal* 43(5): 861–876.

Krivo, Lauren and Ruth Peterson. 1996. "Extremely Disadvantaged Neighborhoods and Urban Crime." *Social Forces* 75(2): 619–648.

Kurwa, Rahim. 2020. "Opposing and Policing Racial Integration: Evidence from the Housing Choice Voucher Program." *Du Bois Review*, October 30 (first view), 1–25.

Lamont, Michèle and Virág Molnár. 2002. "The Study of Boundaries in the Social Sciences." *Annual Review of Sociology* 28(1): 167–195.

Laniyonu, Ayobami. 2018. "Coffee Shops and Street Stops: Policing Practices in Gentrifying Neighborhoods." *Urban Affairs Review* 54(4): 898–930.

Lara-Millán, Armando. 2021. *Redistributing the Poor: Jails, Hospitals, and the Crisis of Law and Fiscal Austerity*. New York: Oxford University Press.

Lauritsen, Janet, Maribeth Rezey, and Karen Heimer. 2016. "When Choice of Data Matters: Analyses of US Crime Trends, 1973–2012." *Journal of Quantitative Criminology* 32(3): 335–355.

Lefebvre, Henri. 1991. *The Production of Space*. Oxford, UK: Blackwell.

Lever, W. F. 2001. "The Post-Fordist City." Pp. 273–283 in *Handbook of Urban Studies*, edited by R. Paddison. London: Sage.

Levine, Marc. 1987. "Downtown Redevelopment as an Urban Growth Strategy: A Critical Appraisal of the Baltimore Renaissance." *Journal of Urban Affairs* 9(2): 103–123.

Liberatore, Federico, Miguel Camacho-Collados, and Begoña Vitoriano. 2020. "Police Districting Problem: Literature Review and Annotated Bibliography." *Optimal Districting and Territory Design* 284:9–29.

Lipsitz, George. 2007. "The Racialization of Space and the Spatialization of Race." *Landscape Journal* 26:10–23.

Logan, John and Harvey Molotch. 2007. *Urban Fortunes: The Political Economy of Place*. Berkeley: University of California Press.

Logan, John and Brian Stults. 2011. "The Persistence of Segregation in the Metropolis: New Findings from the 2010 Census." Census Brief prepared for Project US 2020. www.s4.brown.edu.

Lynch, Mona, Marisa Omori, Aaron Roussell, and Matthew Valasik. 2013. "Policing the 'Progressive' City: The Racialized Geography of Drug Law Enforcement." *Theoretical Criminology* 17(3): 335–357.

MacLeod, Gordon. 2011. "From Urban Entrepreneurialism to a 'Revanchist City'? On the Spatial Injustices of Glasgow's Renaissance." *Antipode* 34(3): 602–624.

Manning, Peter. 1978. "The Police: Mandate, Strategies, and Appearances." Pp. 7–31 in *Policing: A View from the Street*, edited by P. Manning and J. Van Maanen. New York: Random House.

Manza, Jeff and Christopher Uggen. 2008. *Locked Out: Felon Disenfranchisement and American Democracy*. Oxford: Oxford University Press.

Martin, Susan Ehrlich. 1999. "Police Force or Police Service? Gender and Emotional Labor." *Annals of the American Academy of Political and Social Science* 561(1): 111–126.

Massey, Douglas and Nancy Denton. 1993. *American Apartheid: Segregation and the Making of the Underclass*. Cambridge, MA: Harvard University Press.

Mastrofski, Stephen and James Willis. 2010. "Police Organization Continuity and Change: Into the Twenty-First Century." *Crime and Justice* 39(1): 55–144.

McCarthy, Brendan. 2011. "New Orleans Police Adjust Boundaries of 8 Patrol Districts." *New Orleans Times-Picayune*, December 14.

McQuarrie, Michael and Nicole Marwell. 2009. "The Missing Organizational Dimension in Urban Sociology." *City & Community* 8(3): 247–268.

Meehan, Albert and Michael Ponder. 2002. "Race and Place: The Ecology of Racial Profiling of African American Motorists." *Justice Quarterly* 19(3): 399–430.

Melamed, Jodi. 2011. *Represent and Destroy: Rationalizing Violence in the New Racial Capitalism*. Minneapolis: University of Minnesota Press.

Meyer, John and Brian Rowan. 1977. "Institutionalized Organizations: Formal Structure as Myth and Ceremony." *American Journal of Sociology* 83(2): 340–363.

Meyer, Stephen Grant. 2000. *As Long as They Don't Move Next Door: Segregation and Racial Conflict in American Neighborhoods*. Lanham, MD: Rowman and Littlefield.

Miller, Kirk. 2013. "The Institutionalization of Racial Profiling Policy: An Examination of Antiprofiling Policy Adoption among Large Law Enforcement Agencies." *Crime & Delinquency* 59(1): 32–58.

Miller, Reuben Jonathan. 2020. *Halfway Home: Race, Punishment, and the Afterlife of Mass Incarceration*. Boston: Little, Brown and Company.

Mills, Charles. 2014. *The Racial Contract*. Ithaca, NY: Cornell University Press.

Moore, Mark and Margaret Poethig. 1999. "The Police as an Agency of Municipal Government: Implications for Measuring Police Effectiveness." Pp. 151–168 in *Measuring What Matters: Proceedings from the Policing Research Institute Meetings*, edited by R. H. Langworthy. Washington, DC: National Institute of Justice, US Department of Justice.

Moring, Roseann. 2017. "Omaha's 5th Police Precinct Expected to Open by Late 2019 in Elkhorn: Department Plans to Add Dozens of Officers." *Omaha (NE) World-Herald*, October 16.

Movement for Black Lives. 2021a. "Community Control." Retrieved May 25, 2021 (https://m4bl.org).

Movement for Black Lives. 2021b. "The Time Has Come to Defund the Police." Retrieved May 25, 2021 (http://m4bl.org).

Muhammad, Khalil Gibran. 2010. *The Condemnation of Blackness: Race, Crime, and the Making of Modern Urban America*. Cambridge, MA: Harvard University Press.

Nader, Laura. 1972. "Up the Anthropologist—Perspectives Gained from Studying Up." Pp. 284–311 in *Reinventing Anthropology*, edited by D. Hymes. New York: Pantheon.

National Academies of Sciences, Engineering, and Medicine. 2018. *Proactive Policing: Effects on Crime and Communities*. Washington, DC: National Academies Press.

New York Times. 1970. "Berkeley to Vote on Curb of Police." August 16, 46.

Novak, Kenneth and Mitchell Chamlin. 2012. "Racial Threat, Suspicion, and Police Behavior: The Impact of Race and Place in Traffic Enforcement." *Crime & Delinquency* 58(2): 275–300.

Okonta, Patricia. 2017. "Race-Based Political Exclusion and Social Subjugation: Racial Gerrymandering as a Badge of Slavery." *Columbia Human Rights Law Review* 49(2): 254–296.

Omi, Michael and Howard Winant. 1994. *Racial Formation in the United States: From the 1960s to the 1990s*. New York: Routledge.

Owens, Ann. 2018. "Income Segregation between School Districts and Inequality in Students' Achievement." *Sociology of Education* 91(1): 1–27.

Owusu-Bempah, Akwasi. 2017. "Race and Policing in Historical Context: Dehumanization and the Policing of Black People in the 21st Century." *Theoretical Criminology* 21(1): 23–34.

Pager, Devah. 2003. "The Mark of a Criminal Record." *American Journal of Sociology* 108(5): 937–975.

Papachristos, Andrew, David Hureau, and Anthony Braga. 2013. "The Corner and the Crew: The Influence of Geography and Social Networks on Gang Violence." *American Sociological Review* 78(3): 417–447.

Papachristos, Andrew, Christopher Wildeman, and Elizabeth Roberto. 2015. "Tragic, but Not Random: The Social Contagion of Nonfatal Gunshot Injuries." *Social Science & Medicine* 125:139–150.

Pattillo, Mary, Bruce Western, and David Weiman, eds. 2004. *Imprisoning America: The Social Effects of Mass Incarceration*. New York: Russell Sage Foundation.

Peck, Jamie. 2005. "Struggling with the Creative Class." *International Journal of Urban and Regional Research* 29(4): 740–770.

Peck, Jamie. 2012. "Austerity Urbanism: American Cities under Extreme Economy." *City* 16(6): 626–655.

Peck, Jamie, Nik Theodore, and Neil Brenner. 2009. "Neoliberal Urbanism: Models, Moments, Mutations." *SAIS Review of International Affairs* 29(1): 49–66.

Perry, Barbara. 2009. "Impacts of Disparate Policing in Indian Country." *Policing & Society* 19(3): 263–281.

Pettit, Becky and Bruce Western. 2004. "Mass Imprisonment and the Life Course: Race and Class Inequality in U.S. Incarceration." *American Sociological Review* 69(2): 151–169.

Philly Stands Up. 2021. "Philly Stands Up Is . . ." Accessed May 25, 2021 (http://phillystandsup.org).

President's Task Force on 21st Century Policing. 2015. *Final Report of the President's Task Force on 21st Century Policing.* Washington, DC: Office of Community Oriented Policing Services.

Priyadharshini, Esther. 2003. "Coming Unstuck: Thinking Otherwise about 'Studying Up.'" *Anthropology & Education Quarterly* 34(4): 420–437.

Prowse, Gwen, Vesla Weaver, and Tracey Meares. 2020. "The State from Below: Distorted Responsiveness in Policed Communities." *Urban Affairs Review* 56(5): 1423–1471.

Public Safety Strategy Group LLC. 2015. *District Station Boundary Analysis Report.* www.publicsafetystrategies.com.

Quillian, Lincoln and Devah Pager. 2001. "Black Neighborhoods, Higher Crime? The Role of Racial Stereotypes in Evaluations of Neighborhood Crime." *American Journal of Sociology* 107(3): 717–767.

Rahman, Sabeel and Jocelyn Simonson. 2020. "The Institutional Design of Community Control." *California Law Review* 108(3): 679–744.

Ray, Victor. 2019. "A Theory of Racialized Organizations." *American Sociological Review* 84(1): 26–53.

Reardon, Sean and Kendra Bischoff. 2011. "Income Inequality and Income Segregation." *American Journal of Sociology* 116(4): 1092–1153.

Reaves, Brian. 2015. *Local Police Departments, 2013: Personnel, Policies, and Practices.* Washington, DC: Bureau of Justice Statistics.

Regoeczi, Wendy and Stephanie Kent. 2014. "Race, Poverty, and the Traffic Ticket Cycle: Exploring the Situational Context of the Application of Police Discretion." *Policing: An International Journal of Strategies & Management* 37(1): 190–205.

Reskin, Barbara. 2012. "The Race Discrimination System." *Annual Review of Sociology* 38:17–35.

Rhode, Deborah. 2004. *Access to Justice.* New York: Oxford University Press.

Rios, Victor. 2011. *Punished: Policing the Lives of Black and Latino Boys.* New York: New York University Press.

Rios, Victor, Nikita Carney, and Jasmine Kelekay. 2017. "Ethnographies of Race, Crime, and Justice: Toward a Sociological Double-Consciousness." *Annual Review of Sociology* 43:493–513.

Rios, Victor, Greg Prieto, and Jonathan Ibarra. 2020. "Mano Suave–Mano Dura: Legitimacy Policing and Latino Stop-and-Frisk." *American Sociological Review* 85(1): 58–75.

Rose, Dina and Todd Clear. 1998. "Incarceration, Social Capital, and Crime: Implications for Social Disorganization Theory." *Criminology* 36(3): 441–480.

Rothe, Dawn and David Kauzlarich. 2016. *Crimes of the Powerful: An Introduction.* London: Routledge.

Rothstein, Richard. 2017. *The Color of Law: A Forgotten History of How Our Government Segregated America*. New York: Liveright.

Ruch, John. 2019. "Buckhead's Police Zone to Shrink, Boosting Neighborhood Patrols, on March 17." *Buckhead (GA) Reporter*, February 28.

Russell-Brown, Katheryn. 2009. *The Color of Crime: Racial Hoaxes, White Fear, Black Protectionism, Police Harassment, and Other Macroaggressions*. 2nd ed. New York: New York University Press.

Saiger, Aaron. 2010. "The School District Boundary Problem." *Urban Lawyer* 42(3): 495–548.

Samara, Tony Roshan. 2010. "Order and Security in the City: Producing Race and Policing in Neoliberal Spaces in South Africa." *Ethnic and Racial Studies* 33(4): 637–655.

Sampson, Robert and Stephen Raudenbush. 2004. "Seeing Disorder: Neighborhood Stigma and the Social Construction of 'Broken Windows.'" *Social Psychology Quarterly* 67(4): 319–342.

Sampson, Robert and William Julius Wilson. 1995. "Toward a Theory of Race, Crime, and Urban Inequality." Pp. 37–54 in *Crime and Inequality*, edited by J. Hagan and R. Peterson. Stanford, CA: Stanford University Press.

Santana, Deanna J. 2013. *City Administrator's Weekly Report*. City of Oakland. June 7. www.oaklandnet.com.

Santo, Alysia. 2015. "When 'Broken Windows' Meets Tinted Windows." The Marshall Project, August 17. www.themarshallproject.org.

Sassen, Saskia. 2006. *Cities in a World Economy*. Chicago: University of Chicago Press.

Schmidt, Deanna. 2011. "Urban Triage: Saving the Savable Neighborhoods in Milwaukee." *Planning Perspectives* 26(4): 569–589.

Scott, Michael. 2000. *Problem-Oriented Policing: Reflections on the First 20 Years*. Washington, DC: US Department of Justice, Office of Community Oriented Policing Services.

Sentencing Project. 2020. *Trends in U.S. Corrections*. Washington, DC: Sentencing Project. www.sentencingproject.org.

Sharp, Elaine. 2014. "Politics, Economics, and Urban Policing: The Postindustrial City Thesis and Rival Explanations of Heightened Order Maintenance Policing." *Urban Affairs Review* 50(3): 340–365.

Sierra-Arévalo, Michael. 2021. "American Policing and the Danger Imperative." *Law & Society Review* 55(1):70–103.

Simon, Jonathan. 2007. *Governing through Crime: How the War on Crime Transformed American Democracy*. New York: Oxford University Press.

Simonson, Jocelyn. 2016. "Democratizing Criminal Justice through Contestation and Resistance." *Northwestern University Law Review* 111:1609–1624.

Skogan, Wesley. 2006. "Advocate: The Promise of Community Policing." Pp. 27–43 in *Police Innovation: Contrasting Perspectives*, edited by D. Weisburd and A. Braga. Cambridge: Cambridge University Press.

Skogan, Wesley and Susan Hartnett. 1997. *Community Policing: Chicago Style*. New York: Oxford University Press.

Skolnick, Jerome. 1966. *Justice without Trial: Law Enforcement in Democratic Society*. New York: Wiley.

Small, Mario. 2015. "De-exoticizing Ghetto Poverty: On the Ethics of Representation in Urban Ethnography." *City & Community* 14(4): 352–358.

Smith, Douglas. 1986. "The Neighborhood Context of Police Behavior." *Crime and Justice* 8:313–341.

Song, John Huey-Long. 1992. "Attitudes of Chinese Immigrants and Vietnamese Refugees toward Law Enforcement in the United States." *Justice Quarterly* 9(4): 703–719.

Soss, Joe, Richard Fording, and Sanford Schram. 2011. *Disciplining the Poor: Neoliberal Paternalism and the Persistent Power of Race*. Chicago: University of Chicago Press.

Soss, Joe and Vesla Weaver. 2017. "Police Are Our Government: Politics, Political Science, and the Policing of Race-Class Subjugated Communities." *Annual Review of Political Science* 20:565–591.

Spelman, William and Dale Brown. 1984. *Calling the Police: Citizen Reporting of Serious Crime*. Washington, DC: US Department of Justice, National Institute of Justice.

Stoetzler, Marcel and Nira Yuval-Davis. 2002. "Standpoint Theory, Situated Knowledge and the Situated Imagination." *Feminist Theory* 3(3): 315–333.

Stoughton, Seth. 2014. "Law Enforcement's Warrior Problem." *Harvard Law Review Forum* 128:225–234.

Stuart, Forrest. 2016. *Down, Out, and Under Arrest: Policing and Everyday Life in Skid Row*. Chicago: University of Chicago Press.

Stuart, Forrest. 2020. *Ballad of the Bullet: Gangs, Drill Music, and the Power of Online Infamy*. Princeton, NJ: Princeton University Press.

Stucky, Thomas. 2005. "Local Politics and Police Strength." *Justice Quarterly* 22(2): 139–169.

Sunshine, Jason and Tom Tyler. 2003. "The Role of Procedural Justice and Legitimacy in Shaping Public Support for Policing." *Law & Society Review* 37(3): 513–548.

Sutherland, Edwin. 1983. *White Collar Crime: The Uncut Version*. New Haven, CT: Yale University Press.

Swanton, Dan. 2010. "Flesh, Metal, Road: Tracing the Machinic Geographies of Race." *Environment and Planning D: Society and Space* 28:447–466.

Tankersley, Jim. 2021. "Biden, Calling for Big Government, Bets on a Nation Tested by Crisis." *New York Times*, April 28.

Tansey, Oisín. 2007. "Process Tracing and Elite Interviewing: A Case for Non-probability Sampling." *Political Science & Politics* 40(4): 765–772.

Terrill, William and Michael Reisig. 2003. "Neighborhood Context and Police Use of Force." *Journal of Research in Crime and Delinquency* 40(3): 291–321.

Tighe, Rosie and Joanna Ganning. 2015. "The Divergent City: Unequal and Uneven Development in St. Louis." *Urban Geography* 36(5): 651–673.

Tonry, Michael. 1994. "Racial Politics, Racial Disparities, and the War on Crime." *Crime & Delinquency* 40(4): 475–494.

Tonry, Michael. 1995. *Malign Neglect: Race, Crime, and Punishment in America*. Oxford: Oxford University Press.

Tyler, Tom, Jeffrey Fagan, and Amanda Geller. 2014. "Street Stops and Police Legitimacy: Teachable Moments in Young Urban Men's Legal Socialization." *Journal of Empirical Legal Studies* 11(4): 751–785.

US Department of Justice. 2009. *Community Policing Defined*. Washington, DC: Office of Community Oriented Policing Services.

US Department of Justice. 2015. *Investigation of the Ferguson Police Department*. Washington, DC: US Department of Justice Civil Rights Division.

Van Cleve, Nicole Gonzales. 2016. *Crook County: Racism and Injustice in America's Largest Criminal Court*. Stanford, CA: Stanford University Press.

Vargas, Robert. 2016. *Wounded City: Violent Turf Wars in a Chicago Barrio*. Oxford: Oxford University Press.

Vargas, Robert and Philip McHarris. 2017. "Race and State in City Police Spending Growth: 1980–2010." *Sociology of Race and Ethnicity* 3(1): 96–112.

VerHelst, Megan. 2021. "How Biden's $2T Infrastructure Plan Could Benefit U.S. Cities." *Patch*, March 31.

Viteritti, Joseph. 2012. *Choosing Equality: School Choice, the Constitution, and Civil Society*. Washington, DC: Brookings Institution Press.

Vitus, Kathrine. 2008. "The Agonistic Approach: Reframing Resistance in Qualitative Research." *Qualitative Inquiry* 14(3): 466–488.

Wacquant, Loïc. 2000. "The New 'Peculiar Institution': On the Prison as Surrogate Ghetto." *Theoretical Criminology* 4(3): 377–389.

Wacquant, Loïc. 2002. "Scrutinizing the Street: Poverty, Morality, and the Pitfalls of Urban Ethnography." *American Journal of Sociology* 107(6): 1468–1532.

Wacquant, Loïc. 2009. *Punishing the Poor: The Neoliberal Government of Social Insecurity*. Durham, NC: Duke University Press.

Wadman, Robert and William Allison. 2004. *To Protect and Serve: A History of Police in America*. Upper Saddle River, NJ: Pearson Prentice Hall.

Wakefield, Sara and Christopher Uggen. 2010. "Incarceration and Stratification." *Annual Review of Sociology* 36:387–406.

Walker, Michael. 2016. "Race Making in a Penal Institution." *American Journal of Sociology* 121(4): 1051–1078.

Walker, Samuel and Carol Archibold. 2020. *The New World of Police Accountability*. 3rd ed. Thousand Oaks, CA: Sage.

Warner, Sam Bass. 2016. "Evolution and Transformation: The American Industrial Metropolis, 1840–1940." Pp. 63–72 in *The City Reader*, 6th ed., edited by R. LeGates and F. Stout. New York: Routledge.

Weisburd, David. 2008. "Place-Based Policing." *Ideas in American Policing* 9:1–15.

Weisburd, David and Anthony Braga. 2006. *Police Innovation: Contrasting Perspectives*. Cambridge: Cambridge University Press.

Weisburd, David, Stephen Mastrofski, Rosann Greenspan, and James Willis. 2004. *The Growth of Compstat in American Policing*. Arlington, VA: Police Foundation Reports.

Weitzer, Ronald and Steven Tuch. 2005. "Racially Biased Policing: Determinants of Citizen Perceptions." *Social Forces* 83(3): 1009–1030.

Werthman, Carl and Irving Piliavin. 1967. "Gang Members and the Police." Pp. 56–98 in *The Police: Six Sociological Essays*, edited by D. Bordua. New York: Wiley.

Western, Bruce. 2006. *Punishment and Inequality in America*. New York: Russell Sage Foundation.

Westley, William. 1970. *Violence and the Police: A Sociological Study of Law, Custom, and Morality*. Cambridge, MA: MIT Press.

White Bird Clinic. 2021. "CAHOOTS." Retrieved May 23, 2021 (http://whitebirdclinic.org).

Wilkerson, Isabel. 2011. *The Warmth of Other Suns: The Epic Story of America's Great Migration*. New York: Random House.

Williams, Hubert and Patrick Murphy. 1990. "The Evolving Strategy of Police: A Minority View." *Perspectives on Policing* 13:1–15.

Williams, Kristian. 2015. *Our Enemies in Blue: Police and Power in America*. Chico, CA: AK Press.

Wilson, David. 2007. *Cities and Race: America's New Black Ghetto*. London: Routledge.

Wilson, David and Jared Wouters. 2003. "Spatiality and Growth Discourse: The Restructuring of America's Rust Belt Cities." *Journal of Urban Affairs* 25(2): 123–138.

Wilson, James Q. 1968. *Varieties of Police Behavior: The Management of Law and Order in Eight Communities*. Cambridge, MA: Harvard University Press.

Wilson, James Q. and George Kelling. 1982. "Broken Windows." *Atlantic Monthly* 249(3): 29–38.

Wilson, Mark D. 2019. "Austin Police Redraw Response Map to Home In on Entertainment District Crime." *Austin (TX) American-Statesman*, August 16.

Wilson, William Julius. 1996. *When Work Disappears: The World of the New Urban Poor*. New York: Random House.

INDEX

abolition, police, 190
ACLU, 244n29
Adams, M., 186, 193
African Americans. *See* Black people
Aid to Families with Dependent Children, 35
Allan, Roy, 131–32
Alpert, George, 146
Alport, Doyle, 3–6, 82, 90–91
ALPRs. *See* automatic license-plate reader system
American Community Survey, 238n78
antiviolence units (AVU), 122, 144, 163, 164; staffing of, 243n19; West District, 162
Armenta, Amada, 16
Atlanta, redistricting in, 188–89
austerity, 8–9, 182; redistricting and, 190; in River City, 200; in United States, 200
Austin, redistricting in, 188–89
automatic license-plate reader system (ALPRs), 157–58
AVU. *See* antiviolence units

Bachman, Gary, 108, 132, 194; on proactive policing, 123–26
Baltimore, 237n68
Banished (Beckett and Herbert), 11–12
"Becker Principle," 216
Beckett, Katherine, 11–12
Bell, Monica, 159; on segregation, 189–90
Berkeley, 185–86

Biden administration, 200
Black codes, 43
Black Lives Matter, 10, 43–44
Blackness, 148–49; criminalization of, 158; reification of, 185
Black Panther Party, 185
Black people, 74–75; arrests rates of, 245n12; community control for, 185–86; criminalization of, 154–55; in East District, 85; on gentrification, 170; incarceration rates of, 36–38; neoliberal urbanism impacting, 139; policing of, 142, 144, 206–7; in River City, 30–32, 235n8, 235n9, 235n10; stop-and-frisk targeting, 127–28; unemployment of, 35; in United States, 231n2; in West District, 115–16
boundary work, 15
Brayne, Sarah, 158
broken windows policing, 57, 232n33
Brown, Ed, on proactive policing, 127
Brown, Michael, 209
Bruce, Christopher, 56
Buckhead, 188
"Bud-Shell Method," 56
burglaries, 82
Burke, Maurice, 170–72
Burkes, Vincent, 150
business improvement districts, 75–76, 102

CAHOOTS program, 198
Callahan, Alan, 89
Call Log, 93, 95, 105, 113

police shooting, 145
policing and police: of Black people,
142, 144, 206–7; broken windows,
57, 232n33; bureaucratic structure of,
146; centralized, 45–46; community
problem-solving and, 191–93; Cook
on, 175–76; decentralization of, 186;
demographics of, 21; disparities in, 87;
district design, 239n10; in downtown,
101–3; in East District v. West District,
19–21, 86–87, 137–38, 191–92; during
ECD, 98–101; of The Edge, 149–52;
evolution of role of, 43–46; exclusionary, 159; hotspots, 12, 57; incident-
based response model, 12–13; localism
in, 12–13; neighborhood-based, 45–46;
neoliberal urbanism and, 182, 190;
nonracial accounts of, 143–46; order-
maintenance, 11–12; overpolicing,
109–12, 127, 184, 194; place construction and, 183–85; problem-oriented,
12, 23, 28, 46, 48–49, 57, 80, 191, 195;
property values and, 11–12; race construction and, 14, 183–85; of race out
of place, 142–43, 167–69, 184–85; racial
disparities in, 127–28; racial inequality in, 143–44, 154, 183; racialization
of, 10–13; of racialized people, 152–55;
redistricting and, 15, 56, 58–59; relational analysis of, 13–15; revitalization
projects and, 158; segregation and,
17–22, 146, 159; service provision and,
196–98; in United States, 28; urban
growth and, 102–3; urban growth coalitions and, 27–29, 50–51; urban space
constructed via, 14, 43–44; Ward on,
101–2; of white people, 163, 179; work
and balance in, 57–58; zero-tolerance,
12. See also community policing;
proactive policing; service provision;
specific topics
politics, in fieldwork, 220–21
Portland, redistricting in, 188

positionality, in ride-alongs, 218–21
postindustrial cities, segregation in, 9
poverty, in West District, 116–17
preventive patrol, in East District, 88–92
proactive policing, 5, 110; Brown on, 127;
consequences of, 126–29, 138; for crime
fighting, 193; crime produced by, 194–
95; critics of, 129–30; defining, 242n2;
in East District, 122–23; goals and
tactics of, 119–21; Hayes and Bachman
on, 123–26; Lancaster on, 118–21, 128;
limitations of, 126–27; as moral duty,
129; threat identification in, 153; in
West District, 117, 121–23
problem-oriented policing, 12, 23, 28, 46,
48–49, 57, 80, 188, 191; efficacy of, 195
procedural dynamics, 216
Progressive-era, 9
property taxes, 92. See also taxpayers
property values: policing and, 11–12; redistricting and, 33
public-housing, 158
public safety, in Riverside, 172–74
Pulled Over (Epp, Maynard-Moody, &
Haider-Markel), 16

quality of life, in West District, 116–17, 130

race: ambiguity of, 166–67; in East District, 84–85, 148; evolution of categories of, 231n2; in fieldwork, 220; ideological origins of, 233n48; language
of, 148; in mass incarceration, 233n49;
place and, 147–48; policing disparities
and, 127–28; policing in construction of, 14, 183–85; relational analysis
of, 13–15; role of, 146–49; structural
inequalities and, 143; in United States,
220, 232n24, 234n64; urban growth
and, 8–10
race out of place, 25, 84–85, 245n1; consequences of policing, 167–69; in East
District, 142, 158; policing of, 142–43,

ride-alongs, 211–24; candid conversations in, 217–18; civilians during, 221–24; consent negotiation, 211–12; nonparticipant observer status in, 213–15; policework impact of, 215–17; positionality in, 218–21

River City: austerity in, 200; Black people in, 30–32, 235n8, 235n9, 235n10; community-service ethos in, 103–4; creative class in, 238n77; deindustrialization in, 34–35, 40; economic development in, 236n31; history of, 17–18, 30–31; Latino Americans in, 237n51; localism in, 186–87; Native Americans in history of, 234n64; place-making projects, 180; police reform in, 49; racial inequality in, 146, 243n14; racialization in, 159, 160–61; redistricting in, 59–68, 185–90; relational analysis of, 182; revitalization projects in, 41; segregation in, 17, 139–41, 187, 235n17; stabilization planning during 1970s, 238n74; stakeholders in, 5; structural inequalities in, 146; universities in, 158; urban growth coalition of, 41, 53. *See also specific topics*

River City Business Association (RCBA), 41

River City Police Department (RCPD), 1–2, 17, 22, 23, 79–80, 92, 125–26, 154, 178, 181, 207; access to, 208–9; budget, 200; community policing and, 47; community problem-solving and, 191–93; as crime fighters, 193–96; history of, 239n95; officer loss, 200; police districts in, 6–7; relationships in, 209–11; revitalization projects and, 182; roles of, 190–98; service provision of, 196–98; structure of, 48–49, 55

Riverdale Group, 116

Riverside: community-service ethos in, 177; crime in, 172–74; demographics of, 170; diversity of, 171; drug dealing in,

172; in East District, 173–75; economic development of, 170–72; gentrification of, 170; history of, 169–72, 246n3; housing in, 176–77; public safety in, 172–74; reclassification of, 174–77; redistricting of, 169, 178–79; resource allocation and, 174–77; service provision in, 173, 175, 178; symbolic position of, 177–78; in West District, 173, 175, 176; Williams on, 174–75

Riverside Neighborhood Association (RNA), 164, 175; representatives of, 169

RNA. *See* Riverside Neighborhood Association

Roberts, Bonnie, 139–40

Rothstein, Richard, 248n51

Rust Belt, 6–7, 17, 38; history of, 29; segregation in, 29; urban growth coalitions in, 9

Safety Committee, River City, 18, 62, 63, 65, 67, 170, 240n21, 242n12

safety perceptions, Daniels on, 72–73

Sanders, Janice, 71, 95

San Francisco, 187

Sassen, Saskia, 39

Seattle, redistricting in, 187–88

segregation, 6, 24–25, 206; Bell on, 189–90; boundary crossing, 164, 180; differential voice across, 75–77; as dynamic, 169–80; Giles on, 141; industrialization and, 30–34; the local and, 28–29; maintenance of, 159–60; mass incarceration reinforcing, 37; naturalization of, 184–85; policing and, 17–22, 146, 159, 163–64; in postindustrial cities, 9; redistricting and, 140; rigidity of, 164–69, 179; in River City, 17, 139–41, 187, 235n17; in Rust Belt, 29; social welfare reinscribing, 201; urban growth and, 17–22, 29–42; of West District, 138–39; whiteness in, 163–64

Sentencing Project, 236n42

ABOUT THE AUTHOR

DAANIKA GORDON is Assistant Professor in the Department of Sociology at Tufts University.

.

www.ingramcontent.com/pod-product-compliance
Lightning Source LLC
Chambersburg PA
CBHW020248030426
42336CB00010B/665